Up Against the Wal-Marts

Up Against the Wal-Marts

How Your Business Can Prosper in the Shadow of the Retail Giants

Don Taylor

Jeanne Smalling Archer

amacom

American Management Association

New York • Atlanta • Boston • Chicago • Kansas City • San Francisco • Washington, D.C.
Brussels • Mexico City • Tokyo • Toronto

Library of Congress Cataloging-in-Publication Data

Taylor, Don (Donald D.), 1946–
    Up against the Wal-Marts : how your business can prosper in the
shadow of the retail giants / Don Taylor. Jeanne Smalling Archer.
        p.   cm.
    Includes bibliographical references and index.
    ISBN 0-8144-0238-0
    ISBN 0-8144-7916-2 (pbk.)
    1. Success in business.   2. Retail trade—Management.   3. Service
industries—Management.   4. Small business—Management.   I. Archer,
Jeanne Smalling.   II. Title.
HF5386.T319   1994
658.8—dc20   94-31697
                                                                         CIP

First AMACOM paperback edition 1996.

Printing number

10   9   8   7   6   5   4   3   2

To the three most important women in my world: **Helen Lorraine Taylor,** who gave me life; **Sue Ellen Keith Taylor,** who shares my life; and **Christi Lyn Taylor,** who is the light of my life. I love you all.

—Don Taylor

To my husband, **Mike,** and our two wonderful children, **Andy** and **Julie.** They taught me the true value of love, support, and encouragement. And to my mother, **Marie Hickerson Smalling,** who taught me to be inquisitive, and to my father, **Jack Smalling,** who taught me to persevere. My love and appreciation to all of you.

—Jeanne S. Archer

To the three most important women in my world: **Helen Lorraine Taylor,** who gave me life; **Sue Ellen Keith Taylor,** who shares my life; and **Christi Lyn Taylor,** who is the light of my life. I love you all.

—Don Taylor

To my husband, **Mike,** and our two wonderful children, **Andy** and **Julie.** They taught me the true value of love, support, and encouragement. And to my mother, **Marie Hickerson Smalling,** who taught me to be inquisitive, and to my father, **Jack Smalling,** who taught me to persevere. My love and appreciation to all of you.

—Jeanne S. Archer

Contents

Acknowledgments

If we were honest we would admit that our work belongs more to those who helped make it possible than to us. This book is the composite of all who have shared their successes, experiences, and heartaches.

Our thanks must begin with those to whom we owe the greatest debt: the men and women whose successful examples we have sifted and blended into the survival strategies that make up the heart of this book, from the few that we actually mention in the book to the hundreds whose struggles and efforts helped us frame the concepts. You (America's entrepreneurs) are the reason this country is great. Keep up the fight and continue the race. You are proof that small business is alive and well.

Our gratitude must also be expressed to the following:

Andrea Pedolsky, our initial contact with AMACOM books, who, as our first editor, shared our enthusiasm and vision for the book and encouraged us from the beginning.

Mary Glenn, our current AMACOM editor, who picked up our project midstream and guided us as we clarified and polished ideas.

All the troops at AMACOM, who have contributed to the success of our efforts.

Laurie Harper at the Sebastian Agency and Paul Aiken at the Authors Guild for their insight and diplomacy.

Jack Dittrich and Jerry Miller, Don's bosses at West Texas A&M University, whose support and encouragement was vital.

Ann Stanford, David Shipman, and Bill Harrington, Don's teammates, who picked up Don's share of the load as book deadlines neared.

We are grateful to all the people who provided information, resources, and wisdom. These people served as counselors, detectives, and comrades, and this book simply would not have been possible without their help. Our thanks to:

Pat Reed, Murray Provine, and Jack Wilson of the Key America Buying groups, who believed in our message and contributed thought-provoking ideas and discussion.

Buzz Roberts, Glen Brosier, Gordon McOwen, Stan Kennedy, Raul Strum, Robin Muir, Pat Stanhope, Nell Curry, Dottie Nation, Jennifer Blackburn, and Dawna Muir of Principal/Eppler, Guerin and Turner, Inc., who often made their corporate research and expertise available to us on a moment's notice.

Mary Kay Snell and her excellent staff of reference librarians at the Amarillo Public Library: John Birchfield, Art Bort, Katie Anthony, Marian Daniel, Rob Groman, Amarillo, Texas.

Ben Neely, West Texas A&M University, Canyon, Texas.

Sonya Buckner, Council of Small Business Enterprises, Montgomery, Alabama.

Larry Adams, Carolinas-Tennessee Building Material Association, Charlotte, North Carolina.

John Brill, Northeastern Retail Lumber Association, Rochester, New York.

Joe Wildman and C. B. Streeter, Amarillo Hardware Co., Amarillo, Texas.

Stacie White, Threshold Computers, Amarillo, Texas.

Ray Daly, ASCII Group, Bethesda, Maryland.

Dave Ellison, *Fishing Tackle Retailer*, Montgomery, Alabama.

Owen Taylor, writer with *Fishing Tackle Retailer*, Brandon, Mississippi.

Don Pfau, Sports, Inc., Lewistown, Montana.

David Morgan, *Nursery Manager*, Fort Worth, Texas.

Jim Reid, Coulter Gardens, Amarillo, Texas.

Simon DeGroot, National Office Products Association, Alexandria, Virginia.

Gene Hill, Hill's Sport Shop, Amarillo, Texas.

Larry Weindruch, National Sporting Goods Association, Mount Prospect, Illinois.

Mike Mooney, National Buying Syndicate, Fort Worth, Texas.

Jeff Atkinson, *Sports Trend*, Atlanta, Georgia.

John Kirk, *Fishing Tackle Trade News*, Vancouver, Washington.

Willi Bozarth, Land and Sea Pets, Amarillo, Texas.

Barbara Hunter, PIJAC, Washington, D.C.

Tom Crawford, Photo Marketing Association, Jackson, Michigan.

Mike Watters, Cain, Simmons & Watters, Dallas, Texas.

To our families and friends, who endured all the months it took to bring this book to fruition. To their warm and caring support we now return.

Up Against the Wal-Marts

One

Main Street Is Changing

What counts is not necessarily the size of the dog in the fight—it's the size of the fight in the dog.

—Dwight D. Eisenhower

"Bowman's Hardware is closing!" The rumor had spread like wildfire through the small Georgia town just weeks ago. Now the store building stands quietly empty. The auction is over and the owner is gone.

The FOR SALE OR RENT sign dominates the right-side display window. A hand-lettered poster board is taped up in the left-hand window. Its message expresses the bitterness of the former store owner and the area's other failed merchants. It reads: YOU WANTED WAL-MART. SOON THEY'LL BE ALL YOU GOT. GOOD LUCK THEN!

Bowman's is the eighth Main Street business to close since Wal-Mart came to town. The owners are quick to blame the giant retailer for the failures. However, signs of neglect, apathy, and decline were evident on Main Street long before the discounter located at the edge of town.

Bowman's had been the only full-line hardware store in town. Its closing is a blow to the remaining independent owners. For the first time in seventy-three years the big corner store is empty.

Main Street is changing.

Nearly a thousand miles northwest another small town hardware store anchors a similar corner. Jack McNabb's store stands at the corner of Ninth and Main streets in Trenton, Missouri. Although he feels pressure from a nearby Wal-Mart and an aggressive True Value chain store, McNabb is happy to be a survivor.

McNabb's Trenton Hardware is a pleasant blend of the past and present. It's a unique store where you can still buy rope by the foot, nails by the pound, and drill bits one at a time.

The atmosphere hasn't changed much in the past forty years. The wooden floor is oiled and swept often. Fluorescent-light fixtures of 1940s vintage hang four feet below the ornate metal ceiling. The oil stove near the back of the store provides warmth and fuels conversation for the folks who gather there on cold winter days. The sign above the door on the front of the three-story brick building reads: TRENTON HARDWARE—IF WE AIN'T GOT IT, YOU DON'T NEED IT.

McNabb has spent more than forty years in this downtown store, and he can call nearly every customer by name. He's the kind of fellow folks call out of bed when the plumbing springs a leak in the middle of the night. He answers the calls with nary a grumble. He knows his business, his customers, and his competition.

"This is a tough business, and these are tough times," he told us. "But I'll soon have it paid off, and then we'll have some fun again."

In more prosperous times, this store supported the families of five owners. Now only McNabb manages a living. Like the family farmers that make up his customer base, this independent Main Street merchant may be one of a vanishing breed.

Main Street is changing.

Less than an hour's drive east of Flagstaff, Arizona, is another town and yet another hardware store. Casey's is a family owned hardware and builder's supply outlet in the high desert town of Winslow.

Although Wal-Mart is only a mile away, Casey's is booming. Sales have increased nearly 30 percent per year for the past three years in spite of the slow local economy. "We're adding employees, expanding departments, and upgrading our image," said Casey's president, Robert Gondek. "We're watching our prices too. Wal-Mart has fifty or sixty items they advertise pretty hard in this area. We watch those items all the time. If Wal-Mart is at 97 cents on a bag of steer manure, we'll be at 99 cents and load it in your car for you."

As you approach the newly landscaped building you sense that Casey's is a pleasant place. A sales clerk looks up as you enter the store. Instantly her face lights with a welcoming smile as she greets you warmly. You might be a total stranger now, but you won't be one for long. As you walk through the clean well-stocked aisles, other friendly staff offer their assistance. It is a friendly place.

Every item on each shelf is individually priced even though the store uses state-of-the-art bar code scanners at the checkout. Attractive, professionally made signs point out specials and highlight product features and benefits. The store is busy though it's a weekday.

Main Street is changing here as well.

Survival and Success

This book is about survival and success. We want your small business to prosper even if you're right in the shadow of the giants. We don't want you to fail or barely survive. Furthermore, we don't believe you have to. In spite of Wal-Mart, Kmart, Home Depot, and an ever growing host of significant others, you can still build a profitable retail or service business.

Just like David in the Bible, you can stand up against your Goliath. All you need is courage, a few simple weapons, and about 500 small stones. The weapons are our ten survival strategies, and the stones are the business-building tactics we've packed into this book. The modern-day giants do have chinks in their armor. We'll help you direct your shots.

We'll begin with a little history so you can see what happened and how it happened. Then we'll tell you all about the giants.

Don't become discouraged as you read about the success that this new breed of retailers is having. Remember that Goliath had never been defeated before he came up against little David. Read on. We think you will be ready to scrap with the best of them.

Now let's turn back the clock and see what happened on Main Street. We'll go back to nearly forgotten times when the pace was slower and lifestyles were simple.

The Rise and Fall of Main Street

As progress moved across America in the late 1800s and early 1900s, millions of bright men and women opened Main Street stores. They started general merchandise stores, hardware stores, drug emporiums, and specialty shops of all types. They opened shoe shops, clothing stores, gift shops, and fabric centers. As the trade areas prospered, Main Streets flourished.

The Big Three

The first half of the twentieth century saw the arrival and growth of large retail giants. Sears, Roebuck, and Company, J. C. Penney, and Montgomery Ward were the three most dominant chains.

They possessed real retail horsepower and set the standard for other retailers. Interestingly, the big three seemed to coexist easily with the independent merchants. Even the five-and-dime stores like S. S. Kresge, Woolworth's, and Mattingly's blended into, but did not dominate, the Main Street mix.

A New Breed

Then in the early 1960s, a new breed of retailers emerged, led by S. S. Kresge's Kmart, Dayton-Hudson's Target, Woolworth's Woolco, and Sam Walton's Wal-Mart. This new group of discount stores redefined value and variety with low prices and wide inventories.

Kmart, Woolco, and Target experienced aggressive early growth, fueled by the strength of their parent companies. Wal-Mart's early growth was relatively slow, and the company opened fewer than 500 stores from 1962 through 1982.

Surprisingly, there was limited head-to-head competition between these four fast-rising discounters before the early 1980s. Kmart, Woolco, and Target worked regional metro areas, and no one thought Sam Walton's billion-dollar, small-town-only chain was any threat to the huge retailers of the day. In the early 1980s, Sears still dominated the retail landscape while hard-charging Kmart was just beginning to close the gap.

Other mega competitors joined the fray in the 1970s. The category killers entered solid retail markets like hardware, toys, and drugs, and attempted to strip out the entire trade segment. Early successes in this area were Walgreen drugs, Toys "R" Us, and Home Depot. These category specialists now have annual sales in excess of $7 billion each.

The wholesale club concept began in 1976 when Sol Price opened his first Price Club warehouse. From the beginning, these "members only" warehouse stores operated with the "stack it high and watch it fly" philosophy. There are no frills. Floors are concrete, shelves are metal, and overhead is low.

The Predators Circle

The easiest prey for the new breed of discounters and category killers were the independent Main Street merchants who were still doing business as they had for years. They had invested little of their profits back into their businesses and in general had grown complacent. Storefronts reflected the neglect with peeling paint, cracked windows, and general deterioration.

Sidewalks cracked and buckled with minimal repair. Grass grew in the cracks, and litter lingered in the gutter. Parking meters were installed to help control "parking problems," while merchants ignored the message this sent to their customers: You must pay for the privilege of shopping with us.

Owners shortened business hours to accommodate their own lifestyles. Promotions were halfhearted, and few changes were made within stores. Layout, lighting, displays, and merchandising remained virtually unchanged. Only inventory changed, and often that was slow to follow newer trends and changing customer needs.

Business was good enough to allow the owners to relax

and still earn a good living. However, these merchants had lost their first love—pleasing the customer.

The Stage Is Set

With an expanding highway system, customers were becoming more mobile. They were willing to drive an hour or more to shop. They were hungry for new experiences at a time when Main Street merchants were happy with the status quo. The stage was set for a shopping revolution.

The new breed of retailers was more than willing to lead the revolution. They began to grab market share away from the established merchants with wide selections, low prices, and modern merchandising. As business slowed on Main Street, many of the entrenched elite lamented their woes at the local coffee shop. Some went after legal solutions, claiming unfair pricing and competitive practices. Others sought political help with zoning and other "keep them away from our town" efforts. Most did nothing. They seemed paralyzed like a rabbit that freezes in front of a car's approaching headlights. They couldn't run and they couldn't hide.

The small independent owners offered the new breed only moderate competition in most markets. Running profitable but inefficient businesses, the small retailers put little pressure on their suppliers to keep business costs low. Their "mark it up 40 percent across the board" philosophy left plenty of margin for the lean operating discounters.

In addition, small owners had no good source of information on how to combat the new breed. No book like this existed. University professors, home economists, and out-of-work consultants—none of whom had ever run a retail store or made a payroll—scurried around the country defining the problem but offering only superficial solutions. Aggressive merchants were trying new strategies, but no one was sure what was working and what wasn't.

Profiles of the New Breed

The Big-Box Discounters

Today's dominant big three—Wal-Mart, Kmart, and Target— were not the first discount operations. However, they studied early pioneers like Ann and Hope, Korvettes, Zayres, Arlans, and Gibson's to learn their methods. The discount concept was straightforward: Provide good merchandise at low prices, and let the customers help themselves.

The big three all opened their first stores in 1962. No one could have guessed the impact they would eventually have on the retail industry. Wal-Mart, Kmart, and Target's combined sales for fiscal 1994 were more than $110 billion. Many other growing retail chains are watching the big three with awe.

Wal-Mart Stores, Inc.

Sam Walton began his retail career as a Main Street merchant. He owned fifteen Ben Franklin stores when he opened his first Wal-Mart discount store in Rogers, Arkansas, on July 2, 1962. When the store generated sales of $975,000 in its first year, Walton knew he had a winning concept.

This chain grew slowly in the beginning. Limited capital and conservative management curtailed early growth. By 1972, only fifty-one stores were in operation. Wal-Mart went public on October 1, 1970, and continued to grow slowly through the 1970s. The chain had grown to only 276 stores in 1980. However, the 1980s proved to be Wal-Mart's decade of growth as the company opened more than 1,000 stores and exploded into the 1990s.

Wal-Mart became the largest retailer in America in 1990 as it rocketed by number-one Sears and number-two Kmart in the same year. Sales in fiscal 1994 topped $67 billion.

The first Supercenter opened in 1988. In essence Supercenters are expanded Wal-Mart stores with groceries, fast-food courts, and various service businesses. The Supercenters range in size from 97,000 square feet (Wagoner, Oklahoma) to 211,000 square feet (Poplar Bluff, Missouri). Typically, you may find on-site photo finishing, a prescription eyeglass center, a cleaners, a bakery, and fresh flowers.

The Supercenter is the concept of the nineties. Wal-Mart will have nearly 150 Supercenters operating by 1995. The grocery business will play a large role in sustaining Wal-Mart's double-digit growth into the next decade.

Kmart Corporation

The S. S. Kresge Company was sixty-three years old when it opened the first Kmart discount department store in 1962 in the Detroit suburb of Garden City. Kresge was a large company with abundant capital, and it opened seventeen other Kmart stores the first year.

The success of its early efforts, combined with the parent company's financial clout, vaulted Kmart into an early lead among discounters. In 1966, Kresge had its first billion-dollar year and had already opened 162 Kmart stores.

The decade of the 1970s was Kmart's aggressive expansion period. The company opened 271 stores in 1976 alone—more stores than Wal-Mart would open in its first seventeen years! In 1981, when Kmart opened its 2,000th store, Wal-Mart had just 330 units.

The 1980s brought diversification to Kmart. In 1984, the company bought out Home Centers of America, Inc. (now Builders Square) and the Walden Book Company (now Waldenbooks). In 1985, Kmart acquired Pay Less Drug Store Northeast. By 1991, it had further diversified by acquiring PACE Membership Warehouse, Inc., Marko, Inc., The Sports Authority, and OfficeMax. In 1992, Kmart acquired the thirty-one-store Borders Book Shops chain.

Kmart's combined sales climbed to $32 billion in 1990, which was enough to pass number-one Sears. However, it was not a joyous occasion, as Wal-Mart blew by both Sears and Kmart with sales of $33 billion.

Today, Kmart remains a distant second among the new breed as Wal-Mart continues to open up an ever widening lead. The difference between the two largest chains in fiscal 1994 was more than $28 billion.

In early 1994, Kmart announced a major restructuring plan which would close more than 180 Waldenbooks stores and 70 smaller Kmart stores. The company will focus on its new "big box" concept with stores of 110,000 square feet. These stores are bigger and brighter and have upscale boutique areas.

Kmart is also responding to Wal-Mart's huge superstore grocery/discount concept with its own combination stores that cover 167,000 square feet. These megastores are called Super K's and are expected to generate more than $50 million in sales annually per store.

Target

Target is the upscale discount store chain operating as a division of Dayton Hudson Corporation. Dayton Hudson is an old-line retailer with roots dating back to 1881. Its fiscal 1994 sales were a healthy $19.2 billion.

The Target Division was formed in 1962, and three stores opened that year. Target accounts for more than 60 percent of the company's total revenues and generates nearly half its profits. The division consists of nearly 500 stores.

The biggest boxes it builds are called "Greatlands" stores, and they measure in at 125,000 square feet. These oversize Targets contain in-store pharmacies, but do not carry a full line of groceries, as do Wal-Mart's Supercenters and Kmart's Super K's.

Chain Store Age Executive reported in 1993 that two studies, by *Discount Store News* and Babson College respectively, indicated that the Greatlands store concept was not the winner with consumers that Target had hoped for. The studies pointed up the need for a "more dynamic offering of products," and showed that consumers felt that "Target's prices are not as sharp as Wal-Mart's."

Target's image is generally more upscale than either Wal-Mart's or Kmart's. It is successful in attracting a more affluent customer base. However, as Wal-Mart opens more Supercenters and Kmart upgrades its stores, the image difference is evaporating.

Target will most likely remain in the number-three "discounter" position through the decade. It is conceivable that one or more of the category killers will pass the Target division in sales.

The Category Killers

The category killers are an interesting blend of specialty retail and discount store concepts that focuses on a specific retail segment such as toys, electronics, drugs, or computers. Like the big-box discounters, they carry good merchandise at low prices, with fairly low levels of customer service. Notable exceptions are Home Depot and Best Buy, which seem to have a higher commitment to customer service.

Walgreen Company

Walgreen is America's largest drugstore chain. With sales of $8.3 billion in fiscal 1993, the company ranks as the seventeenth largest retail company in America and boasts a total of 1,836 stores.

The chain began in 1901 when Charles R. Walgreen purchased his first drugstore on Chicago's south side. Walgreen founded the chain on the philosophy that every customer was a "guest" in the store.

In 1950, Charles R. Walgreen, Jr., decided to change the merchandising concept to self-service. This decision, along with commitments to change, positioned Walgreen's for expansion into the 1970s and 1980s.

Like Wal-Mart, Walgreen's boasts a high-tech distribution system. The company reports that 97 percent of its stores receive merchandise within two days of placing their orders. They were the first drugstore chain to install bar-code scanners in all stores.

Though an old-line retailer, Walgreen's may be the "newest" drugstore chain in the industry. Seventy percent of its stores have been opened or remodeled in the past five years.

Walgreen's opened 149 stores in fiscal 1993 and plans to open 175 stores in 1995. By 1996, it will open 200 stores annually and expects to operate 3,000 drugstores by the year 2,000.

While many small, independent pharmacists fear Wal-Mart—some to the point of bringing litigation over alleged unfair pricing—Walgreen's may be their worst enemy. Its anticipated expansion rate is more aggressive than Wal-Mart's, and it is taking aim at the health care and beauty aids industry.

Toys "R" Us, Inc.

Toys "R" Us is the fastest-growing and world's largest children's specialty retail chain. This company has shown steady growth since it went public nearly fifteen years ago.

As the name implies, children's toys are the main market niche, although the company also has 211 Kids "R" Us stores which sell children's clothing. Toys "R" Us has more than 160 international locations in Europe and Asia.

Like other category killers, Toys "R" Us aggressively chases market share. The company opened nearly 100 stores in 1993. In fiscal 1994, sales jumped to $7.9 billion for the 1,000-plus store chain. This sales level boosted the company even higher on *Fortune* magazine's list of the "fifty largest retailing companies."

Toys "R" Us is testing new merchandising techniques. The most notable is a Books "R" Us section, which is really a children's bookstore within the main store. Toys "R" Us will develop this merchandising technique in more than 200 locations by the end of 1994.

The Home Depot, Inc.

America's largest category killer is one of the newest kids on the block. Founded in 1978 in Atlanta, Georgia, Home Depot is the largest home-improvement retailer in the United States. Fiscal 1994 sales topped $9 billion, ranking the company in the top twenty on *Fortune* magazine's list of the top fifty retailers.

Home Depot is an interesting hybrid. The average store size is approximately 97,700 square feet, and some stores have nearly 30,000 square feet of selling space outside as well. Their concept is a cross between a warehouse discount store and a full-service hardware store–lumberyard.

Some analysts have compared Home Depot to Kmart's Builder's Square, noting that Home Depot has exceptional customer service. The chain has received national attention for hiring skilled professionals from the building trades to assist do-it-yourself customers.

When we visited a Home Depot store in Phoenix several months ago, store employees were demonstrating three do-it-yourself projects. An electrician demonstrated wiring three-way switches while a former contractor invited interested customers to get hands-on experience laying patio blocks. A plumber showed how to properly install a single-handle faucet.

The U.S. home improvement products market is currently in excess of $100 billion annually. The six largest home improvement retailers hold less than 20 percent of this overall market. There is room for growth, and Home Depot seems well positioned to meet the challenge. The company currently has more than 250 stores and plans to open another fifty or so in 1994.

Best Buy Co., Inc.

Best Buy is an up-and-comer in the consumer electronics, appliances, and home office equipment retail industry. Best Buy has shown strong sales and profits growth since going public in 1985.

Sales increased by 74 percent in fiscal 1993 and jumped a whopping 86 percent in fiscal 1994. The $3 billion company more than doubled profits for the third year in a row.

Best Buy is a warehouse-type category killer with aggressive pricing policies, thirty-minute in-store credit card approval and very low operating expense levels. According to *Value Line, Inc.*, Best Buy's selling, general, and administrative expense ratio is the lowest in the consumer electronics industry.

Best Buy opened thirty-eight new stores in fiscal 1993, bringing the total number of stores to 111. The company will open about forty stores in fiscal 1994. Best Buy's megastore concept utilizes approximately 45,000 square feet. The standard store size is nearly 36,000 square feet.

This category killer is an aggressive advertiser and gives the consumer the best of price and service considerations. Although Best Buy is more than $1 billion smaller than the industry leader, Circuit City, we believe it has an opportunity to leap ahead in two or three years.

Wholesale Clubs

The wholesale/warehouse club concept is one of the newer concepts in retail. This "stack it deep and sell it cheap" concept is dominated by Price/Costco and Sam's Clubs.

This is a no-frills, high-volume, low-margin business. Stores are huge and shoppers must be members. Product lines are limited, and large multiple packaging the norm.

Price/Costco

This new company was formed in 1993 by the merger of two wholesale club pioneers, The Price Company and Costco Wholesale Corporation. The Price Company was founded by Sol Price in 1976. Jeffrey H. Brotman and James D. Sinegal founded Costco in 1983.

The merger makes the new company the largest player in the wholesale club industry, with over $15 billion in annual sales. The chain operates more than 200 stores in the U.S., Canada, and Mexico.

The company's operating philosophy is straightforward. It provides a limited number of products—usually less than 4,000 stock keeping units (SKUs)—in a no-frills warehouse store that averages approximately 120,000 square feet. Members are charged an annual fee of $30 to $35 for the privilege of buying at "wholesale" prices.

The company holds costs down with the following strategies: low-cost land and facilities, direct-from-the-manufacturer purchasing, minimal advertising, and very low labor costs.

Company officials predict that the merger will strengthen both companies. Price/Costco will open nearly fifty new stores in 1994.

Sam's Clubs

The Sam's Clubs are the wholesale/warehouse sales division of Wal-Mart Stores, Inc. In fiscal 1993, the company operated 256 Sam's stores with combined sales of $12.3 billion. This represents a 31 percent increase over 1992 sales.

Wal-Mart opened its first Sam's store in 1983, and has opened more than 130 new Sam's stores in the last three years. The company will build more than sixty new Sam's in 1994, and will relocate or expand twenty others.

Like Price/Costco, Sam's uses a members-only concept that utilizes similar strategies to keep prices low. Wal-Mart's founder, Sam Walton, developed the Sam's Club division after visiting the Price Club warehouse in San Diego.

Sam's stores typically cover 120,000 square feet and turn the inventory more than a dozen times each year. Wal-Mart's research shows that the average member visits a Sam's sixteen times per year and spends slightly more than $100 per visit.

Factory Outlet Malls

Manufacturers selling directly to the general public is the premise of the factory outlet mall concept. Generally targeted toward rapidly developing trade areas, the malls can cover as much as 2 million square feet (nearly 50 acres) and house 400 stores.

Nearly 500 outlet malls exist in the United States, with more being added every year. Manufacturers seem to like the concept because it allows them to showcase their entire product lines and generate higher profit margins.

Developers believe in the concept because in their words, "A rich man enjoys a bargain—a poor man needs one."

Whether this retail fad will become a trend, only time will tell. According to an industry executive, the entire factory outlet industry generated $8 billion in retail sales in 1993. Put in perspective, that's less than 15 percent of Wal-Mart's revenue for the same period.

Why the New Breed Is So Successful

Here are the top reasons why customers are flocking to the new breed of stores. Study these items carefully as they offer some insight you can use to your advantage.

1. *Customers want value.* Every working, middle-class family in America feels the financial pinch of today's economy. The government is taking a huge slice of their paycheck, and they're trying to spend their money wisely. They weigh each purchase carefully and look for stores that give them the most for their money.

Although many chains and independents promise value, no one delivers it more consistently than merchants like Wal-Mart. When a customer spends a dollar at a Wal-Mart store, nearly 80 cents of that dollar is the actual cost of the product.

Compare that to Sears, which delivers only 63 cents in product cost, or some independents, which deliver 60 cents or less. You don't have to be a rocket scientist to figure out that customers will go where they get the most for their money.

Your goal as a small-business owner is to present a fresh package of values that the price-conscious shopper can compare favorably to the megastores. You can be profitable without going head to head with the new breed. We'll show you how changing your purchasing, pricing, service, and promotion strategies can position your business for success.

2. *Customers love choices.* Today's consumers love to have a wide variety of products and services to choose from. The average big-box merchant gives every customer approximately 60,000 choices.

Wal-Mart's Supercenters reportedly carry more than 75,000 SKUs in their combined grocery and general merchandise lines. Regardless of the exact number, there are plenty of options for even the most finicky consumer.

You won't win the variety game by trying to broaden your inventory. That doesn't mean that you can't satisfy your customers by staying close to them and finding out what they really want, and then giving it to them. You'll need to develop a real customer focus to keep your market share. Profitable niches do exist, and we'll help you find them.

3. *Customers love anything new.* We all love new things. It's the American dream. We want to drive new cars, own new homes, try new restaurants, travel to new destinations and sample new experiences. If it's new, we'll try it for just that reason.

The majority of the big-box stores, category killers, whole-sale clubs, and factory outlet malls are new. More than 75 percent of all Wal-Mart stores have been built in the past ten years, in stark contrast to the aging central business districts and Main Streets.

We have worked with several Main Street programs and central business district renovation projects, and we believe in the historical renewal concept. However, we would encourage all involved in such projects to keep the results focused on the customer. When renovation is undertaken with the customer's needs in mind, wonderful things can begin to happen on Main Street. Customers love to see old things renewed.

Kmart, Target, and Wal-Mart are all renovating older stores. Kmart announced an ambitious $3 billion renovation program in the early 1990s. Although the chain has scaled back the renovation program somewhat, it had reformatted more than half of its stores by the end of 1993. The new formats feature upscale merchandising, wider aisles, and expanded product and service mixes.

You will need to consider some renewal as well. It may be as simple as moving merchandise and presenting a new face, or it may require extensive remodeling. *Change* is the key word. We'll point out some companies that are successfully improving their appearance without breaking the bank.

4. *Customers love convenient locations.* You've heard the old retail proverb that "there are three main factors in retail success—location, location, and location." Inconvenient locations are an ingredient in the decline and demise of central shopping districts.

Customers in the nineties demand easy-to-find and easy-to-access business locations. They are less tolerant of limited parking spaces, parking meters, and poor traffic-flow conditions.

Wal-Mart's store location in Anytown, U.S.A., will usually be found close to the major highway intersection of the trade area. In Chillicothe, Missouri, the Wal-Mart sits within 200 yards of U.S. Highways 36 and 65. In Altoona, Pennsylvania, the Wal-Mart is off Highway 22 on business route 220. In

Plainview, Texas, just jump off I-27 at the Highway 70 exit. The most common factor in Wal-Mart's location strategy appears to be the ease of accessibility from anywhere in the trade area.

If your location is less desirable than you would like and you can't move, all is not lost. You will have to work a little harder on other aspects of your business. You'll want to consider some of our low-cost promotion strategies to build traffic.

If parking is a problem, for heaven's sake, don't park company vehicles right in front of your store. Save those premium spaces for your customers. You think this is stating the obvious? You'd be surprised how frequently we see those company vehicles where they shouldn't be.

You will want to put the best face on your store that you can. A coat of fresh paint, sidewalk renovation, some new flowers or landscaping can help overcome other deficiencies.

5. *Customers love long open-for-business hours.* Imagine a Main Street shopping district open twenty-four hours a day, seven days a week. It is not easy to imagine and not likely to happen with a group of independent merchants who can't agree what night of the week to stay open during the Christmas season. However, eleven- or twelve-hour days are common among discounters, and the practice of twenty-four-hour operations is growing. Eight-to-five hours may not satisfy your customers.

The "always open" or "always open late" philosophies translate into customer service in the mind of the consumer. Are you open when your customers want to do business with you? Or are your hours forcing them to turn to the new breed?

What are we suggesting? Not that every store should be open the same hours as the megastores, but that your customers need convenient hours if they are going to shop with you. You should look at this aspect and either adjust or extend your hours to serve your customers better.

6. *Customers want the convenience of one-stop shopping.* Time is a valuable commodity for most 1990s consumers. Single-parent households and dual-income families are the norm today, and the increased pressure of everyone working around tight schedules makes one-stop shopping a real customer pleaser.

The 1950s' idyllic mental picture of an attractive housewife going from store to store to do her family's weekly shopping isn't realistic today. The correct picture is a busy lifestyle like Lynn McGhie's in Lake Zurich, Illinois. McGhie is the mother of two daughters and she combines her management career with the duties of chauffeur, housewife, cook, and maid. "I don't have any free time," she says. "When I shop I have to figure out how to fit it into my schedule. I prefer to go to Wal-Mart, where I can get everything I want. I wish we had a Supercenter; I'd get my groceries there too."

One-stop shopping is a major convenience and time saver. Throw in value and variety and you can begin to understand why the parking lots are filling up at the Supercenters.

7. *Customers don't want hassles.* As a rule, people try to avoid conflict and disagreements. Most customers don't like to argue, and more often than not, customers will walk away before they complain. However, you should not assume that because you hear no complaints the customer isn't feeling hassled.

Here are some of the most aggravating hassle factors.

- *Waiting.* Minutes seem like hours when you're waiting in line. Slow service, too few checkout lines, and poorly trained personnel will force your customers to wait. Waiting is a hassle, and customers will drive across town to avoid a hassle.

- *Poor return policies.* Whether it's broken, doesn't fit, or is the wrong color, customers won't tolerate hassles over returns.

We were conducting a workshop in McPherson, Kansas, when a workshop attendee told us about a return problem he'd encountered. He had purchased a snow shovel at a Wal-Mart store in Salina, Kansas. He broke the handle while scooping snow. Since the store was clear across town, he decided to buy a new shovel at a nearby hardware store. It was nearly twice the price of the original. Later in the week, a friend told him Wal-Mart would replace the broken one. He took it back and they did, no questions asked. However, when he tried to return the unused shovel to the neighbor-hood store, it was a different story. The clerk couldn't take it back. The assistant manager said it looked like it had been used. Finally, the owner reluctantly refunded his money. "I've never been back," he told us. "But I'll bet I've spent $500 at Wal-Mart since. I know if it isn't right, they'll make it right."

- *Out-of-stock on-sale items.* If you advertise a real bargain, make certain you have a good supply. Customers who antici-pate availability may not appreciate a raincheck. Coming back to redeem it can be a hassle.

8. *Customers want a friendly personal touch in a clean, fun place to shop.* Kmart, following Wal-Mart's example, now has greeters in nearly every store. Checkout personnel are trained to use your name if you pay by check or credit card. They try for the personal touch.

Stan Greil is a customer-service professional who travels around the country training employees in the art of giving superior service. He is a frequent shopper at the Wal-Mart Supercenter in Yukon, Oklahoma. He rates the level of service the store provides this way: "This Supercenter is an extraordi-nary customer-service machine. It's clean, friendly, and open twenty-four hours a day. It's a fun place to shop because everyone is focused on satisfying the customer."

Despite Greil's praise, smaller independent merchants have a definite advantage in this area. Wal-Mart associates may be friendly, but few can call many customers by name. Few of them possess real product knowledge.

These are areas where you can excel if you capitalize on your knowledge of customers and inventory. Don't underesti-mate the discounters in this area. You must work twice as hard as you ever have to ensure that your staff is providing what-ever-it-takes service. You can do it. Hundreds of small busi-nesses are keeping their customers by making their stores a shopping experience. You will read about several of these successes in the pages that follow.

Become a David!

We realize we have painted a pretty gloomy picture up till now. But don't despair; there is hope. You can survive, you can win your customers back, you can prosper and grow. We know you can because we've talked with hundreds of independents just like you and they are becoming Davids. They are learning how to counter the giants' strengths. We assume you bought this book so you can learn too.

These new Davids are using the ten survival strategies we describe in the next chapter. They are employing the tactics we've woven throughout the book. We share their stories. You can read about owners just like you—owners who are learning how to overcome the incredible bulk of the new breed. They are becoming smarter, faster, tougher, and more focused on running their business.

These new Davids are improving their businesses. Sales and profits are growing, and in some cases they are setting all-time highs. They may have had their backs to the wall, but they're no longer backing up. They are going forward with determination and vigor. They refuse to run and they won't hide. They are armed with information. They are winning because of their aggressive attitudes and because they are learning how to fight.

So read on friends, gather up some new information, and reenter the battle. You can win. You can prosper and grow. We'll supply the "how to" if you'll bring the "want to."

The Key Is Change

The survivors, the success stories, and the shining stars all have this in common: They are changing the way they think about and take care of customers.

This book is about change. *You cannot do business in the same old way and expect different results.* In the pages that follow, we offer many ideas to help you compete with the new breed of retail giants. To be successful, you must be willing to change. Change is your friend. Embrace it, welcome it, and use it to prosper.

Two

Ten Survival Strategies

Self-preservation is the first principle of our nature.
—Alexander Hamilton

Since 1987, we've worked with more than a thousand small businesses. In gathering information for this book, we visited with hundreds of successful business owners who shared some of the secrets of their successes. The experience and knowledge we've gathered from others, combined with our own "Main Street" years, could fill several volumes.

Our challenge became how to distill all this information into a concise, usable format. As we compared and contrasted the information we gathered in talking to hundreds of successful owners, we found that those who are competing effectively are focusing on making changes that can be summed up by the following ten survival strategies:

1. Focus completely on satisfying the customers.
2. Study the success of others.
3. Gather and analyze management information regularly.
4. Sharpen marketing skills.
5. Increase the customer's perception of value.
6. Position the business uniquely.
7. Eliminate waste.
8. Find something to improve every day.
9. Embrace change with a positive attitude.
10. Pull the trigger and start the battle.

In this chapter we will detail these survival strategies and guide you to other chapters of the book where you'll find examples and suggestions. This way you can focus on critical areas in your business before moving on to other chapters as you choose.

1. Develop a True Customer Focus

All businesses, regardless of type, have one common bond: They exist solely to serve and satisfy their customers. Neglecting or losing sight of this one fact has caused the early failure of millions of small businesses.

All of the successful companies we studied appreciate and understand the worth of their customers. When you develop a true customer focus, your customers will know it. Since all customers go where they are invited and stay where they are appreciated, you'll win not only your customers' loyalty but a valuable asset as well.

In analyzing the assets of businesses, you'll find the only asset with lasting value isn't even listed on the balance sheet. The only asset with lasting value is the customer.

A good example is commercial real estate. We've seen this long-term asset sell for pennies on the dollar of original investment. Inventories are frequently auctioned off at a fraction of their initial value. Savvy buyers often purchase fixtures and equipment for next to nothing from belly-up or bankrupt concerns. We've seen the value of every asset listed on the balance sheet disappear with the speed of biscuits in a boarding house. When the customers take their business elsewhere, the lasting value goes with them.

Understand the Three Customer Laws

There are three customer laws that are as real and consistent as the law of gravity. And, just like gravity, the laws are in force whether you understand them or not.

1. *Customers always go where they get good value.* Value is the *perceived* relationship between quality, quantity, and

price. Value is our customer's perception; that is, it is not what *we* think, but what *our customers* think.
2. *Customers always go where they are treated well.* "Whatever-it-takes customer service" will increase your customers' perception of value and improve their shopping experience at your business.
3. *When the value isn't obvious or when the level of service slips, the customer slips away.* Your customers simply walk out the front door and take their business elsewhere. They don't tell you that they are going; they just disappear. Successful business owners understand these laws and use them to maintain a strong customer focus.

Get Acquainted with Your Customer

As consultants, we've worked with some previously successful businesses that, over the years, had lost their competitive edge. One reason is that the owners and managers were often spending more time in the office and less time face-to-face with customers. A continuing lack of customer contact by a business can be fatal.

Owners learn what's going on in their stores by walking the aisles and talking to customers. Breed & Company, an Austin, Texas, store that specializes in hardware, housewares, and garden products, is a prime example of "management on the floor" success.

Breed's owner, Truman Breed, told us, "One of the reasons we've been successful against the retail giants is that I operate my business from the floor, not from the desk. Our customers like it that the owner is in the store, and it also keeps employees on their toes. You can't run your business from the desk and be successful. You need to get out onto the floor and talk to your customers." Breed averages eight hours on the floor every day.

The managing associates of Wal-Mart's Bentonville, Arkansas, office spend a lot of time in the stores talking to customers. Vice presidents, buyers, regional managers, and CEO alike constantly talk to customers, finding ways to please them even more. It's one tactic that helps them grab market share from others who know less about the people they serve.

As an independent business owner, you have a distinct advantage in this area. Because your customer base is smaller, you can and should be personally acquainted with many of your customers. As pleasant as Wal-Mart greeters may be, there is nothing as nice as being personally recognized by a friendly owner. It's said that the sweetest sound in our language is the sound of our own name. We agree. Smart owners take time to learn customers' names, and other personal information too. You can turn your knowledge into market share.

Identify a Target Customer

The successful business owners begin by determining who their target customers are. You can start this process by analyzing your present customers. The most likely customers to target for future sales are those most like your present customer base. By using demographic information such as age, sex, income level, and buying habits you can draw a portrait of your current customers.

Recently, we helped an upscale ladies' dress shop sketch a composite of their average shopper. Customers were asked to fill out a one-page questionnaire in return for a chance to win a $100 gift certificate. From the 600 responses we learned that the average customer was a female between the ages of 35 and 55. Respondents listed their income levels as more than $35,000, and most preferred using credit cards. Nearly half were single, and more than 80 percent resided within an area that encompassed four zip codes.

The store was able to use this information to mount a very successful direct-mail campaign. Remember, the more you know about your customers, the easier it is to serve them well.

Know *What* Your Customer Wants to Buy

Get to know your customers and focus on their wants and needs. Then you can predict what they will want to buy in the future.

Keep in mind that customers buy only two things. Those two things are "good feelings" and "solutions to problems." When you stay close to your customers every day, you'll know what problems they are trying to solve and you'll know what makes them feel good.

Mats Ola Palm, president and CEO of Volvo North America, recently discussed customers and customer satisfaction with Andrew S. Grove, president and CEO of Intel Corporation. The auto executive stated that his company focused on finding out what the customer wanted and on making sure that the company provided it.

The computer CEO scoffed at the "customer in charge" philosophy and pointed out that computer buyers didn't know what they needed because they didn't understand technology. The computer chief said his company didn't need the customer's input to build faster, more powerful, more complex computers.

Mr. Grove is way off the mark. We do know what we want in a computer. We don't want a model that is faster, more powerful, more complex, and costs more. We want a less expensive, portable model that is truly user friendly and comes with a manual written in everyday English.

Know *Why* Your Customer Wants to Buy

Consumers have many motivations. These motivations are traditionally classified as needs and wants.

Basic needs have been classified by psychologists and sociologists as food, clothing, and shelter. Wants are defined as products or services not required for survival, but advantageous to an improved quality of life.

As our standard of living increased from decade to decade, more wants were satisfied and items once considered luxuries became the norm. Now, most Americans would not consider electricity, indoor plumbing, and telephones as luxuries. Most people would tell you they need those things. As needs and wants become more difficult to separate, motivation becomes increasingly difficult to predict.

Nothing can help you more than having daily conversations with your customers. Part of developing a true customer focus is learning to listen to your customers and understanding why they make the buying decisions they do.

What motivates your customers will vary from business to business and will change from generation to generation. Talk to your customers every day to find out what motivates them to buy. Remember, all customers want value, convenience, recognition, to be made to feel they are important, solutions to their problems, cleanliness, and security.

Know *When* Your Customer Wants to Buy

One of the primary reasons Wal-Mart went roaring through many rural towns in the 1970s and 1980s with great success was it offered many choices to its customers. One of the more attractive options was extended evening and weekend hours.

As more women entered the workforce, the traditional retail hours of eight to five Monday through Friday and a half day on Saturday became an inconvenience. People who were working eight to five didn't have many shopping options.

A thought-provoking 1991 retail traffic study by Richard L. Mistele of the University of Wisconsin revealed that if shoppers are given a seven-day shopping option and have access to stores during extended evening hours, they will follow these general patterns:

1. Some 30 percent will shop from 8 A.M. to 5 P.M., Monday through Friday.
2. Another 30 percent will shop from 5 P.M. to closing, Monday through Friday.
3. The remaining 40 percent will shop on Saturdays and Sundays.

Last year a Kansas Kmart store manager confirmed that this research mirrored his store's sales volume patterns.

The implications are startling for independent business owners. Those who are hanging on to traditional retail hours, even if they open a full day on Saturday, are missing as much as 50 percent of the traffic.

The most significant impact may be that owners who aren't open when customers want to shop force their customers to do business with the competition. Traffic patterns, once they are established, are hard to break.

Know Where People Like to Shop

As we've pointed out, customers love new, clean, convenient, well-lighted stores that offer many choices and extended hours. When given a choice they will choose stores that offer as many of these options as possible. They will avoid stores with limited parking, difficult access, unattractive merchandising, limited business hours, and unfriendly personnel. Are we suggesting that every small merchant move into a new facility? No, but survival will require changes such as upgrading showrooms and investing in new fixtures, lighting, etc.

2. Study the Success of Others

It's simplistic, but true: If you want to be a smart businessperson, study smart businesses. All of the successful companies we studied for this book learned from the good business practices of others. The smart ones ask a lot of questions, keep their eyes wide open, and adapt good ideas whenever they can.

You can steal good ideas from many sources and adapt them to your situation. Three of the best sources are your competitors, your peers, and everyone else.

Study the Competition

Today's successful owners are constantly learning about and from their competition. If you're faced with stiff competition from Wal-Mart, Walgreen's, or Home Depot, find out more about them.

Sam Walton studied his competitors. He read their annual reports and spent time in their stores. He observed, he borrowed, he adapted, and he succeeded.

To learn about your competitors, study all published information. Review their annual reports, SEC 10-K filings, and industry evaluations. Call a librarian or stockbroker for specifics. We have included sources of information in Chapter Nine.

Remember to visit competitors' stores. Look at the way they merchandise different departments, see what they display in high-traffic areas and near the checkout areas, and observe the type of customer who is shopping there. Yogi Berra said, "You can see a lot just by looking around."

Learn From Your Peers

Join or become active in a trade association for your industry. Attend markets, buying shows, and trade meetings. Ask questions, take notes, and listen. Most successful owners use these techniques. They also take time to visit merchants in other parts of the country. By viewing the operations of others, they gather great ideas for merchandising, promotions, purchasing sources, and pricing.

When we were in the lawn and garden business, we once visited a fellow Snapper mower dealer in the Kansas City, Missouri, area. This high-volume dealer displayed a Snapper riding mower standing up. He showed us how easy it was to point out the unit's simple features this way. In addition, the display required less space, which freed up space for other products.

Gather Good Ideas From Everyone

Not all good ideas come from competitors and merchants in your industry. Every person you know is a source of good business ideas. Your clergyman, your barber or hairdresser, owners of unrelated businesses and customers are all potential idea people.

You must adapt a mind-set wherein you consider every situation you encounter as an opportunity to gather ideas to use in your business. When you're looking for ideas, they will come. When they do, steal like a burglar and soak up like a sponge. Adapt those ideas and make them your own.

3. Gather and Analyze Management Information

The new breed of big-box merchants have all invested heavily in technology. The advantage they get from their investment is management information at their fingertips. They know sales figures from yesterday, last week, and last month. They know their current level of orders in progress, inventory in transit, and inventory on the shelves. Their computers allow them to know what's going on so they can make wise decisions based on accurate, timely information.

Contrast that with many smaller independents who, for the most part, don't know their status from month to month. Many of the business owners we've worked with are still getting financial statements once a year, and often they do not understand exactly what the numbers mean. By the time they get the information, most of it is out of date and is of little use other than to offer some historical perspective.

As we interviewed candidates for our success stories it became apparent that those who were thriving and prospering knew a lot about their business. For them, knowledge of their business was a top priority. They have developed systems—sometimes manual, often automated—to monitor the following four areas:

1. Financial information
2. Customer information
3. Industry information
4. Market trends and information

In our workshops, we are often asked what information is most important and how to collect it. We detail the fundamental types of information small businesses need and offer tips on using that data later in the book.

In terms of collecting the information, there is no long-term substitute for technology. We're convinced that the businesses that are able to stand up to the new breed will be computerized. It will take commitment, capital, and time. However, the benefits will far outweigh the effort.

4. Sharpen Your Marketing Skills

Marketing is every activity aimed at attracting and satisfying customers. Marketing spans nearly every aspect of business operations from Advertising to Zeroing in on your target customer. Like all other parts of small-business management, marketing must be focused on the customer.

There are six basic elements often referred to as the marketing mix—that dictate overall marketing success. They are the six P's of *price, product* (or service), *place, promotion, people,* and *positioning.* We believe that these key elements, in the proper relationship, are a necessary foundation on which you can build an effective marketing plan.

The Price Factor

Price is one of the most critical of the six elements. Every person who has an average IQ and even a lick of common sense wants to purchase the highest quality and/or largest quantity at the lowest price.

Although not all products are price sensitive (visible), usually the price is more visible than the quality. For example, we may be considering the purchase of a compact stereo unit and comparing a unit that sells for $500 with another priced at $300. Since they look similar, have nearly identical features, sound alike, and make the same advertising claims, we might assume that the quality is the same.

Since most of us cannot tell the quality of a stereo from looks, sound, or brand name alone, we'll go for low price every time if we perceive little if any quality differential.

The Product Factor

The product element refers to either the tangible products or less easily defined service your business may provide to your customers. If the product element is off, you won't have anything to sell that your customers want to buy. Therefore, you won't have any reason to be in the marketplace. This is why many small businesses are either barely hanging on or going out of business. Regardless of the level of customer support you provide and the low, low price you offer, your products and services must be wanted or needed.

The Place Factor

If you operate a business where the customer must come to you, having the right site may be the difference between long-term survival and early failure. Great locations have kept poorly run businesses in operation for years, while well-managed ventures have struggled due to poor site selection.

Picking the right location is not an exact science, but you can learn from the experiences of others. The late Sam Walton picked out early potential store locations from the air. He studied traffic flows and building patterns for the towns they were considering. Wal-Mart's success in picking the right locations was based on locating their stores to serve a trade area. Walton knew if people had to drive close to or right by his store on the way into downtown they would stop to see what Wal-Mart was all about.

As you evaluate your location, consider items such as actual traffic counts, proximity to competitors, construction trends (growth patterns), cost of land or space, zoning restrictions, tax abatement potential, and insurance costs. There is an old adage that applies to selecting a location: Decide in haste, repent in leisure.

Rebecca Linton, who owns Rebecca's Lingerie in Montgomery, Alabama, made just such a mistake. She selected a store site in a courtyard shopping center that was all wrong for the type of customer she was targeting. "There were a lot of people who would not come to the center because they felt it was above their means," she said, "and that they didn't have the clothes to shop there; much less could they afford to walk into a store. That wasn't what I wanted at all." After moving to a new location, she enjoyed healthy sales growth.

The Promotion Factor

Operating a business without proper promotion is like winking in the dark. You know that you're doing it, but no one else does. All businesses—large or small, home-based or at the mall, cash rich or up against the wall—can gain customers from good promotion.

We don't believe you have to spend a fortune to grow your business. In fact, we've found more than fifty ways to promote your business for next to nothing. These shoestring strategies work because they are focused on the customer. The main purpose of all promotion is to get the right message to the right person at the right time. We refer to these as the three R's of promotion: the right message, the right audience, and the right time.

Like the six P's of the marketing mix, the three R's are basic but necessary. Wal-Mart spends little of its promotion budget on promoting big sale items. Instead it continually hammers home the "best quality at the lowest price" message to its target market.

Wal-Mart has proved that you don't have to spend a lot to have effective promotions. While most large retailers spend 2 to 3 percent of sales on advertising and promotion, Wal-Mart spends less than 1 percent. It can spend less because it has the right products and the right price, and is in the right place to serve its customers effectively. Wal-Mart uses the final two elements in the mix, people and positioning, to round out its marketing mix.

The People Factor

People make up another important spoke in your marketing wheel. Whether you call them employees, coworkers, or associates, people can add to the value perception of your business—that is, if they are friendly, well trained, and customer focused.

If you truly want to distinguish your business from the megastores, people can make the difference. The successful businesses we researched are people smart. They pay above-average wages, teach in-depth product knowledge and customer service skills, and provide a challenging environment to work in. They empower their employees to solve customer problems and make independent decisions.

Wal-Mart is above average in this area. In a recent customer survey of all major retail chains, Wal-Mart associates helped their company achieve a second-place finish in the customer service race. Only Seattle-based Nordstrom's, a legend in the fine art of serving customers, finished higher.

How can a price driven, big-box discounter like Wal-Mart outservice such notables as Saks Fifth Avenue, Bloomingdale's, Dillard's, and Marshall Field's? The answer can be found in the opening paragraph of Wal-Mart's 1993 annual report, ". . . it is their [Wal-Mart associates'] dedication and hard work that continue to make the difference at Wal-Mart."

Large business or small, people make the difference. Don't forget to factor your associates into your marketing mix.

The Positioning Factor

Positioning is the art of locating a niche that matches customer needs with the unique skills and abilities of the business owner and associates. It means finding a place or position where you can excel.

For Lee Sherman, a Tulsa appliance dealer, positioning meant focusing on the narrow market of built-in appliances. "The competition was willing to give us this area," Sherman said. "We saw an opportunity to serve a small, but growing, group of customers, and we jumped on it."

Positioning is also the image of your business you create in the minds of your potential customers. Your goal is to create a unique, positive picture in your prospect's mind. Positioning separates your business from all others. It emphasizes your uniqueness and differentiates your benefits from those of all others.

Every business has a market position or image. How you place yourself in the mind of the customer is critical.

Paying close attention to all factors relating to your marketing mix can take pressure off any single factor. For example, you may be able to skimp a little on the quality (provide less product) if you keep the price low. You may be able to reduce promotion costs if you locate conveniently and provide good value.

5. Change the Value Perception

Your customers define value in their own ways. They weigh the quality or quantity you offer in exchange for their dollars. If you provide a superior product or a large quantity, your customers perceive more value. As customers, it is a judgment each of us makes every time we shop.

Most independent merchants have a reputation for charging higher prices than the big-box merchants. Usually this reputation is justified. Their prices on comparable items often *are* higher. This perception of higher pricing is often perpetuated by the owners themselves as they lament the fact that Wal-Mart is selling at a price lower than their cost for the very same items. In Chapter Ten, we show you a seven-step variable pricing method that will help you change the value perception of your business.

There is no easy, three-step solution to an issue as complex as value perception. One thing we can tell you for certain: The days of taking an across-the-board markup on products are over. By using a variable pricing strategy you can match the discounters' prices on price-sensitive (visible) items and regain that profit margin elsewhere.

You don't have to have the lowest price, but your prices must be close. Recently some discounters and category killers have started guaranteeing "the lowest price" or they'll give you the difference. These low-price guarantees do have an impact on the minds of the consumers.

However, Barry Steinberg, owner of Direct Tire in Watertown, Massachusetts, believes you cannot compete on price alone. Steinberg says, "Competing on price alone is like putting your head in front of a shotgun. . . . You're just never going to win."

We agree with him, but that doesn't mean that you can't earn a profit by staying focused on what customers really want and need, and giving it to them. Hundreds of small independent owners just like you are finding ways to stay close on price, and making up the difference by providing a package of values that the giants can't match.

6. Position for Uniqueness

As we pointed out earlier in this chapter, positioning is the ability to match your uniqueness with the needs and wants of your target customers. This strategy is also known as "niche picking."

There are chinks in the armor of the giants. By positioning your business well, you can carve out a section of the market where you are able to deliver better than your competitors.

To position effectively, you must be different, stand out, and be memorable. You aren't Wal-Mart, so don't try to be just like it. Study its success, learn from it, but position your business in those areas where the megastores can't compete effectively with you. Look for areas where you can say "We're better because. . . ."

7. Eliminate Waste

Thomas Edison said, "Waste is worse than loss. The time is coming when every person who lays claim to ability will keep the question of waste before him constantly. The scope of thrift is limitless."

One of the keys to controlling waste is to plan your spending. Create an annual budget and analyze all expenses against your budget. Constant comparison of actual and budget expenses will allow you to pick up unexpected increases early on. Then you can take immediate steps to control the waste.

The late Sam Walton became the richest man in America in 1985. He learned early in his life the value of eliminating waste. Perhaps the founder of Wal-Mart Stores studied the writings of Cicero, who wrote in 46 B.C., "Men do not realize how great an income thrift is."

Several years ago, as we started to study the Wal-Mart phenomenon, we began to track the company's operating, selling, and general and administrative expenses as a percentage of sales. The percentage has always been low, but according to its annual report, it dipped to a flat 15 percent in fiscal 1994. Contrast that to Sears, Roebuck, whose operating expenses still exceed 30 percent after major cost cutting during the last two years.

Many small-business owners carry operating expense loads of as much as 40 to 45 percent of sales. While many of these expenses are justified, others simply are not. They have become a part of the business and are as accepted as the middle-age spread.

Unfortunately, when you're up against the Wal-Marts, there isn't any room for middle-age spread. The big-box merchants are young, lean, and work hard to stay in shape. Their fitness may be found in their operating expense levels and their inventory turns.

For all of you who have responsibility for managing the bottom line, here are eight elements to consider when eliminating waste:

1. Remember that every dollar saved from your current operating costs goes directly to your bottom line.
2. You must justify *every expense*—every day, every month, every year.
3. You must eliminate nonessential expenses as soon as you identify them.
4. Start with an analysis of your five largest expense categories. Are you getting the maximum return for each dollar spent?
5. Remember, time is money and eliminating time wasters saves you money.
6. You should carefully evaluate any inventory that turns at 50 percent or less than your overall average turns. Clear out slow-moving items unless the profit margin is high enough to justify the slow movement.
7. Watch your spending to control waste. Sometimes a purchase will seem justified initially; then when the backside costs are added in, it isn't such a value. A $2,000 computer may seem a justifiable expense until you add in a $500 printer, $300 modem and $1,200 for software. The backside costs are as much as the initial investment.

8. Remember that when you misspend one dollar you've really wasted two—the dollar you misspent and the dollar you could have spent well.

8. Use the Kaizen Method of Improvement

The Japanese have a word for their informal Total Quality Management process. The word is *kaizen* (ky'zen). Kaizen means "continuing improvement involving everyone."

The successful business owners we interviewed as we did research for this book are practicing kaizen whether or not they know the word. They know their future business depends on how well they managed their last opportunity to satisfy their customer. If the last experience was a positive one for your customers, they'll come back. If it wasn't, they will find another supplier for the products or services they've been buying from you.

We've dedicated all of Chapter Twelve to help you understand the kaizen theory and to give you a list of thought starters. Use this list to find a few areas to start on. Get your employees involved. We believe you won't find it difficult to find something to improve.

9. Embrace Change with a Positive Attitude

Zig Ziglar has said, "It's your attitude that determines your attitude." *Attitude,* according to the dictionary, is "the state of mind with which we approach any given situation." We are in control of our own attitudes. Kmart doesn't control our attitudes, and Best Buy can't make us have a bad day unless we let it. We are in charge of how we choose to compete. The most successful small competitors are keeping a positive attitude.

We know we are at risk of sounding like motivational speakers here, but the fact is that having a positive attitude is one of the common factors we found. If you don't stay positive, your employees know it and your customers will see it too. Most folks won't hang around negative people very long.

Even having a good attitude won't keep you in business if you continue to do business in the same old way. If you are not happy with how your business is doing you will have to make changes.

It seems the longer we've been doing something the same way, the more likely we are to resist change. However, the small-business owners who are prospering in the shadow of the giants have all made changes.

Many change product lines, pricing strategies, store lay-outs, merchandising tactics, and open-for-business hours. Others expand services offered, raise the quality of inventory, and beef up promotion activity. The key to survival is change. Like the kaizen strategy, change is constant and ongoing.

You must not fear change. You will find, as President Franklin D. Roosevelt said, "We have nothing to fear but fear itself." Instead, embrace change. Change is your friend. Keep a positive attitude and you'll find that change can be fun and beneficial to your business.

When you employ the kaizen strategy of continuing improvement, you're embracing change. As you read the remainder of this book, you'll find dozens of suggestions for change.

10. Pull the Trigger and Start the Battle

One of the most successful oilmen in Texas classifies people into two categories: "Ready, fire, aim" folks, and "Ready, aim, aim, aim . . ." folks.

We believe small-business owners are often in the latter group. They go to the workshops, buy the books, listen to tapes, and consider many options, but they take no action. They're in the "ready, aim, aim, aim . . ." category.

Nearly all the successful small-business owners we know are "Ready, fire, aim" advocates. They prefer to pull the trigger rather than wait for the perfect shot. After the shot hits, they can see how far from the mark they are, adjust their aim, reload, and fire again. They may waste a little ammunition, but if they waste time squinting at the target, they'll miss some good opportunities.

There is a point, after you've analyzed the situation, where you've got to take action. You've got to pull the trigger. This book won't help you unless you put some of the suggestions to work. We challenge you to read every line in this book carefully.

Find a few key tactics to implement and pull the trigger. Try something. If it doesn't give you perfect results, adjust your aim and fire again.

Remember, today's decisions are tomorrow's realities. Pull the trigger and enter the fray. Often the hardest step is the first one.

Three

Attracting Customers

Put all your eggs in one basket and watch the basket.

—Mark Twain

One question that haunts every owner of a retail or service business at one time or another is, "What can I do to attract more customers to my store?" The dream shared by all of them is to have plenty of customers, all eager to purchase the products and services they offer. For most, it's a daily consideration; for others it's more like a waking nightmare, the cause of many sleepless nights.

The megamerchants have literally millions of dollars to spend on advertising and knowledgeable, full-time professionals to direct their aggressive advertising campaigns. This is one battlefield where you will never emerge a victor.

But that doesn't mean you have to feel defeated. Maybe the best attitude to take is that of Berlin Myers, Jr. He is an owner of a lumber and building supply center in Summerville, South Carolina, not far from some of the biggest heavyweights in the business: Home Depot, Lowe's, and HQ.

When a Lowe's superstore opened right down the street, he saw it not as a threat but as an opportunity. "I only have one regret: I wish I was closer to it," he said. "They obviously have very deep pockets. They obviously attract a great number of people that I can't attract. They have a wider market penetration, they're able to spend literally millions of dollars in advertising . . . but in spite of what they say, they can't be all things to all people.

"Consequently, there are people who walk out of that store without having their needs satisfied," he continued.

"We'd love to be a position to service that business. They're only as much a threat as I allow them to be."

In this chapter, we'll show you how to position your business for success and give you some ideas you can use to attract some of those customers who are looking for something different from what the new breed has to offer.

We also explore the various aspects of marketing, a critical element of your success. Marketing includes everything you do that attracts customers, convinces them to buy from you, inspires them to keep coming back, and excites them enough to tell others about you.

Know Your Strengths and Improve on Your Weaknesses

Before you begin to draft a plan of attack, make sure you have an accurate assessment of your strengths and weaknesses. Answer the following questions:

1. Do you have *products or services* that customers want to buy?
2. Are you selling them at a *price* your customers are willing to pay?
3. Is your *place* convenient and attractive to your customers?
4. Are the *people* who represent your business (your employees) good ambassadors for your business? Are they friendly, knowledgeable, and skillful?

Do Some Simple Research

You can find the answers to the questions above by doing some simple marketing research. Once you have a thorough knowledge of your customers and their needs, you can build your customer base two basic ways:

1. By finding other customers like the customers you already have

2. By modifying your products and services to better meet the needs of current and future customers

Your methods of marketing research can be as simple or as complex as you want, but don't overlook the easiest method of all, which is *talk to your customers*. Wal-Mart founder Sam Walton walked the floors of his stores, talking to customers and finding out what they thought. You can do the same thing: Walk your aisles and notice what's happening.

Make it easy for customers to tell you what they think—either orally or in writing. Design some simple customer surveys and place them where customers will notice them, or *ask* your customers to fill them out and put them in an in-store box or drop them in the mail. (Provide a postage-paid card.)

These surveys can be as simple as the one shown in Exhibit 1 or a little more detailed, like Exhibit 2. First decide what you'd like to know and then word the questions in simple language to find the answers. Keep the surveys and analyze them daily or weekly.

You can do a little more structured research with a *focus group*, which is merely a discussion session where you talk to current customers (or potential customers) to find out their opinions about your business.

Invite five to ten people to this group discussion and give them an incentive for participating, such as a gift certificate or a lunch. You may want to find an impartial professional to help who is skilled at asking questions and encouraging thoughtful answers. The questions should be open-ended ones, such as "What do you like about our store?" and "What products do you wish we carried?" It's also a good idea to record the meeting, either with an audio- or videotape.

Still another way to get customer feedback is to use a much less structured approach, such as the one undertaken by Phelps County Bank, in the small Missouri town of Rolla. Faced with megacompetition from two big bank holding companies with familiar names, CEO Emma Lou Brent set out to rebuild a different kind of bank that could compete. The staff dissected virtually every aspect of their bank, then began the

Exhibit 1. A simple customer survey.

We'd like to know what you think about our business so we can serve you better. Please answer the following questions.

  1. Did you receive prompt, courteous service?

        _____ Yes _____ No

        Comments: _____

        _____

  2. Was the person who served you helpful and informative?

        _____ Yes _____ No

        Comments: _____

        _____

  3. Were you satisfied with the available selection of products?

        _____ Yes _____ No

        Comments: _____

        _____

  4. Were you satisfied with the product(s) you purchased?

        _____ Yes _____ No

        Comments: _____

        _____

  5. Would you do business with us again?

        _____ Yes _____ No

        Comments: _____

        _____

reconstruction. After the pieces were all back together, they wanted some feedback about what customers thought about their "new" bank. "We really went out on a limb," she said, "by asking customers to tell a story of employees who went out of their way to help them."

The survey/promotion was dubbed the "You bet we can

Exhibit 2. A more detailed customer survey.

Your opinion is very valuable to us. Please check the appropriate answer below each question to let us know how we're doing.

1. How friendly are our store associates (employees)?
   _____ Very friendly   _____ Moderately friendly
   _____ Not friendly   _____ Very unfriendly

2. How knowledgeable are our employees about our products?
   _____ Very knowledgeable   _____ Fairly knowledgeable
   _____ Not knowledgeable   _____ Quite ignorant

3. How would you rate the cleanliness of our business?
   _____ Very clean   _____ Reasonably clean
   _____ Somewhat dirty   _____ Very dirty

4. How convenient are our store hours?
   _____ Very convenient   _____ Reasonably convenient
   _____ Somewhat inconvenient   _____ Quite inconvenient

5. How quickly did we respond to your needs?
   _____ Very quickly   _____ Reasonably quickly
   _____ Somewhat slowly   _____ Very slowly

6. How would you rate our prices compared to other places where you shop?
   _____ Quite expensive   _____ Fairly expensive
   _____ About average   _____ Inexpensive

7. What do you think about our selection of products?
   _____ Large selection   _____ Somewhat large selection
   _____ Fairly small selection   _____ Very small selection

8. Overall, what is your opinion of this store?
   _____ Excellent   _____ Good   _____ Fair   _____ Very poor

9. Will you shop with us again?
   _____ Absolutely yes   _____ Probably yes
   _____ Probably no   _____ Absolutely no

cancan" and illustrated by caricatures of employees doing the cancan. The slogan was "Who have you seen doing it?", meaning providing the ultimate in customer service.

Ask the question in other companies and the responses could be embarrassingly few, but at PCB literally hundreds of responses poured in. Not only did the promotion call attention to the bank's commitment to having fun while providing service, Brent said, but it also was the catalyst for ongoing customer assurance surveys.

Get Your House in Order

There are many things that can make big impressions on your customers—and have a direct impact on their willingness to do business with you. The nice thing is you don't have to have a huge marketing budget to make big strides in these areas:

1. *The hours and days you're open.* The new breed of retail giants has researched when their customers want to buy. To compete with them, you should know when *your* customers want to shop and adjust your hours accordingly. You don't have to match the twenty-four-hour operations of the retail giants, but you must stay open longer than you did a few years ago.

2. *The atmosphere you create inside and outside your business.* Your business has an "attitude," and the customers can sense it as soon as they walk in the door.

3. *How you treat your customers.* Welcome customers with friendly smiles and a helpful attitude.

4. *How you treat your employees and the skills you give them to deal effectively with customers.* Your employees reflect the attitude of your business, and you'd better treat them like they're important too.

5. *How you answer the telephone.* You may be the world's best at attracting people to your business, but if customers encounter a rude or indifferent person on the telephone, their fingers—and their pocketbooks—will keep on walking.

Make A Plan of Attack

You now know a little about your strengths and weaknesses, and you've taken some preliminary steps to put your house in order. It's time to devise a plan of attack.

To paraphrase a line from *Alice in Wonderland:* If you don't know where you want to go, any road will take you there. The same is true in business. Know where you are going, and you can build the road that will take you there.

Draft a marketing plan to analyze where you are, where you want to go, and how you're going to get there. It's not permanent, not carved in stone. It should be a constantly evolving aspect of your business, so review and revise it frequently. Your answers to these questions will be the blueprint of your marketing plan:

1. *What business are you in?* Be specific. Jot down a basic description of the type of business you are in or the service you are selling.

2. *Who are your customers now?* Sketch a profile of them by looking at your current customer records. Computerized businesses may be able to sort data in a variety of categories, and nonautomated businesses can get an idea of their customer base from information pulled from a variety of sources. Categorize customers by:

- Age
- Gender
- Geographic location
- Occupation
- Income level
- Marital status
- Family size: number and ages of children
- Education
- Most common payment method
- Leisure activities

Use the data to paint an accurate profile about your customers, including where they live, how much money they spend with you, and other important facts. You'll have some clues for finding future customers.

What you are building is a profile of your customers that will help you know how and where to reach them. Your description of your customers should be so thorough and well-researched that you could spot a likely target customer on the street.

Many small-business people think that everyone is their target customer. It's just not true. If you own a camping equipment store, you probably won't want to advertise in a women's fashion magazine.

3. *What can you do to add value to the products you sell?* As we entered the 1990s, a sluggish world economy sparked a new rallying cry for consumers: "We want value!" While this doesn't necessarily mean the lowest price, it does mean the best deal for the features they want.

Stress the products and services you offer that will provide added value such as free delivery, in-store financing, an extended service policy, no-hassle return policies, a toll-free number, a frequent-buyer plan, or an excellent service department.

Jim Myers Drug in Tuscaloosa, Alabama, offers a long string of services that he believes provides value for his customers and gives the pharmacy a lot of credibility. He offers free delivery, a convenient drive-up window, twenty-four-hour emergency service, and an education center where customers can get a wealth of information about health topics in general and their medical condition in particular.

His pharmacy was the first in his area to offer customers blood pressure, cholesterol, and blood sugar screenings, as well as a variety of free informational seminars. As a result of these and other effective marketing tactics, sales in Myers' pharmacy have shot up 32 percent in the last three years even within their highly competitive market.

4. *How much money can you invest and how often?* It's an old adage, but a true one, that "you have to spend money to make money," and it's no more true than in setting your advertising budget. When times get hard, you look for ways to cut expenses. It's a perfectly natural reaction. One of the first things on the chopping block is often the advertising budget. Bad idea.

If necessary, find other ways to trim the budget, but don't make the cuts in advertising. Advertising is always a necessity, but it is even more important when business is slow and your customers aren't exactly beating a path to your door. Don't even think of your promotional efforts as expenses. Count them as *investments* in future business. Strive to establish a generous, but realistic budget.

There are many guidelines for establishing a budget, but for small businesses perhaps the best way to set your marketing budget is to base it on a percentage of sales and/or on the goals and the tactics you will use.

Learn what others in your field are doing by checking with your trade associations, but don't spend more than *you* can afford. Set priorities and spend more in situations where you can reasonably expect to get the best results.

5. *How can you reach your customers?* Sit down with your staff and brainstorm some ways that you might reach your target customer. List *where* you will find your customers as well as what *tools* you might use to reach them. What publications are they likely to read?

If you own a building supply company, you can reach target customers at a home and garden show. If you own a pharmacy, many of your target customers have recently been in a physician's office. Target them there with a short brochure about your quick, accurate filling of prescriptions and your delivery service.

As you explore with your staff ways to reach your customers, let your imaginations run wild and encourage everyone to suggest ideas without rejecting any of them. A sixty-second television spot during the Superbowl might not be feasible this year, but maybe you'll get some useful, more practical ideas that you *can* use. Be creative; then narrow the choices, make your selections, and fit them into your budget.

6. *Who are your competitors?* List them by name. What are their strengths and weaknesses? Research your competition by visiting their stores. Know what they are selling, what type of customers are in their store, and what prices they are charging for the same merchandise that you sell.

Watch what your competitors like Wal-Mart are offering. Beyond the "everyday low price" that they're touting, they offer a wealth of marketing ideas that can work for even the smallest businesses. You just have to know what to look for. They have greeters who meet you at the door with a smile and a warm welcome. The shopping carts they offer will make it easy to buy large quantities. Their large, easy-to-read signs direct you to the area you're looking for. If you pay by check or credit card, they'll make a point to call you by name when they say their final thank-you.

These actions are not done accidentally. Wal-Mart knows that people love to be acknowledged, that people who take carts tend to buy more, and that we all love to hear the sound of our own names.

7. *Why should someone buy from you instead of your competition?* What advantages do you have over the competition? What makes you unique? If you don't have clear, concise answers to these questions, how do you expect your customers to know?

Fisher Office Products, a company in Boise, Idaho, accomplishes this with its one-page flyer outlining the advantages of shopping at Fisher's instead of the discounters. (See Exhibit 3.) Such head-to-head comparisons can be very effective in showing customers the hidden benefits of doing business with you.

Look at all the things that make you special in the eyes of your customers and tell them what benefits you give them that make their lives easier, more fun, healthier, more exciting, tastier, safer, or more satisfying.

If your marketing program is effective enough to get your customer's attention, remember that he or she is tuned in to only one station: WII-FM—the call letters for "What's In It For Me." Sell the benefits.

Perfect the Fine Art of Niche Picking

A good way to effectively compete with the retail giants is to position yourself where the competition isn't. In other words, find your niche—that section of the market where you are uniquely positioned to deliver better than your competitors.

The implications of positioning for small businesses are:

Exhibit 3. A retailer's flyer informing customers of the advantage of patronizing the retailer rather than discounters.

	RETAIL STORE		DISTRIBUTION CENTER
	825 W. IDAHO ST.	P.O. BOX 1616	575 E. 42ND ST.
FISHER'S	83702	BOISE, IDAHO	83714
OFFICE PRODUCTS	FAX 208-343-6009	83701	FAX 208-378-4606

A **BASICNET** DEALER   **(208) 378-1200**

TO OUR VALUED CUSTOMERS:

There's a lot of talk these days about low-price items at discount stores. With big advertising budgets, these national chains tempt you to their stores with products priced at cost. But the hidden costs can be substantial.

We thought a comparison chart would be useful to calculate the true cost of your office products. We appreciate your business and will continue to serve the Treasure Valley as we have for over 50 years.

FISHER'S VERSUS DISCOUNTERS COMPARISON CHART

	Discounters	*FISHER'S*
Liability Risk	Substantial. Employees drive their cars, which may not be insured for business use, and also risk injury when lifting heavy items.	None. Your employees stay in the office, we do the driving, hauling, and lifting.
Labor Cost	High. You pay your employees to drive to the discounter, find and select products, then wait in line to pay.	None. We fill your orders and deliver. Emergency orders are processed immediately.
Placing Orders	Cumbersome. You must call an 800 number and talk to someone unfamiliar with your business and your location.	Easy. Call local number and talk to one of our customer service representatives; fax your order; schedule a regular visit from an account manager; or we will install a terminal for direct access to our computer.
Delivery	High fee charged, except for large orders. Or your employees can load, transport, then unload. High fee for furniture, and you assemble.	Free. No minimum—including furniture, and we assemble at no extra charge.
Returns	You return product. If manufacturer supplies warranty, you contact manufacturer.	No Hassle return policy. Call, we pick up and resolve problem. We take responsibility for every item we sell.
Sales and Support Staff	You must serve yourself, usually very few, if any, experienced personnel.	Knowledgeable sales staff. Career employees specializing in machines, furniture, and supplies. Factory-trained technicians available to install, service, and repair all office machines.

Exhibit 3. (continued)

	Discounters	FISHER'S
Special Orders	Not encouraged.	Up to 60,000 items to choose from. We research sources for special items.
Pricing	Low on advertised specials.	Overall low prices, not just on advertised specials.
Usage Reports	None.	Free monthly, quarterly, annual, detailed usage reports—even by department.
Ownershp	Out of State.	Local.
Buying Power	Fisher's has more BUYING POWER through its $1.5 billion buying group than ANY other office products buying group in the country.	

- Position yourself where your competition isn't.
- Target markets that are too small for the retail giants.
- Target markets that value service above price.
- Target areas where your competition doesn't do well or products that your competition doesn't sell.
- In short, *find the need and fill it.*

Barry Steinberg, who owns Direct Tire, a tire and auto service business in Watertown, Massachusetts, carved out his niche by targeting customers who want to be a little pampered and will pay a premium for the privilege. "We let the public know that we are more expensive," he readily admits. "We can't compete with our competition in the arena of price and still have loaner cars, employees who dress nicely in suits, and serve coffee and croissants. We can't compete in the arena of price, and they cannot compete with us in the arena of customer service."

Finding your niche takes a lot of hard work, knowledge of your customers, careful planning, commitment, and patience. The key is: Do your marketing research and learn what your customers want and what your competitors don't have. Then find a way to communicate to your customers that you're better than anyone else.

Capitalize on Trends

As you define how you're going to position your business, consider the trends that have developed in the marketplace over the last few years. Lifestyles have changed, needs have changed, and customers have changed.

Here are some growing markets which have come about as a result of changes in our society:

- *Women.* One of the most significant social changes that has occurred in our country during the last century is the increase in the numbers of women in the workforce. In 1900, one woman in five was employed outside the home. During the 1940s, one of every three women was employed. Today, roughly 60 percent of women are working outside their homes.

More people are now employed by women-owned businesses than by the *Fortune* 500, according to *Working Woman* magazine. The trend is likely to continue as women are opening new businesses at a rate about double that of their male counterparts.

Opportunities open up when you consider these statistics. The purchasing power of women is growing along with their stature in business, and many of the buying decisions are now made by them. Speak to them.

- *Older people.* This over-fifty group, which a famous talk-show host refers to as "seasoned citizens," is the fastest-growing segment of the population.

According to recent statistics, more than 63 million people are in this age bracket, and the number will explode as baby boomers reach the "big five-oh." Don't forget older customers in your marketing plans, as a substantial number live in households with incomes of $50,000 and more. And much of that income is discretionary.

Savvy business owners are finding ways to target this important group, but watch how you refer to them. Use the term *older* or *mature*, not *elderly* or *senior citizen*. In your photographs, show them as *actively* old—healthy, vibrant, well educated, and well traveled.

You might be surprised to learn that the magazine with the largest circulation in the United States is *Modern Maturity*, the member publication for the American Association of Retired Persons (AARP). Its circulation is more than 22 million.

▪ *Ethnic groups.* Many small-business owners recognize the huge purchasing power that rests in the hands of ethnic groups. The Hispanic and Asian markets have combined purchasing power of more than $215 billion.

In the future, ethnic groups may well command an even higher portion of market share. New population projections from the Census Bureau indicate that by 1995 fertility rates in order from highest to lowest will be (1) Hispanics, (2) Asians, (3) African-Americans, and (4) whites.

▪ *Kids.* Kids wield a lot of purchasing power. They're really a threefold market. As a *current market,* they have billions of dollars to spend. *American Demographics* reported that parents given preteens as much as $14.4 billion a year to spend as they wish.

As *influencers,* they influence decisions—more than $130 billion worth—on everything from breakfast cereals and hamburgers, to sneakers, toys, and family vacation destinations. As a *future market,* it may be worth it to build loyalty for future business because cultivated customers are more loyal.

Kids love clubs. They love to get mail. They're concerned about the environment, so address that in your marketing, if it's appropriate. Marketing experts also suggest you make sure that clubs are free, fun, and accessible.

Food businesses have been quick to capitalize on the kid market. You don't have to look much farther than McDonald's with its playgrounds and in-store promotions. When it's time to eat a hamburger for lunch or dinner, where do you think the kids want to go?

How can you capitalize on the kids' market? For small-business owners, it might be as simple as designating one area of the store FOR KIDS ONLY. Equipped with toys and perhaps bounded by a plastic "fence," kids can play contentedly while their parents shop.

Look at clubs, giveaways, and fun when targeting kids, and remember, if the kids are happy, parents may spend more time in your store.

▪ *Busy people.* Everyone's in a hurry these days, with almost every waking moment filled with working, commuting, families, socializing, and exercising. Victims of "time poverty" are looking for value, speed, and convenience.

A study by Yankelovich Partners found that consumers no longer need the latest gadget or gizmo and are showing less and less interest in shopping. The study also found that retailers were driving customers away. While there were some disturbing facts revealed, there are some opportunities for small retail and service businesses to position themselves to provide the things that large price-driven competitors don't have. Findings that emerged from the study indicate that today's consumers want speed, value, and convenience. Moreover, many will not tolerate poor service. For example, 62 percent of those surveyed said they had left the store without buying something because sales clerks weren't available. Almost as many, 60 percent, left without a purchase because the sales clerk couldn't answer a question they asked.

What are the implications for retail and service businesses? Small businesses can win by having enough skilled, knowledgeable, helpful salespeople to help customers. Be efficient, be convenient, anticipate the customer's needs, and recognize that people want to be pampered just a little.

 • *Entertainment seekers.* As customers become bored with the typical shopping experience, they are looking for a dose of entertainment along with their merchandise.

While providing entertainment is a natural for toy stores like F. A. O. Schwarz, the book industry has joined the ranks of retailers who provide fun and games. Big chain bookstores—led by Borders (owned by Kmart) and Barnes & Noble, Inc.—are luring customers with an entertainment package that includes coffee shops, games, concerts, and lectures. No longer just suppliers of reading material, these stores are positioning themselves as neighborhood retail destinations.

How can you make *your* store more fun, more entertaining, more of a pleasant experience?

 • *Community partners.* To the benefit of everyone involved, large and small businesses alike are finding new and unique ways to give back to their communities. In addition to the personal satisfaction that comes from being involved in worthwhile projects, there are business benefits.

Employees at McWhorter's Stationery in San Jose, California, are encouraged to get involved in the community, and the company has several programs that benefit schools and organizations. As McWhorter's president, Steve Andrews, told us, "these programs let everyone know that you're trying to give something back to the community that you serve. With that, very often, the local people are going to support the people who are supporting their cities and their schools."

A recent survey suggests that one third of the public is more influenced by a company's social activisim than by its advertising.

Do you feel strongly about a community project or environmental cause? If so, there are several ways to become a good "partner," such as sponsoring educational, social, and cultural programs. In the bargain, you'll build a positive image of your business in the eyes of your customers.

Put Your Promotion Plans on the Calendar

As the saying goes, no one plans to fail, they just fail to plan. Consider your promotion plans as part of a year-round program with a well-organized month-by-month schedule for action.

As you prepare your promotions calendar, refer back to your marketing plan. Consider who your customers are and when they'll likely be thinking of buying the products you sell. Look back on your past sales figures or consult your trade associations to determine the heavy buying times.

Lead the heavier sales months with heavier advertising. During the slow times, find other products or other methods of reaching your customers to get them into your business.

Thelma Decker of T&M Appliance in Clinton, Missouri, believes in the strategy. She keeps a detailed record of sales figures by month and by product category, covering a two-year sales history as well as projections for the current year. She knows what sold when and has a blueprint covering *when* to spend money advertising which products. "You don't advertise for air conditioners in December," she said, laughing.

The important thing is to know when your customers are likely to buy and plan to put your name in front of them so that when they're ready to make the buying decision, they'll think of you.

Choose Your Weapons

We've noticed that many owners of small businesses fall into two extremes. There are those who love advertising. And then there are others who feel like Berlin Myers, Jr., who runs a lumber and building supply center in Summerville, South Carolina. He says, "If there were one thing I'd like to give up and never touch again, it would be advertising."

Since you can't win the advertising wars with the mega-merchants and their multimillion-dollar advertising budgets, think about advertising niches where you can excel.

Two methods that some businesses are using to attract customers utilize special events and direct marketing, or direct mail.

Special Events

Special events can be effective not only in drawing new people to the store, but also in helping customers associate your business with something besides a constant plea to buy. As Jim Baum, the winner of the 1993 National Retail Federation Small Store Retailer of the Year award, told us, "The approach is to try to come up with events that are not sale-driven events, in other words not price-driven. They may have price features in them, but they are not a sale."

Baum owns Hanover Linens and Baum's, a women's apparel store in Morris, Illinois, and believes that special events have a definite place for small retailers trying to compete with the retail giants.

Baum's hosts at least two large nonsale events each year, interspersed throughout the year with smaller ones. Each spring, Baum's hosts a "Come Fly a Kite" promotion, complete with kite flying demonstrations and free kites.

The other is a "Vegas Days" celebration that features casino-type gaming where winners receive "Baum's Bucks" they can use to buy merchandise in the store. As Baum says of special events, "We think it sets a tone for the store, and you simply cannot scream 'sale' all the time."

Far to the west in Scottsdale, Arizona, is Peter Barbey, owner of Houle's Books, who is trying to maintain market share despite an influx of the book giants, Borders and Bookstar. One way he's found that works to generate traffic, build customer goodwill, and set him apart is to host special events.

Most of his special events are author signings, but he also hosts talks by film critics and other types of functions. "You have to get creative, take advantage of different situations," he says, and with more than fifty events a year, some drawing more than 2,000 people, he's doing just that.

Direct Marketing—Databases

Direct marketing is the fastest-growing category of advertising and it is an area with a lot of potential for small businesses willing to make a technological leap. Using a computer database, you can find out a lot about the buying habits of the customers you have and build repeat sales by staying in contact with them.

Described elsewhere as "relationship marketing," the idea is to target the *individual* in your messages. The Yankelovich study mentioned earlier echoed this thought when it named "the need for personalization" as one of the things today's shopper craves.

The basis for this trend of individualizing your messages was cited by John Naisbitt and Patricia Aburdene in *Megatrends 2000:* "The great unifying theme at the conclusion of the twentieth century is the triumph of the individual."

Seeking to connect with these individual customers, retailers are increasingly packing their databases with information about customers' buying habits and future needs and then using the information to provide frequent buyer programs, preferred customer coupons, newsletters, and customized messages.

Take the Java Coffee & Tea Co., in Houston, Texas. Phone the company and identify yourself by name and before you've finished the sentence, the employee accesses your name on the computer and knows what your address is and when (and what) you last bought from Java. Its system allows the company to manage an effective frequent buyer program. It can also tell who hasn't ordered in a while, and to those thirsty customers it will send a *personalized*, handwritten postcard expressing concern over their absence.

Charles Tannehill owns TS Cyclesports in Wichita, Kansas, and faces competition from the likes of multiple Wal-Marts, Sam's, Targets, Toys "R" Us, Sears, and twelve independents. He's staking the future of his business on database marketing. "Information is the new currency," he says he believes that database marketing is a way to establish relationships with customers.

The possibilities for database marketing are virtually endless, and Brady's Clothing for Men in San Diego takes the concept to a high level. Brady's invites customers to complete an information card that asks not for just the basic name-address-telephone information but also for preferences on colors, designers, styles, and sizes. The information card covers information on birthdays of customer and spouse, favorite hobbies, radio stations, and magazines.

Brady's sends customers on the mailing list preferential information about sales and special events, as well as highly personalized messages. For instance, if Brady's finds itself with an abundance of size-40 shorts, employees can search the database for men who wear that size and contact them with a special offer.

Scornful skeptics scream that direct mail is costly and has a low response rate. But what we're talking about here isn't the shotgun approach to direct mail; rather, it's a personalized communication from a retailer to the individual.

Done right, database marketing tells your customers that you know them, remember them, and care about their interests and desires. Done right, it helps build a positive, long-term relationship and generates sales. In fact, research has shown that of all small businesses that use direct mail, fully 85 percent say it helps them get new business.

Use some care and give customers the option of remaining an anonymous customer. Case in point is a story told in *American Demographics:* "A few years ago Neiman-Marcus mailed an offer to men who had recently purchased expensive jewelry. These purchases were news to some of their wives, and the result of that mailing was angry customers."

In addition to maintaining close contact with current customers, you can also attract new customers by using mailing lists generated from databases other companies own. That's just what Debbie Kramer did. She's the owner of Ebaugh's Gifts, which is just a short distance from Wal-Mart in McPherson, Kansas.

Using a service, she sends a customized Christmas catalogue to current customers as well as a targeted group in specific zip codes in nearby areas. "It was a big investment for me for advertising, but one I'd have to give the most credit to because from the time I did the first one in 1991, my sales in November and December went up about 25 percent from what we had in the previous year," she said. "I have to think it's because new customers came in that had never been here before and they continued to come."

Make Your Weapons Hit the Target

Every day, consumers are bombarded with thousands of commercial messages everywhere they turn—on radio and television, in the newspapers and magazines, on billboards and bus and subway placards, at restaurant tables, and in their mailboxes. "Buy me," "Choose me," the messages scream. Most people tune them out. So how can you make your messages stand out in the crowd?

All of your promotion materials must:

• *Build an image.* What image of your business do you want to portray? Casual and friendly? Sleek and sophisticated? Trendy and upbeat? Whimsical and elegant? Your marketing materials should reflect the image you want to portray. Carry it through on your business cards, letterheads, envelopes, signs, statements, and brochures. Be consistent.

- *Attract attention.* With so many messages screaming at your customers, your message must be unique. Some retailers will do about anything to get attention—from waddling down the aisles in duck suits to driving around town in a graffiti-splashed van. Some messages grab your attention because they are unexpected or amusing.

- *Be memorable.* Barry Steinberg designed a billboard for his tire and auto repair company, Direct Tire, in Watertown, Massachusetts. The billboard said simply, "We fix it so it brakes."® Though he hasn't used the billboard in more than five years, when he asks his customers how they heard about him, many of them still answer, "We saw your billboard on the Mass Turnpike." They still remember the now trademarked ad more than five years later!

- *Communicate the benefit.* Once you get the customers' attention, they will filter the information through the screen that asks, "What's in it for me?" They are interested in buying only two things: good feelings and solutions to problems. Use the words *you* and *yours* frequently. Understand and address the needs of your potential customers.

- *Be relevant* to your business or service. Have you ever watched an advertisement on television and then said to yourself, "That was interesting, but what were they advertising?" Attention for attention's sake is of little value. Don't get so drawn into being different that customers don't realize what you are selling.

- *Be frequent.* One of the most important aspects in your plan is *repetition*—put your company name, products, and services in front of the customer often, and when they're ready to buy they'll have a greater chance of thinking of you. Studies show that consumers recognize something only after seeing it as many as twenty-five times!

- *Target the audience.* From your market research and marketing plan, you know who your potential customers are.

Speak directly to them. Try to "narrowcast" rather than broadcast your message.

■ *Be simple and straightforward.* Use simple words and phrases and choose your words carefully. Don't use big words if short ones will work. You're talking to friends, so write the same way you talk. Use contractions.

■ *Invite action.* Many businesses produce marketing materials that are terrific in every way, except for one key element. They don't ask for action. What action do you want the customer to take? Call you? Stop by? Mail something? Make it clear what action you want your customers to take. Then deliver what you promised to give them. Remember the adage "Underpromise, overdeliver." Make sure your business name is prominent. Include your address and phone number and the hours you're open.

Before printing or producing your promotion materials, let an impartial person look at them to check for clarity. Whatever you do, stay focused on your purpose and don't try to cover too much ground.

Use All Your Resources

Small-business owners frequently feel frustrated that they have limited resources of time and money, particularly as it relates to promoting their business. That makes it even more important to cultivate and utilize all possible resources to the fullest. Here are some suggestions:

1. *Form partnerships with your distributors and buying groups.* Work closely with your distributors and buying groups to get new ideas. As Thelma Decker, whom we mentioned earlier in this chapter, said, "The people that we deal with, the distributors and the buying groups, are our partners. If we don't take advantage of their expertise and their abilities, and let them in to help us, I think we're missing the bet. As business owners, we are so busy with our noses to the grindstone or in our little focused world that . . . we sometimes have tunnel vision . . .

and can't see what's coming at us. They can take a six-page document and condense it down to one paragraph and say, 'This is what you need to know.' "

Successful small-business people tell us they get many ideas for promotions (and other topics) through this type of partnership.

2. *Form partnerships with other businesses.* In Montgomery, Alabama, Rebecca Linton and Betty Roberts own separate businesses that target female customers. Linton owns Rebecca's Lingerie, which sells intimate apparel and serves a growing customer list of mastectomy patients. Roberts owns Focus on Fashion, an upscale women's clothing store which also carries wigs and, consequently, has a large market of women with cancer.

After meeting at a chamber of commerce function, they realized that they had at least two things in common: They shared a specific group of customers (those with cancer), and wanted to do more advertising for less money.

The owners pooled their resources and jointly produced a brochure, with each one taking one half of it. Though the stores operate in separate locations several miles apart, there are now two businesses promoting that aspect of their business instead of just one. And it works. Rebecca refers customers to Betty, and Betty does the same for Rebecca.

3. *Use all your co-op money.* Aledia Hunt Tush, owner of Mr. CB's, a marine sporting goods store in Sarasota, Florida, cites this as one of her most important success tactics. She says, "Many retailers don't want to go to the hassle of meeting co-op requirements, but if you don't, it's like throwing money away."

Photo store owner Ken Dumminger, in Fremont, Ohio, agrees, and co-ops with his photo suppliers to offer seminars and other promotions throughout the year.

4. *Get help when you need it.* When you're out of ideas or if you *know* it's time to add a little more pizzazz to your promotion materials, you may want to consult with specialists such as advertising agencies, writers, graphic artists, photographers, or media buyers. There is a very fine line between an effective

promotion and one that falls flat, and sometimes it's very difficult to tell where that line will be. An expert can help.

Consult with other business owners for recommendations; then ask to see portfolios from those you are considering. To make sure you are comparing apples to apples, give each marketing expert your budget and ask what they have done for clients within that budget. Before proceeding, talk frankly about fees and expectations. Then cooperate; offer constructive criticism, but trust their talents.

Maybe you don't need a full-service agency but only need help on limited projects. In that case, consider using an agency just for the essentials such as brainstorming for ideas, editing promotion materials, and targeting publications.

Ready, Fire, Aim

We told you earlier about the philosophy based on the premise that it's cheaper to experiment than to philosophize. The idea is to make a plan, try it, and if doesn't work after a reasonable length of time, modify the strategy, reaim, and take another shot.

We're not saying it's a good idea to approach your marketing in a haphazard manner, but don't be afraid to experiment. Monitor what works. Ask your customers, "How did you hear about us?" Strengthen what's working and modify what isn't.

In the next chapter, we make it easy for you to do a little experimenting with fifty-three suggestions for low-cost promotion tactics.

Four

Low-Cost Promotion Strategies

I know that half the money I spend on advertising is wasted;
but I can never find out which half.

—John Wanamaker

We've heard sad tales and bad tales from enterprising
owners of small businesses who would agree with Wanamaker's words. One appliance store owner told us he had wasted
more than $50,000 on advertising before he discovered what
worked—and he discovered what worked strictly by trial and
error.

What works and what doesn't will depend a lot on *your*
specific products or services, *your* community, *your* competition, and *your* skills in how *you* promote your business.

As you develop promotion ideas, remember to keep these
important points in mind: The cheapest advertising you can
get is by word of mouth. Foster good relationships with all
people—employees, customers, and friends—by treating them
with respect, honesty, and compassion.

Become active in your community. You will reap big benefits by expanding your network and through the personal
satisfaction of participating in a worthy cause. Like a stone
thrown into a pond, your connections with other people will
have a rippling effect.

Always remember to keep your current customers happy.
It's much cheaper to keep the customers you have than to
develop new ones.

In this chapter, we offer fifty-three low-cost ideas that have worked for a variety of businesses. Copy them, adapt them, and experiment with them.

Fifty-Three Low-Cost Promotion Strategies

1. *Invest in high quality, colorful, unique business cards.* Have some printed for all of your employees and encourage them to pass them out to everyone they meet. This will help build those important relationships between your employees and customers and spread the name of your business throughout the community.

Consider your business cards as "mini billboards" that may be the first direct contact that a potential customer has with your company. Be creative and try for unusual designs. Some cards are larger than the traditional size (3½ by 2 inches) and fold out to a width of 5 inches. These can serve as "mini brochures" and list the services or products you provide. Some attention-catching business cards we've seen:

- Thin wooden cards, for a plywood manufacturing company
- Distinctive *and waterproof* plastic cards, for a fly fishing shop
- Cards with a tear-off section that's an admittance ticket, for an amusement park
- A card that is actually a photograph, for a photography store

2. *Create a good, ten-second introduction to describe yourself and your business.* Make it fifteen to twenty-five words and practice it until it rolls off your tongue, so that you can deliver it smoothly when you need to introduce yourself. For example, when the owner of one auto repair shop passes out his business card he says, "Hello, I'm Skip Burroughs with Mastercraft Automotive. We specialize in finding and correcting problems no one else can."

3. *Network.* One of the best sources of ideas and contacts is to network at trade shows, chamber of commerce meetings, and community functions. Doing so will help you remain

competitive and keep you up to date on developments in the business world.

One client approached us for help when his business was dwindling. One of the first questions we asked him was how active he was in his community, and we anticipated the answer: He had stopped going to community functions and chamber of commerce activities and admitted that people told him they thought he had retired.

When you develop new contacts you will, at the very least, broaden your base of resources for future information. Network for the sake of meeting interesting people—don't cultivate friends and contacts solely for what it will do for you. But remember that networking can also build business: We all like to do business with people we know.

4. *Develop a clean, crisp, distinctive logo for your business.* Use it on your business cards, letterhead, invoices, and integrate it throughout your signs and printed materials. A good logo can enhance your business image, increase your name recognition, and create an identity.

5. *Use every advertising weapon at your disposal.* Use your business letterhead, envelopes, return labels, forms, and invoices to carry your message. Don't underestimate their importance.

Many small-business owners think of these items as merely office supplies, but in truth these are powerful marketing tools. They represent you and your business even when you are not around. Virtually every piece of paper that leaves your store or office is a potential marketing weapon. Mention your commitment to service, quality, and convenience for your customers, or the unique benefits you offer your customers.

6. *Attend trade shows and industry meetings.* One consistent trait of the successful business people we know is that they regularly attend trade shows and meetings related to their business. Away from the everyday duties of running your business, it's the one time where the focus is completely on what you can do to improve it. Put your networking skills to work and you'll make valuable contacts while learning new skills.

7. *Start a "customer suggestion of the month" program.* Offer $25 gift certificates to the customer whose suggestion is chosen as the best. Three good things happen with this promotion:

1. You reward present customers (it's a way of saying thanks).
2. You get good suggestions on how to better serve your customers.
3. You learn what your customers are thinking.

8. *Stage a fun event or happening at your store.* Lee Sherman at Hahn Appliance in Tulsa, Oklahoma, pokes fun at a local talk show host with the "John Erling Meltdown" he stages every year in August. Sherman has an ice sculpture made of the radio host and embeds a tiny appliance (representing his appliance store) in the sculpture. Customers guess how many hours and minutes it will take for the sculpture to melt. The correct guess wins a freezer full of gourmet ice cream. Erling talks about it on his show and does a live remote the day of the event. It gets people talking and coming by to join in the fun.

During "Vegas Days" at Baum's, a women's apparel store in Morris, Illinois, customers can play blackjack, roulette, and slot machines in a minicasino set up for the occasion. Winners earn "Baum's Bucks," which are merchandise certificates they can spend in the store.

If customers hit a particular space on the "Wheel of Fortune" game, Baum's donates $500 to the United Fund. According to Baum's president, Jim Baum, the special event generates customer traffic and excitement.

9. *Start a club.* When Phelps County Bank started a club for "mature adults," the response was overwhelming. Echoing what we told you earlier in the marketing chapter about taking care how you address this important group of customers, one of the new members said he didn't want to be called a senior citizen and asked how PCB defined a *mature adult*. The satisfying response was, "Someone who doesn't throw their food."

The club you form is more likely to be successful if you make sure it's fun, involve the members from its inception, offer adequate rewards for membership (discounts, preferred customer mailings), keep in close contact with the members, and solicit their input.

10. *Write an article for a trade publication.* Editors are on the lookout for well-written, timely articles. Select publications catering to your field of expertise, and take a close look at the types of articles they run. Make sure your article fits the format. Call the editors or associate editors with specific questions about their guidelines and what sorts of photographs (if any) should accompany the article. To build your credibility and name recognition, post reprints of the article in your store or distribute them to selected people.

11. *Invite everyone you do business with to do business with you.* We know a menswear shop that has business cards printed with an offer of a discount on the reverse side of the card. To get the discount, the buyer must present the card at the shop. The owner asks every employee to hand out the cards, and offers an incentive for doing so.

Whenever the employees buy a car, a hammer, or a doughnut, they pass out a business card to the seller and say, "Shop with us." At the end of each quarter, the owner pays a bonus to the employee who has had the most cards returned. One employee's bonus was $500, and store sales increased by more than $13,000 that quarter.

12. *Package a slow-moving item with a fast seller to move out the former.* Keep in mind that your "slow mover" must be a real value or it will slow sales of fast-moving items.

13. *Develop a mailing list of your customers.* Use a computer for this if possible. By having an accurate mailing list, you'll open doors to all sorts of marketing possibilities. Read Chapter Three for more detail on database marketing.

14. *Steal and adapt good ideas from others.* The legends of retailing all were cat burglars of good ideas. Buy out-of-town papers and scan the ads for design ideas. Look closely at direct-mail pieces you receive. Any ideas there? Visit the stores of your competitors and notice what they're doing and the things they're advertising. Watch big companies and small companies to see what tactics they are using to promote their businesses. The key words are *steal* and *adapt*.

15. *Become an expert on a subject involving your business.* Communicate your expertise to radio and TV talk show hosts, newspaper editors and columnists, magazine publishers, and other public figures. You may be called upon for a quote for a publication or program, which can mean big-time publicity for you and your company. You'll even seem like more of an expert if you can quote a few pieces of obscure trivia.

Associations and clubs are always looking for good, entertaining, and informative speakers. Your chamber of commerce may have a list of local organizations. Develop a professional-looking letter or flyer offering your services and send it to them.

16. *Establish an internal ad agency, and earn 15 percent in the bargain.* The author of *Guerrilla Marketing,* Jay Conrad Levinson, offered this tip. Advertising agencies earn money by receiving a 15 percent discount from printers, publications, and broadcast stations. Why not have your internal "agency" get the benefit of that instead of an outsider?

In most cases, Levinson says, you'll only need to tell the advertising medium that you're an in-house or internal agency for your business. In some cases, you'll need to give it a separate name, establish a separate checking account in your "agency's" name, and print some stationery—minimum fees for each. From then on, you'll be paying that 15 percent to yourself instead of an outsider.

17. *Always say thank-you either orally or in writing.* Showing your appreciation to current customers will help make them future customers. In a world that has become very impersonal, a handwritten thank-you card makes a great impression on a customer.

18. *Send birthday cards.* Most of us like to be recognized on this special day. (A client mentioned to us that the card he got from the appliance store he patronizes was the only birthday card he received.) Offer customers a discount if they bring the card in during a specified time period or let them know there's a special gift waiting for them.

19. *Use "messages on hold" to carry your advertising message via the telephone.* These can be great to advertise your special services, or the expertise of your employees. Direct Tire's

message in Watertown, Massachusetts, tells callers about the special services it offers and that all its technicians are "Automotive Service Excellence" certified. Sounds impressive.

The added benefit for the customers who must be placed on hold is that they hear the message *you* want them to. We know store owners who switched to their own customized "messages on hold" when customers mentioned they heard a competitor's advertisement while listening to the radio that was being played through the telephone.

20. *Exhibit at trade shows or community fairs.* You're looking for exposure, not necessarily sales. Take advantage of the opportunity to acquaint prospective customers with what you have to offer. Be creative with your displays and have a drawing for a free product or gift certificate to your store. Capture the names for your mailing list.

Many communities have "business-to-business expos," where a variety of businesses can display their products and advertise their services. If you don't have such a program, talk to your chamber of commerce and try to organize one.

21. *Send special-event notes or cards congratulating customers for a promotion, wedding anniversary, graduation, or other special event.* Ask your employees to keep their ears tuned to conversations and assign an employee to scan the newspaper daily for news about your customers which might merit a congratulatory note.

22. *Sponsor a drawing for free merchandise.* Entry forms could be a brief questionnaire capturing essential information such as names and addresses (which will tell you where your customers come from) and also information about whether they intend to purchase the type of product you sell within the next sixty days. You'll get valuable information to help you target your advertising.

Charles Tannehill held a drawing for free hi-tech sunglasses in his bicycle and fitness shop, T. S. Cyclesports, in Wichita, Kansas, and was amazed at the response and also at how much data he collected to add to his database.

23. *Donate your services or products to a nonprofit organization for a fund raiser or special event.* Putting your name and your

products in front of the public will have a positive effect and show you are a supporter of your community.

24. *Host how-to classes or seminars*. Such strategies are widely used by the retail giants. Some of them regularly host free clinics on topics ranging from plumbing to tiling, thereby creating a market for their services.

Mr. CB's bait and tackle shop in Sarasota, Florida, regularly hosts seminars featuring local boat captains who pass out fishing maps and teach would-be anglers where the fish are biting and what type of bait they're hungry for. After the seminars, participants hop aboard a boat to try out the techniques learned in the seminars.

Owner Aledia Hunt Tush claims the benefits aren't just financial. "I don't expect to make a lot of money when we do the seminars," she says, "but it builds traffic and builds the respect that customers have for us."

25. *Send a note or letter to someone whose work you admire*—a writer of an article whose opinions you agree with, or an artist whose work you enjoy. It's always nice for people to hear a word of praise. (This book's coauthor, Don Taylor, values the letters he's received from distinguished retailers, including the late Sam Walton, congratulating him on his newspaper columns.) The benefits are that you build rapport and may build business since we all like to be associated with people who are doing more than just peddling their wares.

26. *Seek out informal partnerships with noncompeting businesses and arrange to work together in mutually beneficial ways*. Phelps County Bank in Rolla, Missouri, did this with a small marketing firm in town that was building their business and needed some good references. Said CEO Emma Lou Brent, "One of the smartest things that we have done consistently is to form partnerships with other small businesses where we can benefit each other."

27. *Use as much co-op advertising money as you can*. Take advantage of the matching funds that manufacturers offer to help you advertise their products. By some estimates, as much as 50 percent of co-op allocations aren't being used.

Be sure to use your logo, keep the name and image of

your business prominent in the advertisement, and comply with all the co-op regulations. These record-keeping requirements may be time consuming, but co-op will make your advertising dollars go farther.

28. *Develop an effective Yellow Pages ad.* Many small-business owners develop their Yellow Pages ad using the basic format suggested by the sellers of Yellow Pages advertising. While this approach may be adequate, it won't make your ad stand out from the others, particularly if you're in a very competitive market. (Remember one of the rules is "attract attention.")

Get ideas by going to the library and looking at Yellow Pages ads in some out-of-town phone books. When you travel out of town, do the same thing.

Look at the ads of your competitors and then make sure yours is different. People turn to the Yellow Pages to discover specific information, so give it to them—lots of it. List what you offer (products, services, and benefits), grab their attention with a strong headline, and use graphics or a photograph.

29. *Investigate remnant space advertisements.* This is advertising space in regional editions of national publications "left over" after major advertisers have bought space. Magazines are put together in four-page units and sometimes not enough ads will be sold to fill the unit, so remnant space is sold very cheaply to fill the section. Call the advertising department of the magazine directly, well in advance of the publication date.

30. *Find a way to connect your products or services with a famous person or local personality.* Skiers have raised this tactic to an art form. Right after coming down the slope, the first thing they do is pull off their skis and pose, the name of the skis prominently shown. Wouldn't you love to have your name so prominently exhibited?

Ruth Hanessian, president of the Animal Exchange in Rockville, Maryland, uses this tactic in her newspaper ads, which feature photographs of people running for public office posing with her products (pets).

These advertisements, which she did against the advice of her former advertising agency, have proven very successful. So much so that she often gets calls from candidates—before they announce their campaigns—to arrange the photo session.

If you'd like to steer away from the political arena, keep tabs on interesting or famous people who will be visiting your town or find someone who's doing something that's bound to get media attention. Invite them to come to your store and, with their permission, notify the press.

31. *Offer free services to add value to the products you sell.* This one element can be the deciding factor in whether a customer decides to buy from you or your competition. Appliance dealers might offer free delivery and free hookups, like Hahn Appliance does in Tulsa, Oklahoma. Debbie Kramer, owner of Ebaugh's Gifts in McPherson, Kansas, will provide free gift wrapping and free delivery—with no price minimum. If you're a man looking for a special outfit, George Wilder at The Locker Room in Montgomery, Alabama, will bring the store's customized showroom-on-wheels to your door with selections in your size.

32. *Make a long-lasting impression with specialty advertising* (caps, writing instruments, calendars, mugs, paperweights, notepads). Two big advantages of using this medium: Your name stays in front of the consumer a long time; and chosen well, your advertising can generate a good response because everyone loves a useful, attractive, free gift.

There are thousands of types of specialty advertising. Whatever type you choose, make sure to imprint your logo, name, and address and be sure to keep your selection relevant to your business and appropriate for your customer. Your image is at stake: Select items that are durable, high-quality, and useful.

33. *Offer something for free.* Fisher's Office Products in Boise, Idaho, includes Tootsie-Roll candies with every order it delivers. It's a free unexpected bonus for customers, and they love it.

34. *Find a win-win opportunity to become a civic partner.* McWhorter's Stationery in San Jose, California has a successful back-to-school program it instituted throughout its twenty-store chain. During August and September, customers who purchase products at McWhorter's can rebate 10 percent of their purchase cost to a participating school of their choice. In

a win-win situation, McWhorter's donated $68,000 to local schools and enjoyed a hefty revenue increase for the two months the promotion ran.

The key is to find a partnership where everyone benefits and then gain the support of all the players involved. Though McWhorter's program got off to a relatively slow start, three years of heavy promotion finally paid off for everyone. According to McWhorter's president, Steve Andrews, "People are asking about it all the time and in virtually any meeting we go to, people will ask about the program . . . and how they can enroll."

35. *Offer progressive reductions.* The owner of a Missouri garden center was overstocked with garden tractors and displayed one of them in his store in a highly visible location. He promised to reduce the price by $10 every day until it sold. The local radio station picked it up as a news story, and every day the disc jockeys asked, "How low will it go?"

Shortly after the tractor sold, other customers came in offering to buy the tractor at that day's price, which the store owner was happy to do with the remaining tractors. It generated interest and cleared inventory.

36. *Start a frequent buyer program by copying the airlines' frequent flyer programs.* For small-business owners, this type of program offers incentives for loyal customers to continue to buy from you and rewards them for doing so. The "prize" might be a discount or their next item free, depending on the products or services you sell.

Before the book superstores arrived in his area, Peter Barbey started a frequent buyer program in his Arizona book store, Houle's Books. The program was very effective in building customer loyalty.

One of the ways to build your business is to get your current customers to buy more from you. Done well, this type of program will do it.

37. *Set up merchandise displays in nearby vacant buildings.* Many cities have vacant buildings badly in need of tenants, or at least decoration. By displaying your products in these facilities you reduce the ugliness of empty buildings and promote your business much like a billboard.

The display must reflect positively on your business, so make sure your display is attractive with a nice background. Include a big sign with your business name and address.

38. *Create a killer business presentation.* The owner of a bus leasing company charters his bus for special trips. To promote the service, he created a funny, entertaining slide show that was so well done, he's had many requests to present the program to service clubs. The audience enjoyed the entertainment and it brought great exposure to the company—all at no cost.

39. *Use your dressing rooms (if you're in the clothing business) or your rest rooms to promote unadvertised specials, to post current advertising, and to reinforce your mission statements.*

40. *Set up truly unusual displays in your store windows.* If they're zany or interesting enough they may attract enough local interest to be newsworthy.

41. *Create a float for your local parade.* Whether it's for July 4th, homecoming, your city's birthday celebration, or the kickoff event for your county fair, parades can be a great way to get exposure for your business. Your image is at stake, so make the float unique and memorable.

42. *Sponsor or cosponsor a race or event such as a bike-a-thon or walk/run.* These events, if promoted well, can attract a lot of attention. Those who participate will link your business to a worthwhile cause.

Well ahead of time, discuss promotion plans with event organizers and request a copy of the names and addresses of participants for your mailing list. The benefits will be twofold: You'll build name recognition and show your community spirit.

43. *Sponsor or cosponsor a sports team.* Have your name printed—possibly with your slogan—on the back of the shirts. Whether it's your son's baseball team, your daughter's basketball team, or an employee's volleyball team, you'll earn appreciation and recognition by sponsoring a team. (We've heard from many people that this is one thing that some of the retail giants refuse to do.)

44. *Draw people into your store with a fun contest.* Thelma Decker's pumpkin decorating contest at her T&M Appliance

store in Clinton, Missouri, won an award from the North American Retail Dealers Association.

Each October she gives away pumpkins to contest participants, and after they're decorated the pumpkins are put on display in the store where visitors can cast their vote in several categories for their favorite pumpkin.

Considering the attention it attracts and the store traffic it generates, it's not surprising that the contest helped spur the best October sales figures in the history of the company.

45. *Enter contests.* Associations, chambers of commerce, and a variety of other organizations offer contests in many fields. Investigate the qualifications and apply for the ones that fit you and your business.

Winners are often honored with concrete evidence that they are the best in the field, which can only help your marketing efforts. The story may get picked up by local or national publications, ever widening your sphere of influence. Don't miss this opportunity on the local—or broader—level to boost your image.

46. *Send postcards.* The Java Coffee and Tea Co. in Houston sends customers a postcard when they haven't shopped or ordered in a while. It's an attractive, handwritten card that is addressed directly to the customer and says simply, "We haven't seen you in a while. Let us know if you need anything."

Even though we've been in the marketing business many years and familiar with the computer programs that allow businesses to track inactive customers, it was still somehow flattering to think that they noticed our absence! According to co-owners Bill Lawder and Bill Boyd, they send the cards to keep the company in the minds of their customers, and when customers call or come in they say, "Thanks for sending the note." They told us sending the postcards is very profitable and definitely worth the effort.

47. *Plan a festive holiday party.* It's a nice way to say, "Thanks for your business" while generating sales. Debbie Kramer hosts a holiday open house at her gift shop, Ebaugh's Gifts, in McPherson, Kansas. In what has evolved into a fun

social event, she times the open house to correspond with the arrival of her Christmas gift catalogue. It's been so successful that her customers begin calling in October to make sure they're on the mailing list and to put the date on their calendars.

48. *Make full use of a toll-free hot line or support line.* Building long-term customer relationships is what modern-day marketing is all about, and one way that all types of businesses are discovering they can do this with out-of-town customers is to keep in touch via a toll-free line.

An attractive selling point for the computer systems that Joe Wolf sells at his store, CompuSystems in Washington, Missouri, is his offer of free and toll-free technical support *forever*.

Do your customers know that you'll always be available to answer their questions about the products they buy from you? It's a great selling point and a good way to turn them into lifetime customers.

49. *Send messages to your customers via fax,* but get their permission first. A natural for a computer store selling technology, Wolf instituted a way to reach his customers with advertisements or special offers by sending flyers over his automated fax machine.

Once or twice a year, he hires temporary help to call representatives of every business in the community to update fax information and verify that they would be willing to see promotional faxes from time to time. CompuSystems sends no unsolicited faxes, and the program has been a great success. About 97 percent of the businesses they call express interest in receiving the faxes, and almost all of those become customers.

50. *Be the first.* It's one way to differentiate you from the competition and to make an important impression on your customers. Most people remember that Charles Lindbergh was the first to fly across the Atlantic, and Neil Armstrong the first to walk on the moon. We remember firsts, and we sometimes forget those who come in second.

One of the ways that Jim Myers Drug in Tuscaloosa, Alabama, has competed with the retail giants was to be the *first* to offer a variety of services, such as free screenings for blood pressure and blood sugar and free delivery of prescriptions.

51. *Provide tip sheets for your customers.* These can range from instructions on how to install a faucet (a hardware business) to how to plant a perennial garden (garden center), to how to take care of your new guinea pig (pet store). Today's customers are hungry for information. Give it to them.

52. *Volunteer for high-visibility assignments such as making presentations, chairing committees, or organizing events.* Being visible in the community through such activities will make you visible in the marketplace. Everyone likes to do business with people they know and respect.

53. *Write a letter to the editor or do a guest editorial.* This can be a dynamic marketing device if you communicate well and can offer a reasonable solution to a problem instead of just articulating it. Presenting yourself well in the newspaper will help you gain some respect as a person who is taking a leadership and advocacy position on an important topic of local interest. Pay attention to the publication's format and guidelines and write clearly and concisely. Laminate or frame the printed piece and display it in your store.

Five

Delivering Whatever-It-Takes Customer Service

> There is only one boss: the customer. And he can fire everybody in the company, from the chairman on down, simply by spending his money somewhere else.
>
> —Sam Walton

We'd be willing to bet that if you asked people what they'd most like to change about the places where they shop, the answer you'd hear most often is "service." Fed up with salespeople who are rude, indifferent, or invisible, customers are singing the "I Can't Get No Satisfaction" blues all the way to a competitor's store.

One of the most common mistakes that a business can make is to forget the reason it exists: to serve the customer. Without customers there simply is no reason for your company to exist. Yet many business owners seem to have lost sight of the value of customers as *individuals*, and employees have become too busy or too scarce or too indifferent to give customers much attention.

You have a key advantage over big-box merchants and discounters in that many customers want more than just a transaction. They want someone to care about them and help solve their problems—someone who offers not just an item, a thing, but who also offers knowledge, concern, and attention. Smart businesses utilize that information to look upon each customer transaction as not just a one-time event but as an opportunity to build a long-term relationship.

The good news is that people like you in small businesses are much better positioned than the megamerchants to give customers the kind of service they are seeking and to build that type of relationship.

Customers come where they're invited and stay where they're appreciated. When your customers have so many options about where and how they spend their time and money, it's crucial to the success of your business to provide not just good service but great, "I'll gladly pay more for that" service.

Service like George Wilder provides for his customers at The Locker Room, an upscale men's clothing shop in Montgomery, Alabama. Wilder and his staff of long-term employees offer relationship-building services that the big stores can never match.

With the hectic lifestyles of today, his customers don't want shopping to be a chore, so Wilder strives to make their experience in his store fun, pleasurable, exciting, and easy. And if customers don't have time to come to the store to shop, they can call him. After finding out what their needs are, Wilder makes several selections in the customer's size and delivers them to their door in his custom-built van. Tastefully decorated with antique fixtures, wall sconces, and furniture, the van is really a showroom on wheels.

Service like Thelma Decker provides for her T&M Appliance customers in Clinton, Missouri. If a customer can't program the VCR or the remote control, she'll go to their home and show them how to do it. She said, "Sometimes it's not even the VCR that we sold them." It may just be a need that the customer mentioned while in the store looking for a television or a refrigerator. Decker confesses they don't have a lot of calls to do those things, but adds, "If you do enough of those through the years, it makes you feel good and the P.R. is just unbelievable."

Pull your car up to Tony's Auto Parts Store in Pella, Iowa, and one of the four owners will be ready "right away to poke our head out the door and take a look at it," says one of the owners, Bob Bokhoven. "We don't get involved in doing the work, but we'll be happy to take some time and tell you how to go about it. We're a friendly place and base a lot of our business success just on plain having friendships with the people who come in here." It's no surprise that with an attitude like that, their business has seen steady growth, even with a Wal-Mart nearby.

Have you ever wondered why you don't hear more examples of superlative service? Many people can—and love to—recite horror stories about how they were treated in a place of business. In fact, complaining about bad service has become something of a catharsis for today's consumers. Customers have come to expect the worst and are surprised when companies go out of their way to offer superior service. Therein lies the opportunity for small businesses!

What Happened to Good Service?

It would be easy to update the litany of that famous commercial a few years ago that asked, "Where's the beef?" The new question, echoed by customers everywhere, would be "Where's the service?" And the answer, all too often, would be silence.

What's happened? We think there are seven basic reasons for the general decline in customer service:

1. Businesses have overlooked the importance of service in a race to save labor costs and keep prices low. The result is not enough employees to really service customers.

2. Managers have put too much emphasis on doing routine chores like paperwork and inventory. This attitude forces employees to look at customers as interruptions to their work, rather than the reason they are working.

We know a woman who, having witnessed an automobile accident, rushed into a store and frantically requested to use the phone to dial 911 for emergency assistance. After listening to the woman's story about the accident, and hearing her request, the store clerk acidly responded, "I'll be with you in a moment" and went back to chores of filing invoices. The woman's second plea for help similarly went unanswered.

Finally, a manager overheard the conversation and made the call. How can things like that happen?

3. Managers have forgotten the importance of walking the floors, finding it all too comfortable to sit behind a desk. Truman Breed, owner of Breed & Co. in Austin, Texas, knows that one of the big reasons his hardware, garden, and houseware business has been so successful is that he operates it from the floor, not from the desk.

4. As everything has become more automated, from buying airline tickets to getting a check cashed, to talking on the telephone, the importance of each person-to-person encounter has taken on a greater significance. Make the encounter pleasant and efficient and the customer will find fewer reasons to shop the competition, automated or not.

5. Frontline employees who have face-to-face customer contact often receive less training in customer service than in how to run the computer or the cash register. What does that tell employees about where the company places its priorities?

6. Employees aren't given adequate incentives or rewards for taking care of customers. Good employees don't come cheap. The successful companies we know all pay their employees more than the going rate and provide adequate incentives to keep good employees happy.

7. In this scenario, customers are at fault too. They don't always regard companies for good service. Jim Chick, president of Chick's Sporting Goods in Covina, California, provides an example: "One of my competitors actually tells his customers that he has no service level at all," Chick says. "I've had people overhear them tell customers, 'Go up to Chick's and get fit for your ski boots, then come back and we'll beat their price by 30 bucks.' It's shocking how many people will do that."

Maybe we'd all get better service if we would reward businesses for good service, not only with our business, but also by letting the manager know when an employee has done a good job. Everyone thrives on compliments, and it would be good motivation to continue the good work.

These Basic Truths Apply

Now that you know what some of the problems are, what can be done about them? The answer depends on your own willingness to change or improve the things you are doing now. As you begin the process, keep in mind that in today's highly competitive marketplace, customer service is often the deciding factor in a customer's decision to do business with you or another company.

As we move through the various steps involved in creating a new standard of customer service excellence, consider these basic truths:

- The quality of service customers get directly affects their willingness to do business with you.
- Most people will pay a premium (up to 10 percent or more) for good customer service.
- Customers who have had pleasant shopping experiences are much more likely to buy again, so your marketing costs will be lower.
- It costs five times as much to gain a new customer as it does to keep an existing customer.
- *Service* is the difference between selling something and creating a customer. As costs skyrocket and profit margins dwindle, the name of the game in the future will be building loyal customers who will come back to shop again and again.
- Happy customers will tell their friends, so you will spend less on advertising.
- Some experts estimate that businesses lose as much as 30 percent of their potential revenue because of poor customer relations.
- The biggest reason customers will quit doing business with your company is poor service.

Write the Script for Whatever-It-Takes Customer Service

The essence of good customer service is really very simple. Treat customers with respect, go beyond what they expect, and make the experience of dealing with you as easy and satisfying as possible. It's not exactly rocket science; it's more like the Golden Rule.

How can something so simple be so difficult to accomplish? Try thinking of customer service as *great theater*. Draft a script that covers your philosophy of customer service as well as your expectations for delivering it to customers.

Make sure your employees understand the value of each customer. The customer is the reason the business exists and is the only asset that has lasting value. Customers generate the profits that pay the bills and are the only reason the employee has a job.

Develop procedures that help you meet the needs of your customers. Evaluate each policy by asking, *How will this benefit our customers?* If you don't have a good answer to that question, it's not a good policy.

How are your merchandise return policies? If you require employees to get four signatures and a notarized statement, you'll irritate customers who are looking for a company that values their time and their opinions.

We suggest that you include the pointers below when you draft your script.

Fifteen Ways to Create Whatever-It-Takes Customer Service

1. *Find good employees, train them well, and treat them like superstars.* (We pack all of Chapter Six with helpful hints on how to do this.) To your customers, your employees *are* your company.

2. *Constantly monitor how you're doing.* Ask your customers what they think. Listen and react to the answers. McWhorter's Stationery, an office supply company based in San Jose, California, hires "mystery shoppers" to shop their stores and write reports on what they have found. President Steve Andrews

reads every report and offers a $25 bonus to any employee who scores 90 or above (on a scale of 100), and every report with an 80 or above is posted in the employee lunchroom.

If you don't like the idea of mystery shoppers, develop some other way to measure customer service performance. We give you some ideas later in the chapter.

3. *Keep employees informed.* A customer finds nothing so irritating as taking the time to go to a store that advertises a special on a certain item only to find the employees know nothing of the sale or the location of the advertised product.

4. *Find something to do every day that surprises, excites, or delights a customer.* If you're lucky enough to be able to shop at Nordstrom's—the famous Washington-based department store which sets a high standard for service—and find they don't have the brand you're looking for, don't despair. The clerk might just run to the store down the street and get it for you.

5. *Make customer service everyone's job.* One of the pet peeves of every customer is that irritating and overused retort, "It's not my job."

6. *Be reliable, keep your promises—and keep your word.* Don't promise what you can't deliver, and deliver more than you promised. In other words: Underpromise, overdeliver.

Elizabeth Brooks needed to take her car in for its checkup and called the dealer to inquire about the costs. The employee explained what the charges would be and what services would be performed. Elizabeth delivered the car to the service department and again clarified the charges. When the work was completed, the casher totaled the order, which was several dollars more than had been quoted. The explanation given for the higher costs was that the people on the telephone and the people at the service desk were working from old price lists. After some negotiation, the dealer reluctantly lowered the charges to what had been quoted, and it was a lose-lose situation for everyone. Elizabeth lost respect for the dealership, and the dealership lost a customer—all over a few dollars.

7. *Apologize when you make a mistake and explain how you'll make it right.* How different the scenario in item 6 would have

turned out if the cashier had said simply, "We made a mistake, and we'll correct it."

8. *Don't hesitate to say "I don't know" but always follow it with the words "but I'll find out."* One of the big keys to success in the years to come will be the ability of your employees to share their *knowledge and expertise.* In a study by Yankelovich Partners, 55 percent of the people surveyed said they like a great deal of information before they purchase an item.

The retail giants know the value of providing knowledge. That's why Home Depot sponsors free clinics for shoppers on plumbing, construction, and tiling. They don't just supply knowledge; they create a future market for their products. You could do the same.

9. *Learn your customer's name and use it.* When a customer pays by check or credit card, even the megastores take note and call the customer by name when they say thanks. It works. Everyone likes to hear the sound of his or her own name.

10. *Say thanks to your employees.* A feeling of being appreciated is a powerful motivator for employees. Don't ever miss an opportunity to praise.

11. *Say thanks to your customers.* An Austin, Texas, car dealer appreciated the many referrals one of its customers had made to the dealership and honored the customer with its "top salesman" award—a gold-plated golf putter.

12. *Be courteous, friendly, and welcoming.* A pet peeve of many customers is being ignored and made to feel unimportant.

We once went to a doughnut shop in a southern city, and behind the counter was an attractive, enthusiastic woman who, oblivious to the early hour, greeted each customer with a bright smile and a cheerful welcome. It seemed that each customer was a favorite friend.

Since we had never met the woman, we were curious to see how she might address us, as total strangers. As we stepped up to place our orders, she said, "Good morning! How are y'all doing today?" It confirmed that she wasn't friends with all those who preceded us; she just made them feel that way!

Make each person feel as if he or she is the most important person on the premises at the time.

13. *Be efficient and value your customer's time.* No one has the time or the patience to wait to check out or exchange merchandise. A sure sign that you value your customers is to show them that you value their *time*. In this hurried, frazzled gotta-get-there-quick age, time is one of the most valuable commodities that any individual has. If customers must wait, give them an idea of how long the wait will be.

14. *Give your employees the authority to solve problems, and teach them how to do it.* Jason and Stephanie Blakely checked into the hotel that was going to be the site of their family reunion. Beyond a facade of beauty, it was clear that the hotel's customer service policies needed some repair.

Murphy's Law took over as soon as they arrived, and nothing went according to plan. The reservations had been lost, and once they got a room it wasn't what they'd requested months earlier. The meal was a disaster. Things went quickly from bad to worse. After getting no answer when he called the front desk, Jason methodically went down the "Call us if you need us" list of phone numbers the hotel provided. No one answered.

In frustration, he went downstairs to the desk and calmly stated his complaints. The response from all personnel, one after another, was, "I understand." Frankly, he didn't care if anyone understood. What he wanted was *someone who would take action.*

Your customer service training policies must go beyond teaching employees to understand to teaching them to also react.

In a well-managed business, employees take the responsibility to help the customer. Customers are looking for two things—solutions to problems and good feelings. Don't be the cause of their problems, and make them have good feelings about doing business with you.

15. *Be accessible:* Is it easy for people to enter your business? Can people in wheelchairs easily navigate your aisles

and offices? Do you have trained personnel on hand to answer telephone calls?

Set the Scene

You've written the script. Now it's time to set the scene. There are plenty of small—and large—details that must be in place before the customer ever enters the store. According to a major retailing study by Arthur Andersen, success in business requires more than just doing five or ten big things right; it requires doing hundreds of little things right. As Jim Baum, owner of Baum's, a women's apparel store in Morris, Illinois, puts it, "Whoever said 'retail is detail' was right on target."

Pay Attention to First Impressions

As Will Rogers said, "You never get a second chance to make a first impression." It's important to remember this and to ask yourself what image you are projecting about your business.

Pretend you are seeing your business for the first time just the way a new customer would. What kind of impressions is your business making on the customer? Ask yourself, *Would I do business with me?* Walt Disney continually challenged his employees to engage all the senses. You can do the same.

What do your customers hear? If the first customer contact is over the telephone, what do customers hear when they call?

Now that many businesses are cutting payrolls, the first voice customers hear may not be a real person but an electronic traffic director leading the caller through a series of instructions and beeps. Though great for efficiency, it's annoying for many of us who like the personal touch of a real voice at the other end of the line.

If the first customer contact is in person, what do your customers hear when they walk into your business? If there is music playing, is it low, pleasant, and calming—or loud, pulsating, and annoying? Your music should suit your clientele and convey the atmosphere you intend it to.

What do your customers see? Look critically at the outside of your business. Is everything neat, clean, and well lighted? Are the trees pruned, and is the grass cut or overgrown and unkempt? Is the building freshly painted and attractive? What about the signs? Is the outside sign eye-catching and easy to read?

Now look critically at the inside of your business. Is it clean? Are the carpets vacuumed or the floors swept and mopped? Are the windows clear? What about your in-store signs? Are they effective in directing customers quickly and conveniently to the products they seek? Are the mannequins in good repair and well dressed? Is the merchandise folded or neatly arranged? Are the counters free of dirt, dust, and fingerprints?

Jonathan Gray frequently stops at fast-food restaurants to grab an early-early breakfast before he goes to work. This morning, feeling adventurous, he tries a restaurant he hasn't been to before. He pulls up to the drive-up window after giving his order to the faceless voice behind the speaker. As he sits in his car waiting for the nourishment that will help him through his day, he inspects his surroundings. The ledge on the drive-up window is dusty and dirty, covered with the grime of too many spilled milkshakes and smashed packages of ketchup. Buzzing flies pay their last respects to their dead relatives lying on the ledge. Hardly appetizing. Jonathan, who might have become a regular customer under more favorable conditions, won't be back. Would you?

Similarly, a garden shop that welcomes patrons with weeds and wilted flowers won't make the impression that it can help customers create beautiful gardens.

Make sure your business is clean, bright, and attractive.

What do your customers smell? Researchers are just beginning to understand how aromas can influence emotions, evoke memories, and alter moods. What mood do you set in your business by its smell? Some businesses apply themselves to appealing favorably to customers' sense of smell much better than others. Texas Photo Store owners Corlis and Myrle Metcalf are well aware of the strong scents that their photo processing chemicals produce. Not wanting to offend customers with the smells, they began to strategically place attractive bowls of potpourri around and burn scented candles. When so many customers came in asking "What smells so good?" they decided to stock a line of sprays, candles, and potpourri. The products are great sellers.

For some—like a soap retailer or a coffee shop—evoking pleasant smells is just a matter of *being* what you are. For others, it might be a matter of *concealing* what you are—a garden shop with a large line of "natural" fertilizers, for instance, or a business with strong chemical smells.

What do your customers taste? Grocers and food specialty stores have long realized what a powerful marketing tool it is for customers to sample products before they buy them. How many times have you walked into the grocery store to buy just one item and found a pleasant person offering you a sample of some delectable treat? Many of us can't resist buying the product we are sampling.

Clothing stores often offer small cookies or snacks for their customers as a form of hospitality and an unexpected extra. It works.

What do your customers feel? As soon as a person comes into your business, he or she begins developing an opinion, even if it's done unconsciously. Your employees are a major factor in creating the mood, the atmosphere of your business. How are they doing?

Cast the Parts

After you have written the script and set the scene with some help from the clues above, it's time to find and rehearse the people who will play the parts. Hiring the right employees is critical. Not everyone is qualified by personality, skills, or intelligence to serve customers.

Peter Barbey, who owns Houle's Books in Scottsdale, Arizona, recognizes there's a big difference between the type of person who will be good at handling customers and one who will be much better suited to back-room work. For customer service people, Barbey said he looks for "the type of person who smiles naturally when talking to me, who seems to lead a life that is somewhat balanced, and who genuinely likes people."

If you hire the right people for your frontline positions and train them with the skills they will need to deal with the public, you'll be way ahead of the megastores, which are sometimes characterized by poorly paid, poorly trained, and poorly motivated employees.

Good employees will be ambassadors for your company in surprising ways. That's just what happened one snowy, frigid night several years ago when we were on a ski trip in Colorado—and the event was memorable. Riding up the mountain in a gondola, we settled in for a long ride in close quarters with strangers. In such instances, the conversation often turns to the question, What do you do?

Our fellow rider, who was an employee at the Keystone Resort, began to describe with great enthusiasm what a great place it was to work. "Our policy is to do whatever it takes to provide whatever the customer wants. And that's just what we do," he said.

We learned three things from him:

1. It was a business dedicated to serving the customer.
2. As an employee, he was enthusiastic about doing it.
3. Excellent customer service is a great marketing technique.

Who wouldn't want to stay at a place with such a commitment to customer service?

Rehearse the Players

As you begin "rehearsals" (the training process) impress upon each employee the importance of treating each customer as an invited guest and a welcome necessity to the success of the business—and to their paycheck.

Employees become frustrated when they must deal with a situation for which they have no training. So role-play with them the customer service process from the time the customer first walks in the door or contacts your business. Go through all the interactions and the transactions that will occur up until the sale is made and the customer leaves, eager to tell other people about the outstanding service.

Discuss not just actions, but also attitudes. All customers deserve to be treated with respect and made to feel important, not as though they've been given a bit part in a bad play.

It's Show Time—The Customer Who Comes Into the Store

Use the GOALS—A process to train your employees how to deal with on-premises customers. This process should start, if possible, at your front door.

G: Greet the customer and call him or her by name, if possible. Many of the discount stores have greeters posted at the door to smile a friendly hello and say a few words of welcome to the store. One of the things that people like about Wal-Mart, for instance, is being greeted at the door. It sets the tone for a positive encounter.

While the stereotype of the retail giants is "low prices and no service," that's not always true. Some of them are realizing their weaknesses and trying to improve. As Lee Sherman, president of Hahn Appliance in Tulsa, says:

> You go into the discount stores and you're greeted at the front door by very friendly, courteous people. The stores look nice. They're clean, they're well marked. They're doing all the things small businesses used to do before they became too complacent. That's why I have a receptionist at my front door. To the best of my knowledge, I'm the only independent retailer in Tulsa that has a receptionist at the front door.

Like Hahn's, most customer-focused businesses strive to greet customers within ten to fifteen seconds of the time they walk into the store. Sherman doesn't want anyone to be in his store more than fifteen seconds without being greeted. And if everyone's busy, someone still looks up and says, "Welcome, come in. Somebody will be with you in a moment."

O: Offer to help the customer. Use open-ended questions like "How may I help you" or "What can I help you find?" rather than "May I help you," which invites a yes or no response.

A: Appreciate the customer. Each employee must recognize the value of your customers and show them that they're important.

L: Listen to the customer. What has been called the forgotten skill is important enough that Lee Iacocca has said it can make "the difference between a mediocre company and a great one." When you truly listen to your customers, you'll learn more about them and their needs and you'll make them feel more important.

S: Service the customer's needs. Train your personnel to discover what the customer needs and then find a way to service those needs.

A: Ask the customer to come back, and make sure you have given him or her good reasons to do so.

It's Show Time—the Customer Who Calls On the Telephone

With extra time in short supply, people are relying more and more on the telephone to reduce shopping time. Whether they're looking for an auto part, a book, or a television, many of your customers are likely to make their first contact with you by phone.

These first impressions are critical. Every time that telephone rings, the person who answers it (and preferably it's a real person, not an electronic device) may gain a customer, keep a current one, or lose a potential one. Unconsciously, callers make a decision about you on the basis of the attitude of the person on the other end of the line. The question those callers may be asking is, *Is this the business I want to do business with?*

Do you ever pay attention to how your telephone is answered? Some people answer the telephone with such a long string of words that it's impossible to understand what they're saying. A few basic commonsense rules apply for training employees to handle call-in customers (of course, you may also find them helpful for improving your own phone manner):

- *Answer the phone promptly, but not immediately.* While it's annoying for the caller to wait while the phone rings six or seven times, it's startling if the phone is picked up before it reaches the end of the first ring. Such a quick pickup may also give the impression that you're desperately waiting for someone, anyone, to call.

- *Speak the greeting clearly and at a normal speed.* Briefly identify the name of your business, then ask a question like "How may I help you?" or "How may I direct your call?"

Your company greeting should be short, simple, and clear. Identify yourself to the caller. That will help the caller put a name with the voice and will set the tone that yours is a friendly, personal business.

- *Speak with a smile in your voice and with enthusiasm.* Some businesses even suggest putting a mirror near the telephone and visually checking the smile before answering! Change the pitch of your voice and add inflection.

- *Answer the caller's question or request.* This may seem ridiculously simple, but it's amazing how many people simply don't follow this rule. If your potential customer asks for the parts department and gets the garden department, he or she may wonder how many other mistakes are going on.

- *If the caller must be put on hold, use one of the "messages on hold" services,* so that the caller will hear a message about your company that you have selected. If callers hear a radio station while on hold, they may also hear your competitor's advertisement.

- *Avoid irritating phone habits.* Don't mumble, interrupt the caller, eat while on the phone (particularly apples, celery, or ice cubes) or carry on two conversations at once. Focus your full attention on the person on the phone—and remember that everyone who calls is a potential customer.

Who's Your "Audience"?
The New Customer of the 1990s

If you've been in business for a number of years, you've probably noticed a shift in customer attitudes. In short, Americans feel more stressed about almost every area of their lives, from money to marriage to planning for the future.

Today's overstressed customers are showing less and less interest in shopping, and they have issued the challenge to American business: Make shopping for products and services easier. With decreasing free time, they don't have time to wait and they certainly don't have patience for inferior merchandise. They don't tolerate errors, and they want policies and products that meet their needs, not the business owner's. The stress is showing. Customers are frustrated, distrustful, and likely to give you a piece of their minds.

The good news is that if you take the time to listen to customers' complaints and solve their problems, you will give them what they want: someone to care whether they're satisfied or not. Listen to the unspoken question, *How easy can you make it for me to do business with you?* Your answer, if you want to build your business, had better be the one they hope to hear.

Build a business environment that is pleasurable, easy, and fun—and they will come. Follow the techniques described throughout this book, and you can show them you care about them and keeping their business. But no matter how hard you try, you'll find a reason to use the information below.

Listen to Your Critics

By any measure, Breed & Co. is a well-run store that's dedicated to pleasing customers. Its products may be hardware, lawn and garden materials, and items for the home, but what it really sells is *service*.

The president, Truman Breed, says, "A day doesn't pass that we don't have a customer come up and tell me that they've had a fantastic shopping experience." The store's goal is to greet each customer as soon as he or she walks in the door and to give all customers that pleasant shopping experience.

But even in the best-run businesses, there will be mistakes and irritated customers. So accustomed are Breed's customers to being helped immediately that on those rare occasions when it doesn't happen, some customers will voice their complaints in no uncertain terms. For example, one lady who felt neglected stood in the middle of the floor and yelled, "Won't someone please help me?" How did the employees respond? Breed answers, "You'd better believe that about fourteen people instantly dropped everything they were doing and descended on her." Sometimes, as in that woman's case, you'll hear the complaints, and sometimes you'll have to solicit them.

How to Diffuse Angry Customers

It's good to hear complaints from your customers. It's a lot less fun than hearing compliments, but probably more valuable. By voicing a complaint, the customer is giving you a chance to correct the problem and salvage the relationship and all the business that may come in the future.

The ones to worry about are those people who are "silent, but deadly." As the famous retailer Marshall Field said, "Only those hurt me who are displeased but do not complain. They refuse me permission to correct my errors and thus improve my service."

Consider the following statistics:

- For every customer who bothers to complain, there are twenty-six others who remain silent.
- The average "wronged" customer will tell eight to sixteen people. More than 10 percent will tell more than twenty people.
- 91 percent of unhappy customers will never buy from you again.

Smart companies encourage feedback from customers and even solicit it. What happens in your company when a customer has a problem? In terms of generating repeat business, what happens *after* the sale is frequently much more important that what happens *before* the sale.

Unfortunately, it doesn't take much to ruin a business relationship that may have taken a great deal of time, effort, and money to build. You may have a beautiful store, great displays, and quality merchandise, but if you don't consistently treat your customers well, they will beat a path to your competitor's doors.

Two of the biggest sources of customer complaints are rude and indifferent service, and promises which weren't delivered. Even in a business that strives to provide customers with excellent service, there will always be people who have complaints.

Remember that you have basically two problems to solve: dealing with the customer's emotions, and solving the problem. When someone has a complaint remember to *keep your cool*. When someone is angry it's easy to get defensive, but it only makes matters worse. The person with the cool head will control the situation. Then follow the ALERT method to resolve the complaint.

A: Acknowledge the problem and apologize. By admitting that there is a problem, you begin to diffuse the angry or upset customer. By apologizing, you make him feel that he has some power in finding a solution. Introduce yourself and get the customer's name and address if you can.

L: Listen to the answers after you invite customers to tell you what happened. You cannot solve a problem you don't fully understand. Allow them to vent some steam if they need to. By listening carefully, you show customers you're concerned. Don't interrupt what they are saying but offer empathetic phrases like "I see what you mean" or "I understand."

E: Engage in a fact-finding dialogue. Now that the customer has vented some steam, your open-ended questions will help get the facts while the customer does most of the talking. What happened? What should have happened? How did it happen? What does the customer want to happen now? Remember, your purpose is to gather information, not assess blame or find fault.

R: Restate the problem as you understand it and record the information. Take notes and verify facts. Unfortunately, not all problems can be solved on the spot, so you may need the information in the future. Taking good notes shows your commitment to finding a solution and will serve as a long-standing record.

T: Thank the customer for sharing the problem with you—and take action. As difficult as it is to take criticism, the only way to solve a problem is to know about it. You want to create an atmosphere where customers know that you want to hear from them if their needs aren't satisfied.

Ask the customer to propose a solution. Ask "What would you like us to do?" or the ultimate disarmer, "What would it take to make you happy?" If the request is realistic, do it. If not, explain what you *can* do. If the customer doesn't know what he or she wants, suggest some options. Once you agree on the best solution, take action, and follow up. Thank the customer again for advising you of the problem and for his or her understanding.

Keep in mind that the most important ingredient in the problem-solving process is courtesy. Your attitude should convey genuine concern and consideration. Stay friendly and pleasant. Don't interrupt and don't correct. It doesn't really matter how right you are if you lose a customer who may tell twenty or more people about the experience.

Bad luck for you if that dissatisfied customer happens to be a writer for a national publication. When that happens—and it has—the "unsatisfied customer" won't tell just twenty other people, but 2 *million* or more. Maybe we should treat each customer as if he or she could possibly write a damaging article . . . or produce an exposé on national television.

And for a final note, remember what your mother told you, "You can't please everybody." Unlike some experts, we don't believe the adage that "the customer is always right." No one, for instance, has the right to be rude or abusive to you or your employees.

If a customer is being unreasonable, evaluate your options and consider an offer to refund the person's money and an invitation to take his or her business elsewhere, or possibly consider sending a gift as a token of apology.

At Southwest Airlines, when the facts don't justify what the customer is asking for, the airline sends a little "we're sorry" gift, such as a pen or potpourri, as a gesture of goodwill. The gift is accompanied by a letter saying, "I hope you accept this gift in the spirit in which it's being sent."

Do the customers accept the demonstration of goodwill? As Colleen Barrett, Southwest's executive vice president for customers, told *Working Woman* magazine, "Most of the time they do. But every now and then we'll get one of the gifts back with a note: 'Keep your damn pen.'"

Get Feedback from Your Other "Critics"

Every time you get feedback from a customer, it gives you an opportunity to improve something about your business. The most successful companies we know are diligent about monitoring customer opinions. Choose methods that best suit your needs and budget, but make your effort to solicit customer opinions an *ongoing* one.

Here are a few ideas:

• *Customer visits.* As you walk through your store, ask your customers "How are we doing?" Encourage feedback.

• *Customer surveys.* Design simple, easy-to-read surveys and post them in a prominent location. Invite customers to fill them out and drop them in a box in your store or use a postage-paid card. (We give you some examples in Chapter Three.)

• *Focus groups.* Invite a small group of people—usually five to ten—to come to your store and share their opinions and suggestions about your business. The session might last an hour or two and should be led by a professional who is skilled in communications and getting people to give honest opinions. Provide refreshments and give each participant a thank-you gift, such as a gift certificate, for participating. It's best to videotape or audiotape the meeting. Listen carefully to what your customers are saying and don't become defensive.

• *Employee surveys.* The ones who know your customers best are your employees, and they hear firsthand the comments being made. Establish a system for employees to note customer opinions, but do this in conjunction with other programs since some may be reluctant to reveal criticisms of management or of their own work.

Inspire a Standing Ovation

In theater, if actors and actresses have a good script, do their job superbly, and have interesting sets, the payoff will be a standing ovation and a long run. Audiences will leave the theater raving about the performance and encouraging their friends to see the play.

In business, if your employees do a super job and you have quality products to sell in an attractive, comfortable setting, you too will be successful. You'll keep your existing customers happy, and their enthusiasm will generate other business through word-of-mouth referrals. But each encounter with a prospective customer or an existing one must be treated as an opportunity to acquire a new fan—or lose a current customer.

As Stanley Marcus, that impressario of retail, says, "Nobody owns anybody anymore. This is show business, folks, and you're only as good as your last performance."

Strive to do whatever it takes to satisfy your customers so they will keep coming back for encores and you'll be assured of many repeat performances.

Six

Who's Minding Your Store? *Everybody!*

You can dream, create, design, and build the most wonderful place in the world, but it requires people to make the dream a reality.

—Walt Disney

One big advantage that small businesses have over the giants is that for a large segment of the population, there are things that factor into buying decisions besides low prices and huge selections.

Though price and selection are important ingredients, this large group of customers is also interested in things like service, knowledgeable personnel, and a place where they can go to find people who are willing to take care of their needs.

As one person told us, "If I go somewhere and they've got what I want and I like the person and I'm treated well, I'll keep going there to shop with them and I'll tell everybody about them—even if costs a little more."

To compete with the megastores, you must have products or services that people want to buy. To distinguish yourself from the giants you must have knowledgeable people devoted to providing superior service and helping customers *solve* problems, not make problems.

Fisher's Office Products is a company in Boise, Idaho, which has managed to post impressive revenue increases despite the competition from such office products giants as Office Depot, Costco, and OfficeMax. Fisher's president Gary Mahn recognizes the importance of developing good people who are pleasant to be around. "People like to do business with people they like, particularly in this business," he said. "The only thing we offer is service, and service is our people."

To strengthen the value package you offer your customers, don't just give them the same things they get from the super-stores, give them *more:* Give them personal attention and services only people can offer.

In our consultations, interviews, and research, one thing we hear consistently from the owners and managers of small retail and service businesses is their plea for advice on how to find, train, and motivate employees who will help build the kind of business that can compete with the retail giants.

How do you do this? There are five steps:

1. Create a working environment where people enjoy working.
2. Find the right people to work there.
3. Train them to cultivate customers and to perform effectively.
4. Motivate them to be productive.
5. Manage them well.

Creating the Atmosphere for a Winning Team

The New Workplace

Have you ever dreamed of having someone help run your business? The ideal "someone" would help keep an eye on the success of your company, help make those difficult decisions, and be as concerned about your business as you are.

That notion doesn't have to be just a dream; it can be a reality if *you* make it so. That someone—or those people—may already be on your payroll. Owners and managers are finding that getting employees to think and act like owners is the single biggest factor in the success of their businesses.

Employees are changing. They want more than just a paycheck. They want recognition, satisfaction, and a sense that their efforts contribute to a bigger picture.

Bosses are changing. Not so many years ago, the "boss" was the person with absolute authority. He—most of them were men—was the person who made all the decisions, barked all the orders, and who demanded that his "troops" be obedient, unquestioning, and submissive. If they weren't, they were quickly dismissed.

The fallout was employees who didn't make a move without the boss's OK and a workplace that didn't utilize the talents and contributions of employees, leaving them frustrated and unfulfilled.

That style just isn't effective anymore. The authoritarian figures with the "do it my way or the highway" attitude have been replaced in many successful companies by a totally different mind-set. Rather than a dictatorship, there is teamwork: employees working together for the good of the company. Rather than an employer who is concerned only with the bottom line, there is a coach who truly cares about his or her employees and inspires and leads a team of productive employees to new levels of creativity and innovation.

Take, for example, Emma Lou Brent, the CEO of Phelps County Bank, an independent bank in Rolla, Missouri, which won recognition by *Inc.* magazine in 1992 as one of the best small companies to work for.

Faced with stiff competition from two big bank holding companies with well-known names, Brent realized she had to build a different kind of company so her bank could deliver a high level of service that would make it successful. Now the bank has nudged aside the competition to take over first place. Says Brent:

> We basically started with education and employee training because we felt that was our weapon, the only weapon we had for the future if we were going to stay independent and small and be successful. The only way we are going to be able to do this is to have a whole staff of thinkers.

After receiving lots of education and training, employees were given ownership of their jobs and the freedom to act on their own judgment. "We said, 'You know what to do, so just go do it. You don't have to ask anybody,' " says Brent. "Now they call that 'empowerment.' "

The E Word: *Empowerment*

This new approach to management, which involves giving workers the training and authority they need to manage their own jobs, has several labels—self-management, participative management, or self-directed management—but the most common one is *empowerment*.

Companies that empower their employees:

- Trust the judgment and abilities of people.
- Bring out the best in people by training them and supporting them.
- Build employee trust by treating employees with honesty, openness, and integrity.
- Give people ownership of their jobs and the authority to use their best judgment in performing them.
- Hold employees accountable for their work.
- Allow them freedom to take risks and make decisions without fear or humiliation.
- Ask them what changes might result in better performance and then implement those changes.
- Teach employees to work in teams and give the teams power.

For the company, empowerment can greatly improve performance. For the employee, it means a happier, more satisfying work environment. For the customers, it means there is always someone who has the power to take care of their needs.

Customers don't have to wait for a refund while the customer service representative gets a manager's approval. If the customer has a complaint, an empowered employee moves to resolve it.

It's important to match the right individuals to the right positions and give them information, authority, and responsibility to do their jobs. You can expect motivated employees,

Exhibit 4. How to build an employee-centered workplace.

- Match individuals with the positions in which they're likely to thrive.
- Create a work environment that is stimulating and fun.
- "Empower" your employees.
- Share information with others and encourage communication and teamwork throughout the organization.
- Look for results more than the processes to get there.
- Respect individuals.
- Form partnerships with your employees and make them feel a part of the business and its decisions.
- Listen to employees and respect their suggestions.
- Be positive and enthusiastic.

better quality of work, higher job satisfaction, and lower turnover. Exhibit 4 summarizes how you can empower your employees by developing an employee-centered workplace.

What Do Employees Want?

When workers were asked in a 1991 Gallup poll what they valued most in a job, the answers surprised a few people. While many employers thought that high income would have topped the list, the research proved otherwise. (That answer was eleventh.)

Workers in different occupations will give different answers to the question, so maybe the best way to find out what *your* employees want is to ask them. Some of the answers that you're likely to hear most often:

• *Interesting work.* This rated high in the Gallup poll, second only to *good health insurance and other benefits.*

• *Fair wages.* When employees come to work, they feel that they are striking a bargain. The unspoken feeling is that "I will do a fair day's work for you if you treat me right and pay me fairly." It's very difficult to expect creativity, loyalty, enthusiasm, and commitment when you're paying less than the job requires.

Are you paying your employees enough? Our successful

businesses typically pay well above the industry average for similar jobs.

■ *To be included in the decision-making process.* Successful companies, we found, regularly get input from their employees.

■ *A caring environment.* In the intense struggle to survive against the mass merchandisers and super competition, it may seem superficial to say that the way to get more out of employees is to truly care about them. But, think about it: Whom would you work harder for—the boss who really cares about you or the one who believes you're only a ticket to the bottom line?

■ *A job that's fun.* Even in the most demanding jobs, don't overlook the importance of having some fun. It's not inconsistent with operating a serious, profit-making business. Robert Levering and Milton Moskowitz noted in their book *The 100 Best Companies to Work for in America* that they are seeing companies now where having fun seems to be part of the corporate mission. Why not?

■ *To feel valued for the work they accomplish.* Recognition is one of the easiest, and most important, motivators. Catch your employees doing something right and praise them for a *specific* behavior or results.

■ *A job that's satisfying and significant.* You will hire and retain better employees if they enjoy their work. And if the workplace is enjoyable, you'll find that absenteeism will dip, as will claims for disabilities related to job stress.

Hiring a Winning Team

Of all the decisions that a small-business owner must make, one of the most crucial is hiring the right people for the job. People are your company's greatest asset, but mistakes in finding the right ones can be costly.

According to their latest figures (1992), the Employee Management Association in Raleigh, North Carolina, found it cost an average of $443 to recruit a new hourly worker and almost $6,900 to recruit a professional or management employee. Add in the mishire's salary, fringe benefits, and time and expenses involved in training and the costs skyrocket. If you add the intangible expenses such as lost opportunities, the cost of a bad hire can amount to seven times the tangible costs, according to some estimates.

As the competition gets tougher and tougher, it's more crucial than ever to have productive people in your organization. Your success is defined by the people you employ. How can you find the right ones? You can look at job experience and education. You can interview them and test them. But when it's decision time, it all comes down to instinct, a gut reaction.

At McWhorter's Stationery in San Jose, California, a prospective full-time employee goes through a series of interviews and a battery of tests. After this careful screening, the final hiring decision is based on the answer to one basic gut-reaction question. That question, says president Steve Andrews, is, "Would I like to have Thanksgiving dinner with this person?"

You may have different deciding questions in your situation, but before you get to that final question, there are six key steps that will help you find the right employees.

1. Define the Skills the Job Needs

Writing a job description is perhaps the single smartest thing you can do to ensure good results in hiring. The best job description goes well beyond just a list of job duties. It includes the desirable traits that the person should have, and what the results of hiring the right person might be.

Outline the physical and mental tasks involved and the qualifications necessary for the job: training, knowledge, skills, and personality traits. As a starting point, define the traits possessed by the most successful person who held the job.

By going beyond a surface description, you'll improve your chances of finding someone who will bring more to the job than just the technical skills. You can train people, but you can't change their personality. Here are some of the traits to look for:

Eight Traits of Good Employees

1. *High self-esteem*. This trait is described by experts as the greatest single predictor of success in any activity, and people who have it tend to be risk takers and to be productive. They tend to say, "If life hands you lemons, make lemonade."

In contrast, when self-esteem is low, employees will spend time reading help-wanted ads and daydreaming.

2. *Good communication skills*. Rebecca Linton, the owner of Rebecca's Lingerie in Montgomery, Alabama, defines this as "the person who has a twinkle in their eye and who *talks*. They can be a quiet person, but they need to be able to talk."

Good communicators will look you straight in the eye, volunteer information, and listen attentively too. As Jim Chick, president of Chick's Sporting Goods in Covina, California, says, "It's very easy to give people product knowledge. That's not the hard part. The hard part is teaching them to be aggressive and to want to wait on people, communicate with people, listen to what the customer wants, and try to fulfill their needs."

3. *Self-motivation*. These people are goal oriented, know where they want to go, and have a plan to get there.

4. *Dependability*. It's essential to find employees who possess this basic trait. Dependable people will do what they promise to do, are on time, and produce work that is consistent in quality. They show up.

5. *Energy and dedication to hard work*. Thomas Jefferson said, "I'm a great believer in luck, and I find the harder I work, the more I have of it."

Direct Tire's owner Barry Steinberg, who thrives in Watertown, Massachusetts, amid competition from national tire chain stores, is such a believer in the importance of this trait that he interviews prospective employees three times, at three different times of day. He's looking for people who have a high energy level throughout the day.

6. *Perseverance*. Those with this trait will do whatever it takes, for as long as it takes. Thomas Edison would never

have perfected the light bulb if he had given up after one hundred tries.

7. *Enthusiasm.* People who are genuinely enthusiastic are more likely to succeed. Charles Schwab says, "A man can succeed at almost anything for which he has unlimited enthusiasm." So convinced of the importance of enthusiasm was coach Vince Lombardi that he quipped, "If you aren't fired with enthusiasm, you will be fired with enthusiasm."

8. *A sense of humor.* People with the ability to take work—but not themselves—seriously can be a great addition to a team. A company named as one of the best to work for in America says to potential employees:

- "Tell me how you recently used your sense of humor in a work environment.
- "Tell me how you have used humor to defuse a difficult situation."

2. Plan an Effective Search

The search for employees is carried out on two levels: to satisfy immediate needs, and to satisfy future needs. Your hiring duties will be easier in the *future* if you have laid the following groundwork:

1. *Be a company where people want to work.* If you have a good reputation for paying well, treating people right, and nurturing employees, it will be much easier to find people to hire.

2. *Recruit all the time.* Have you ever been impressed by an employee in a restaurant, store, bank, or other business and thought, "Boy, I'd love to have that person working for me?" When that happens, don't just conclude your business and leave. Introduce yourself and tell the employee how impressed you are. Explain that you periodically have openings in your business and would like to keep his or her name on file. The worst that can happen is he'll be flattered to know his good work has impressed someone but won't be interested in a job

now. The best thing is that you'll be building a resource file of people who may fit in well with your company.

A specialty chain store we know has refined that type of recruiting. Its managers have cards saying, "I was impressed by your service. If you're ever looking for a job, please call me."

3. *Constantly build a pipeline to future employees.* Through your network of contacts, put out the word—before you need someone—about the types of employees you are looking for. This widens your sphere of influence and, when you need a key employee, your "sphere" may know just the person for you.

When you need an employee *now:*

1. *Consult your network.* It's easier to analyze a few good prospects who come highly recommended by people you trust than to search for a pearl from a stack of applications and resumes.

2. *Place a help-wanted ad in your newspaper or trade publication.* As you develop your advertisement, keep in mind that you are "selling" the job and the company to prospective employees. Make the ads brief, but make the job and the company sound exciting and interesting. List qualifications, but avoid using discriminatory terms such as *boy, youthful,* or *girl Friday.*

3. *Ask for referrals from current employees.* Often your present employees are great resources for finding future employees.

4. *Retain an employment agency or head hunter.* Though there will be expenses involved, agencies can do some of the initial screening for you, which may save time and money in the long run.

5. *Consult placement offices, colleges, or technical schools.* For some job requirements, these can be excellent sources of employees.

6. *Post the job with your state employment commission.*

7. *Look at your interns.* If you have an internship program, it may be an ideal source for future employees.

8. *Send direct mail to your customers or network.* Don't miss out on the opportunity to tell your customers that you're a growing, successful business and are looking for employees who will take care of them.

3. Interview According to a Plan

While some business owners are extremely competent in many areas, many of them are ineffective at interviewing. Your skills in asking the right questions and listening to the answers are important in the selection of the right employee.

The interview process takes place on two levels. "Horizontal" information such as education and work experience is easy to uncover. "Vertical" information plumbs the depths of the candidate's personality, capabilities, and potential.

Knowing the legal issues surrounding hiring practices can save you from a variety of nightmares. Know which questions you can and can't ask on applications and in interviews. Exhibit 5 provides some guidelines for appropriate and nonappropriate questions, as well as helpful hints for preparing for and conducting job interviews.

4. Check References

As the job market tightens, applicants have been known to stretch the truth in their desperation to find suitable employment. This makes reference checking all the more important to verify identity, education, employment history, and other information the candidate supplies.

Recently, the threat of lawsuits has changed the willingness of past employers to give out information, making it more difficult to check information. For former employers, the risk is giving out information that could put them in court for a defamation suit. For you, the risk of not investigating the candidate's past is negligent hiring. If you hire a delivery person who burglarizes a customer's home, you could be guilty of negligent hiring.

Develop a thorough application form that requires complete information from candidates, including full name, Social

Exhibit 5. Questions you can and cannot ask during preemployment interviews.

Topics you *cannot* ask about include:

1. Age or date or place of birth (or nationality).
2. Place of birth (or nationality) of mother, father, wife, or other close relative.
3. Religious affiliation (denomination, name of church, pastor, etc.).
4. Color of skin.
5. Whether naturalized or native born.
6. The name of any relative other than father, mother, husband, or wife and minor children.
7. Names of clubs, societies, or lodge memberships.
8. Original name, if it has been changed by court order.
9. Birth certificate or records of baptism or naturalization.
10. To see a photograph.
11. Citizenship (name of country).
12. Native tongue.
13. Marital status. Don't ask if they're married or where their spouse works.
14. Maiden name.
15. Child care arrangements.
16. Arrest records.

Topics you *can* ask about include:

1. Applicant's place of residence and the length of time as a resident of this city or state.
2. Whether applicant is a U.S. citizen.
3. Applicant's work experience.
4. *Convictions* of any crimes.
5. Membership in the armed forces of the United States.
6. Whether applicant is between the ages of eighteen and sixty-five.
7. Any physical or mental impairments which would prevent the applicant from doing the job.

Helpful hints for the interview:

1. Draft a description of the company and its mission, and a description of the job you are hiring for. Some companies show candidates a video or ask them to read a brochure or report about the company.
2. Prepare your questions in advance, drafting them to ferret out job traits that fit the description you have written.

Exhibit 5. (continued)

3. Familiarize yourself with the person's application data before your interview.
4. Ask open-ended questions which explore past experiences.
5. Here are some specific questions to ask:

   - What qualities do you have that would help you in this job?
   - Tell me about your past jobs and your responsibilities there. What did you like and dislike about them? (This will be an indication whether the job you are hiring for is a good fit for the candidate.)
   - Describe the three times in your life when you did work that made you truly proud. What did you learn from those accomplishments?
   - Tell me about three setbacks you've experienced and what you learned from them. (These last two questions will give an indication whether the candidate has the ability and willingness to learn from experience—a critical factor in finding a good employee.)
   - We are a growing company. Suppose you were being hired today: Describe the type of job you hope you'd be doing in five years and what you'd be accomplishing.
   - What did you like and dislike about the people you worked with in previous jobs? Whom did you admire, and what traits did they have? (This may give some clue about how important relationships are to the candidate and whether he or she is a team player.)
   - What do you consider are your strengths, and what are your weaknesses?
   - Why did you leave your last job? (Use caution with the candidate who badmouths a previous employer.)
   - Tell me about situations during your last job that caused you to miss work. (This question will give a clue as to the candidate's dependability and whether he or she assumes responsibility to get to work.)

6. Listen carefully to the answers to all questions. Let the candidate do the talking. Experts say that candidates should do at least 75 percent of the talking.
7. Pose follow-up questions or requests, such as, "That's interesting; tell me more about that . . ." until you have your answers.
8. Immediately following the interview, jot down some notes that will jog your memory at decision time. What did the candidate look like? What were your impressions? Ask yourself, "Should I hire this person?" then sort the materials into stacks of yes, no, and maybe.

Security number, driver's license number, address, employment history with months and years of employment. Include on the application form a request for the names of past supervisors and their current telephone numbers.

Look for any unexplained gaps and ask potential employees to sign a release giving you permission to confirm the information. Before checking references, ask the candidates if there is anything they would like you to know about and give them the opportunity to explain.

5. Use Preemployment Tests

Preemployment tests can run the gamut from psychological exams, personality assessments, skill-based tests, aptitude tests, and achievement tests, to integrity tests and drug testing.

There are good tests and bad tests, and none of them works in all situations. A debate is raging about whether certain tests are predictors of a candidate's success or weapons of discrimination.

The consensus is that tests should not be the sole basis for hiring. How do you choose the best tests for your situation? Check with others in your industry, your trade association, or a local university professor of industrial psychology.

6. Make the Hiring Decision

Now that you've completed all the steps above, it's time to make the hard decision. Reread the job description you've written. Review the application materials from the "maybe" stack and see if you can now sort them into either the "no" stack or the "yes" stack. If you need to follow up with additional questions or another interview, now is the time to do it. If other people on your staff have had a part in the interviewing stage, consult with them for their opinions.

Even with the best screening process, nothing takes the place of good judgment and a thorough understanding of the job requirements. Base your decision on the answers to these questions:

1. Does the candidate have the skills and knowledge necessary to perform the job?
2. Does the candidate have the traits necessary to succeed at the job?
3. Will the candidate be a good addition to your team? Ask yourself, *Would I like to be around this person?*
4. Is the candidate motivated and trainable?

The hope is that you'll be able to choose someone who appeals to you. If not, don't hire anyone yet. Keep looking. It's been reported that Home Depot hires only two people for every one hundred who apply. Truman Breed, president of Breed and Co., sums it up when he says, "We keep looking until we find the right one."

Training a Winning Team

The first step in building your "dream team" is finding the right employees, and the second crucial step is training them. While many small companies make the effort to find and hire good employees, few will invest much time or money in training. Then they wonder why employees don't measure up to expectations.

It's like investing the time and effort to select and plant a beautiful rose bush, then depriving it of water, fertilizer, and sunlight. You'll likely get thorns, but not very many roses in full, glorious bloom.

Training is an ongoing process. Just as the rose needs constant nutrients, your employees will grow into better, more productive employees if they are constantly nurtured, evaluated, and trained. Exhibit 6 will help you to get the training process started.

Resources for Training

In any training program, it's important to start with a clear idea of what you hope employees will learn. Is it to upgrade job

Exhibit 6. What employees want and need to know.

- *The company's mission.* Employees must understand the company's vision and purpose. Do they know what the mission of your business is? Instead of just dumping a new employee into the job, take the time to describe your company philosophy and your expectations.

- *The company's attitude toward customers.* If new employees learn nothing else, they must learn your philosophy toward taking care of customers. What do you expect from your employees? Remember, your actions will speak louder than your words.

- *The skills necessary to perform their jobs well.* If you're lucky, new employees will bring to their jobs the skills necessary to perform their jobs well. But you'll still need to train employees in the skills necessary for your particular systems.

- *How to handle customer complaints.* In even the best-run businesses, customers get irritated. Train each employee how to deal with an unsatisfied customer. (We cover how to handle this in detail in Chapter Five.)

- *Knowledge about your products and services.* This goes beyond just knowing where something is. It includes what the product does, its features, and the benefits it offers the customer. The companies that will prosper during the 1990s and beyond will give their customers this information.

- *How to be problem solvers.* Customers don't just buy what you have to sell. Customers buy what you know. They want *people who can solve their problems.*

Home Depot is a good example of a company that has put this practice into action and become the industry leader for supplying information to its customers. Employees will gladly tell the customer not only where to find a new faucet, but also how to replace it.

For small businesses, this is also a good way to build customer satisfaction. The successful small businesses of the future will provide knowledge and expertise.

---

skills, learn new techniques, or just become more motivated? Set specific objectives for training.

First-class training programs don't have to cost a lot of money, but they do require some creative approaches. With these ideas in mind, turn to:

▪ *Other employees:* On-the-job training is the most widely used method of training. Your best trainers may be among your current employees.

▪ *Books, audiotapes, videos, and professional journals.* Start a training library and encourage employees to spend time there or give them specific assignments. You might develop a simple form for employees to use that asks them to describe what they have learned.

Consider holding weekly discussion groups to share information. Even those who don't read the books or watch the tapes will benefit by the sharing of information and ideas.

▪ *Seminars.* With a wide variety of cost and quality, many seminar companies offer expertise on a range of topics. The important things to remember here are to be sure employees share their knowledge with others and be open to integrating new suggestions they've learned. Schedule "minitraining" sessions during lunch hours or in the first or last hour of the day.

Seminars can be great for stimulating enthusiasm and generating excitement, but if new suggestions are greeted with apathy or negative attitudes, that can kill all the benefits.

▪ *Schools and colleges.* There is a wealth of knowledge available at local learning institutions. Call local colleges, universities, or technical schools and inquire about experts in the field of choice. Community colleges in particular strive to build partnerships with businesses and may have training programs already in place.

Consider asking employees to share in the costs of the training. Direct Tire's Barry Steinberg requires his employees to be certified in certain areas. He pays for training if they pass the test, and the employees pay for the training if they fail. It's an incentive that works!

Don't overlook training as a marketing ploy. In its marketing messages, Direct Tire proudly proclaims that its mechanics are certified in Automotive Service Excellence.

▪ Your local chamber of commerce may also have the names of *qualified speakers or trainers.* If not, they should be able to provide you with the names of people who might have those names.

- *Pool resources.* Do you know of other business owners who might benefit from the same type of training you think you and your employees need? Hire a good speaker or consultant or schedule a workshop and share the expenses with another company.

- *Promote continuous improvement as a company value.* If you publicly congratulate employees who have learned new skills or trained others, you'll encourage other employees to follow suit.

Motivating a Winning Team

What would you give to have your employees arrive at work happy, enthusiastic, and ready to give their best at their jobs all day long?

Surprisingly, it may be easier—and less expensive—than you might think. Most small-business owners mistakenly believe that the best employee motivator is money. Not so, say the experts. We should stress here that if employees aren't receiving satisfactory wages, they'll keep their eyes peeled for a better job and will hit the road as soon as they find one. It's hardly the situation that breeds employee loyalty. However, once their basic economic needs are met, money isn't the most powerful motivator.

We still have much to learn about what does motivate people to become good employees, and it will vary from person to person and company to company. (Bill may be thrilled to have a steady job with a dental plan, while Susan cherishes a flexible schedule that allows her to be on hand for the important events in her children's lives.)

While it's difficult to assess a definite relationship between employee satisfaction and company success, the successful small-business owners we know all agree that their company *is* their employees and that it is in the best interest of the company to make sure employees stay happy and satisfied.

What makes employees want to work harder and smarter? The answers will vary from employee to employee, and the best way to find out is to just ask. You may find they have relatively simple—and easily filled—requests. Just don't make the assumption that what motivates *you* will also motivate *them*. The following tips will help you to motivate your employees.

Twelve tips for motivating your employees

1. *Give your employees the tools and resources to do their jobs effectively.* Nothing can be so frustrating and defeating as making an employee struggle with equipment that is outmoded and ineffective. Investing money in equipment to help your employees get the job done efficiently is always a good investment—as long as they have the proper training to utilize it. When crushing deadlines loom, bring in temporary employees.

2. *Constantly tell your employees how important they are, and show it in small and large ways.* Aledia Hunt Tush, who owns Mr. CB's, a marine sporting goods store in Sarasota, Florida, understands how important her employees are to the success of her business. "I will never take credit for this store by myself," she says. "My employees are extremely important and anyone in business who doesn't understand that had better go back to school." How does she communicate that to her employees? "I tell them all the time," she says.

3. *Celebrate the special days in the lives of your employees.* Birthdays top the list, but employment anniversaries are important dates to remember too. Whether you give your employee a holiday on his or her special day or a card or small gift, the message you send is, "You're important enough for me to remember your special days."

4. *"Praise publicly and criticize privately,"* as the adage goes. Catch your employees doing something right and praise them—publicly! If you must criticize, stay focused on the actions or behavior you object to. Tell them briefly, but specifically what changes you want.

5. *Look for tangible ways to let employees know how important they are.* A note of thanks, fresh baked cookies for all to share, seasonal small gifts are all good—and economical—morale boosters. Even those inexpensive Valentines like the kind we

used to trade in third grade, accompanied by sweetheart candies, can be fun and effective at the proper time. Be creative!

6. *Be sensitive to the family and personal responsibilities of your employees.* Companies that breed loyalty and commitment have made tremendous strides toward helping employees deal with the delicate balancing act between work and personal life. Some offer flexible schedules; others offer job sharing. The common denominator is understanding and cooperation, and the reward is employees who lead balanced, fulfilling lives and are willing to give 100 percent to their jobs.

7. *Match the person to the job.* It's become clear over the years that the old adage that "anybody can do anything if they really put their minds to it" is simply not true. People who work in a job they're not well suited for because of knowledge or temperament will be prone to stress and poor job performance. We're not saying that employees can *always* avoid jobs they don't like, but you'll get amazing results if you pair the person to the position they are best suited for.

8. *Give all employees a business card and encourage them to give the cards to identify themselves and your business.* You may be surprised what benefits this subtle form of marketing can yield and how proud some employees may feel to be considered important enough to have their own cards.

9. *Keep the lines of communication open.* Keep employees informed and convey to them the role they play in the company's success. Hold frequent meetings, even if they're informal.

10. *Set doable goals and encourage competition between departments.* Contests can spur energy and enthusiasm. Post the results daily. Recognize the winners, but be sure to encourage and congratulate the teams that didn't win, too.

11. *Don't forget to have some fun.* How sad it would be to work in a job where there was no laughter and no humor! Having fun doesn't have to be inconsistent with a profit-making business. One business we know actually has a group of employees who are assigned the task of coming up with offbeat activities to generate fun and laughter for the employees. Among the ideas they've come up with are Hula-hoop

contests, a telephone booth stuffing contest, and a bubble gum blowing contest.

12. *Start a bonus or profit sharing plan if you can.* Employees who have a stake in the success of their company will work harder to ensure its success.

By instituting a profit sharing plan, McWhorter's Stationery has developed more committed employees and given them a stake in the success of the company. "If you walk in and the lights are on in the bathroom, or if there's garbage thrown away that could be recycled," says McWhorter's president, Steve Andrews, "or if the door's open and the air conditioner's on, that's profit-sharing dollars just going right down the tubes." The employees know it and make appropriate changes.

The costs of bonus or profit-sharing plans will likely be outweighed by the increase in employee loyalty and motivation. Take into account the high costs of continually advertising for, interviewing, and training new employees and the even higher costs of poorly motivated employees.

Whatever tactics you use to motivate your employees, be sure to monitor their satisfaction and encourage suggestions. This leads us to the next section.

Managing the Winning Team

Getting Feedback from Employees

You probably have a suggestion box somewhere in your store asking customers what they think about your products and services. If you're smart, you constantly monitor these suggestions and make appropriate changes.

Do you give your employees the same opportunity to make suggestions? They are the people closest to your customers and the products and services you sell. Getting employee input can be helpful in deciding how to serve those customers as efficiently and effectively as possible. But getting their input won't happen unless you have trained your employees to *listen and ask.* (See Exhibit 7.)

You wouldn't be reading this book unless you were eager to learn new ways to make your business run better. Have you asked your employees for their ideas? Ask them, *If this were your company and your money, would you be doing things the same way we are?*

There's no better way to get employee input than to just ask for it. But don't get defensive about their suggestions. If, as the adage goes, you're afraid of finding skeletons in the closet, don't open the closet door. But if you think you can be objective and open-minded about your employees' opinions, then don't hesitate to ask for them. Your employees may have the key that will unlock the doors to a more profitable, productive business.

Hold frequent staff meetings to share company information and ask for input. What are customers saying about your new products? What do they think about the new displays? What type of marketing is drawing them into the store? Your employees know, if they're asking the questions.

Some retailers use a suggestion box to elicit employee input, and some schedule brainstorming meetings. Others post a large piece of paper on a wall, and employees are invited to jot down an idea or suggestion.

Whatever your format, you'll be sending a clear signal to employees that you feel they are part of the team and you value their input.

Employees hold a wealth of knowledge and ideas. Companies have saved thousands of dollars by implementing their suggestions. Some companies even offer incentives to stimulate employees to make recommendations. Regardless of how you

Exhibit 7. Rules of the employee suggestion game.

- Don't get defensive about ideas.
- Write down all suggestions.
- Don't reject them automatically because they aren't *your* ideas.
- Listen attentively to any suggestion and think of why it's *good* before you consider why it's *bad*.
- If a suggestion can't be implemented, explain why.

stimulate ideas from employees, remember that employees' number-one complaint about their jobs is that their bosses don't listen to them.

When It Isn't Working: How to Fire Fairly

Change is a fact of life in every business, and it's important to accept the fact that no matter how hard you try and how carefully you plan, your business won't be a great place to work for everyone on your payroll.

In a small business with few employees, the decision to fire someone can send ripples through the entire organization. How do you know when it's time to fire? We suggest you use the MOP Test to determine if your employee's actions are putting you and your company in jeopardy.

M = *morale.* Is the problem employee having a negative influence on the morale and attitude of others?

O = *operations.* Is the problem employee affecting operations, causing a decrease in productivity or an increase in costs?

P = *profits.* Are profits dropping because of the employee's actions? Are you losing customers, sales, or orders? All of these will eventually lead to a profit decline.

If you answered yes to any of those questions, ask yourself if you can change the employee's behavior or if it's time to fire him or her. If you elect to fire an employee, know your responsibilities.

Maybe you have an employee whom you're not ready to fire, but you do believe holds some promise. To salvage this employee, consider the three-step "progressive discipline" method.

1. *Counseling.* Counsel with the employee, addressing behavior that is unacceptable. Tactfully point out improper activities and suggest some steps for improving them. Be positive

and encouraging, praising all strengths, but stress that the undesirable behavior must be stopped.

Many times, this first step is the only one that you will have to take. Good employees will often work hard at changing unsatisfactory behavior once they're aware of what they're doing. Be sure to make notes of your discussion. Date and write the details of the conversation. If you don't see any improvement after counseling, go to step 2.

2. *Written reprimand.* Put the problem in writing. Clearly state deficiencies or improper behavior and review the counseling discussion. Issue written guidelines, with a timetable, to correct the behavior. Date your notes and get the employee's signature. It's possible to salvage the employee at this point, but the chances are growing slimmer.

3. *Final warning.* Make this blunt and to the point. Restate your previous discussions and written reprimand. Stress that this is the last chance for improvement. Point out that failure to meet your demands will result in termination. Detail your demands in writing, ask the employee to sign it, and put a copy in his or her personnel file.

If you don't see immediate improvement at this point, fire quickly and don't let the situation drag on. Remember your employee has rights and feelings. Here are some suggestions:

- Never fire without being ready. Have the employee's final paycheck ready on the day you fire, including back pay, earned vacation, and severance pay, if applicable. If you provide insurance benefits, the employee has a right to keep them in effect and you must tell him or her that.
- Don't fire in anger.
- Expect the worst, including anger, tears, verbal abuse, and more.
- Keep the firing to yourself and do it in private.
- Do it yourself. This is one task you shouldn't delegate.
- Fire only as a last resort.

Some things we'd fire for "on the spot" include:
- Dishonesty
- Any illegal activity such as theft

- Violent behavior or blatant disregard for the safety of others
- Substance abuse
- Sexual misconduct

Many people have noted positive changes taking place in the American workplace. With the suggestions offered in this chapter, we hope you'll be able to hire and keep the best employees so your business can *be* the best.

Seven

Sharpen Your Selling Skills

Everyone lives by selling something.

—Robert Lewis Stevenson

Faced with tremendous competition from the retail giants, it's important to realize two things:

1. The selling skills of every employee will be a large factor in the success or failure of your business. Their skills—to provide service and to generate sales—will also be a major advantage that you have over the retail giants.
2. To your customers, the salesperson *is* the business. It follows then that if the salespeople are good, the business is good. And if the salespeople are bad, in the minds of your customers, so is your business.

Perhaps you have a successful advertising program that is effective at bringing customers to your store. Great! But before you can turn shoppers into buyers, you've got to focus on turning employees into a motivated sales force.

The Sales That Slipped Away

A recent study by Yankelovich Partners sponsored by Master-Card International found that 62 percent of shoppers leave a store without buying because sales clerks weren't available. *That would never happen in my store,* you say?

Perhaps you have sufficient salespeople to service your customers, but maybe they're unavailable, or unwilling, or unable to give service. Could that be happening in your store?

If you're not happy with your sales figures, maybe some things are happening in your store that you *don't* know about. Here are five reasons your salespeople may be losing sales:

1. *Apathy.* Marie Jackson entered a bookstore, uncrowded on a Saturday morning, looking for a particular book. When she couldn't find it on the shelves, she approached three clerks who were standing behind the checkout counter, engaged in an animated but private conversation.

After she waited long and patiently for the clerks to acknowledge her presence, one of them finally offered assistance, and Marie asked about the book she was seeking. He replied, "I'm sorry, we don't have that in stock," without offering to order the book or to call another bookstore in the chain to locate it for Marie. Then, with much more enthusiasm than he showed for Marie's request, he rejoined the other two clerks in the still ongoing conversation. The situation was bad for Marie, but worse for the bookstore. The fact is that the book was on the shelf all along, and when Marie left, it remained there, unsold. Could this be happening in your store?

2. *Misjudging your customer's intent to buy.* Still dressed in her office attire, Julie Sampson entered the motorcycle store with her two children and their grandfather. They were looking for a birthday gift for Julie's husband, who was planning to buy a new motorcycle in a few weeks.

Five clerks stood behind the counter, ignoring the newcomers to the store. (A businesswoman, two children, and a grandfather perhaps were not the shop's typical customers.) Several minutes passed while Julie and her children browsed through the merchandise and selected their gifts. Still no one offered to help.

They heard the low rumble of a motorcycle get louder as it approached the store. Then the door to the shop opened and in walked a man and a woman, arms linked, both dressed in the black-leather uniform of the serious motorcyclist. The clerks descended upon them, eagerly offering assistance.

Disgusted with such preferential treatment, Julie and her family left without buying anything. She also suggested to her husband that he purchase his motorcycle and any products he might need from another dealer.

The clerks misjudged the buying potential of Julie and her family and lost not only that day's sale, but also the chance for future business with them.

Could this be happening in your store?

3. *Lack of product knowledge.* Andy and Amy Geoffrey went into a gourmet kitchen shop looking for a utensil they needed for a dinner party they were hosting Saturday night. Not finding it, they asked a clerk, who replied hastily that she had no idea what they were talking about.

The kitchen tool was not a particularly obscure item for a kitchen shop, and Amy, a business owner herself, told the manager she was surprised that the salesperson didn't know what it was. "That's one of our new people," the manager responded. "She's just been here three months." In our opinion, ninety days is more than enough time to become familiar with the merchandise.

The Yankelovich study found that 60 percent of shoppers asked a question that the sales clerk couldn't answer. Could this be happening in your store?

4. *Rudeness.* After a grueling day in her high-pressure job, Sharon Michelson rushed to the department store to do some late-night shopping for her son, Richard. She found the style of shirt she was looking for, but couldn't find the proper size. Two sales clerks were busy counting inventory and doing paperwork and never looked up to offer assistance.

As the hour got later and her patience grew thinner, Sharon gave up finding the shirt and approached the counter with just one of the four items she was hoping to buy. She stood at the counter a few moments while the clerk finished totaling the numbers on the sheet in front of her. When Sharon cleared her throat, the clerk looked up and with exasperation threw her pencil onto the counter. With a pointed look at her watch, she glared at Sharon and icily asked, "You don't want to *buy* that, do you?"

Could this be happening in your store?

5. *Failure to suggest other items.* Ready to begin the next step in his remodeling project, Ryan Benson went to the building supply store and purchased several sheets of Sheetrock. He had never installed Sheetrock before and guessed at the items he would need. No one in the store offered suggestions for any products or expertise that might help Ryan do the job more efficiently. Once he got home, he found that his efforts at installation left quite a bit to be desired.

He returned to the supply store and this time sought advice. An experienced, well-trained sales clerk offered simple solutions to Ryan's problems and demonstrated the tools and techniques necessary to do the job effectively. Ryan bought every tool the clerk suggested and hurried home to complete the project.

If someone had taken an interest in Ryan's needs on the first visit, it would have saved his time and the clerk's time and resulted in faster, increased sales.

Could this be happening in your store? Don't miss an opportunity to sell customers something they need—even if they don't realize they need it.

Exhibit 8 offers some pitfalls that you and your salespeople should avoid like the plague.

Six Steps Toward Selling Success

We are all interested in finding the quick fix, the easy answer, the "secrets" to anything. In selling, as in many other endeavors, there's no such thing. It happens one customer at a time. Put another way, sell the one you're with.

There have been countless articles written, videos produced, and seminars presented to help salespeople hone their skills. The *tools* of the trade may have changed—more people use cellular telephones and laptop computers to track and

Exhibit 8. Twenty selling mistakes you must never make.

1. Don't ever stretch the truth. Honesty isn't the best policy; it's the *only* policy.
2. Don't believe that you don't have to sell. (You do, all the time.)
3. Don't believe that selling isn't a service. (It is.)
4. Don't forget to put yourself in your customer's shoes.
5. Don't believe that there are born salespeople. (There aren't; selling is a skill that can be learned, and it improves with practice.)
6. Don't underestimate the value of product knowledge.
7. Don't believe you have to be highly educated to be successful in sales.
8. Don't believe your selling skills can't be improved with education. (They can.)
9. Don't ignore the "ready to buy" signals.
10. Don't forget to ask for the sale.
11. Don't ever get into arguments with your customers. You might win the argument, but you'll lose the sale.
12. Don't forget to say "thank you" when customers do business with you, or when they say nice things about you, or when they recommend your products or services to someone else, or when they complain.
13. Don't ever say "I don't know" without adding, "but I'll find out."
14. Don't say "I'll find out" without doing it.
15. Don't make any sales presentation without being prepared.
16. Don't underestimate the value of every sale you make, no matter how small. Customers who are satisfied with a small purchase they make today may come back tomorrow for a large one—and tell their friends to come in too.
17. Don't believe you can't win an old customer back.
18. Don't treat all customers alike. (They aren't.)
19. Don't believe that just because you're good friends you'll be assured of the sale.
20. Don't take any customer for granted.

follow up on sales—but with few exceptions, the basic selling *techniques* haven't changed much over the years.

What has changed is what customers are looking for. In today's fast-paced world, the customer is looking for value, speed, and convenience. As Tom Peters says, "If you give something worth paying for, they'll pay."

How do you show your customers that your business has

something worth paying for? By ensuring that your salespeople are trained to discover what the customer needs and to find a way to meet those needs.

Here's a six-step customer-needs-oriented selling system designed to get and keep customers:

1. Lay the groundwork.
2. Approach and relate.
3. Make the presentation.
4. Overcome the objections.
5. Close and supplement.
6. Follow up and make them customers for life.

Each of these steps is explained in detail in the sections that follow.

1. Lay the Groundwork

What we have found in our research and consultations is that successful businesses prepare their employees to be good salespeople in three main ways: training, goal setting, and motivating. Zig Ziglar, one of the world's best-known experts on selling, says in his book *Ziglar on Selling:*

> Looking back over my career as a salesman, sales manager, and sales trainer, I have no doubt in my mind that the most successful sales professionals continue to have the attitude of the beginner. The selling pro who gets to and stays at the top of the profession is an "experienced rookie." By that I mean when we approach sales as an ongoing learning experience, we are continually learning the "little things" that make the "big difference" in our careers as sales professionals.

Maybe you've been in business thirty years and think you know everything there is to know about selling. Maybe yes, maybe no. The danger of taking that approach is that your skills and those of your staff may become stale and your attitudes may become a little tired.

Keep your techniques fresh and hone the skills you do have by hosting ongoing training programs. You'll build a stellar sales force if you excel in three main areas: knowledge, attitude, and techniques. Remember the acronym KAT:

1. *Knowledge.* Know your products or services, your customers and their needs, your industry, and your competition.
2. *Attitude.* Be friendly, outgoing, confident, helpful, honest, and enthusiastic and you will find that selling becomes easier.
3. *Techniques.* Develop techniques that enable you to learn the customer's needs and then present the products and services that will satisfy those needs.

Study the "secrets" of successful businesses and you'll find that most of them have regular, ongoing training programs addressing those three areas.

Take Lee Sherman, who owns Hahn Appliance in Tulsa, Oklahoma. In addition to informal training sessions, he schedules a general store meeting for all employees once a month. The meeting includes a general sales training session and a "product specific" training program hosted by a manufacturer's representative. At the meetings, employees gain new knowledge about products they sell and learn new techniques for selling them. Sherman believes these sessions help build a knowledgeable, cohesive sales team. As an added bonus to boost morale and foster teamwork, after the meeting he treats all the employees and their "significant others" to a meal at a local restaurant.

Your industry associations and buying groups can be helpful sources of training materials for your employees. Look into training programs at your local colleges and universities. Chambers of commerce host courses designed to improve skills in a variety of areas. Contact seminar companies to provide training for groups. Pool your resources with other businesses, if necessary.

In addition to emphasizing and upgrading training, laying the groundwork means setting goals. Management guru Peter Drucker has said, "Management by objectives works if you know the objectives. Ninety percent of the time you don't." Most successful salespeople set goals. Do you set realistic sales goals for you and your employees?

Jim Chick, the owner of Chick's Sporting Goods in Covina, California, does. "You've got to set expectation and performance levels for people and continuously be asking them for a little bit more," he says. "If you set a higher goal, you're going to get a higher performance. And if you as a manager didn't tell them that you expect them to perform at this level, and they don't get there, you're the one to blame, not them."

How do you motivate them to reach those goals? One study suggests that retail salespeople who are not reaching their sales goals may not be getting adequate incentives to do so. The key is to find the incentive that motivates your individual employees. For one employee it might be cold, hard cash, but for another it might be free merchandise, a special gift, or an extra day off.

Chick believes that his company's commission-type incentive helps them develop and hold on to good people. Some businesses use group-based incentives that tie awards to department performance rather than individual sales. Some companies spark sales by using a combination of individual and group incentives. Another method is to base pay on either an hourly wage or a percentage of sales, whichever is greater.

Still other companies reward individual employees for their achievements. The risk of individual-based rewards is that one employee may shoulder aside another employee to get first crack at a customer and ignore tasks that also need to be shared equally.

The bottom line is that while some stores report sales increases of dramatic amounts once they've instituted a commission program, others say that paying on commission diminishes the importance of the small-purchase customer. Ignore that customer today, and you'll lose any chances for the next big purchase they want to make. (Remember the motorcycle story earlier in the chapter?)

The key of any incentive program is to find the one that works best for your business and your employees.

2. Approach and Relate

One of the most powerful techniques you can use to help build sales is to sell the *relationship*, not the product. As Lee Iacocca, former chairman of the board of the Chrysler Corporation, puts it, "Make someone like you." The point is, if your customers like *you*, there is an automatic transference to what you sell.

By doing so, you'll not only cement long-term personal bonds, but also make them your customers for life. It's one big advantage you have over the retail giants. While they sell price and selection, you'll be selling *relationships*.

You begin the process as soon as your customer has the first contact with you, whether it's over the telephone or when he or she walks through your doors. First impressions are important. What you aim to do in those first few seconds is to establish rapport and build trust.

In person, this means make eye contact, smile, and deliver a good opening line that offers to help and invites further conversation. In other words, zap that old line "Can I help you?" right out of the vocabulary of your salespeople. Typically, the customer responds, "No, just looking, thanks," which is a conversation stopper.

Probably the best opening line we've heard lately is, "What can I help you find?" That question does two things: It delves for a need, and it offers help. It's a good start.

Over the phone, put a smile in your voice, be helpful and friendly. When you make a telephone call and are lucky enough to reach a person rather than an electronic device, it's a breath of fresh air if the person you speak to is friendly and nice. That reflects positively on the company.

Take the example of Millie Gang at Baum's, a women's clothing store in Morris, Illinois. The day we called, Morris was in the middle of one of the worst snowstorms in its history, but Millie volunteered in a typically chatty Midwestern manner that she was keeping warm in her "CUDDLDUDS" clothing—which, of course, was available at Baum's.

By the time we concluded our conversation, we had a positive feeling about Millie—which transferred to Baum's—and were ready to go there to meet her and check out the store she claimed had "everything a woman could want."

After you establish a baseline for a relationship, it's time to find out what the customer needs. You have to find out what the customer wants before you can sell, and you must be able to frame good questions and listen for the answers to be successful in selling.

Employees in computer stores often do a poor job of (1) speaking a familiar language and (2) deciphering what a customer needs. Computer store owner Joe Wolf, at Compu-Systems in Washington, Missouri, is an exception. He puts it this way:

> Before the sale, we evaluate their needs. We go as far as to go out and see what equipment they already have and get a feel for what they're lacking. We take time with them and show them the different programs that are available.
>
> We try to address the whole customer's needs, from "What do you need?" to "This is what we can fill it with and this is how we're going to service you afterwards." It's not just, "Come in, pick up a box, and we'll see you later."

While his counterparts are selling "boxes" or RAMs and ROMs and megabytes, Wolf is filling the needs of his customers by asking them questions and listening to the answers.

Getting the answers to the following questions will help you find out more about your customers' requirements and give you some clues about structuring your presentation.

- What benefits are your customers looking for in the products or services you're selling?
- What do your customers like—and dislike—about the product or service they have been using?
- Are there any "hot buttons" or special requirements?
- How knowledgeable are your customers about the prod-

uct they want to buy and how much information do they want? Do they want to know how many megabytes the hard drive has or just that it will run the programs they have now with room for expansion in the future?

In any case, always make it clear to your customers that you want to help them buy the *right* thing.

3. Make the Presentation

Garey Alimia, the New Orleans owner of A-1 Appliance, a seven-store chain, believes in the FAB method of making the presentation: Sell the Features, Advantages, and Benefits (or more accurately, but less easy to remember, the FBA method):

Know the features. According to the Yankelovich study, 55 percent of shoppers want a great deal of information before they purchase an item. With your well-trained staff of sales professionals who have a high level of product knowledge, you'll have a big advantage over the mass merchandisers.

One of the big complaints that customers have about the retail giants is that salespeople can't do much more in the sales presentation than read the features off the description sheets—which customers can do themselves. By knowing your products thoroughly, you'll add value to the products you're selling. Alimia believes that's important. "Our people can tell you everything you want to know about any product we sell," he says.

After listening to your customers and discovering what they're looking for, direct them to the products or services that you offer that will best meet those needs.

Describe the features, such as "a two-speed, seven-cycle washer," but go to the next step. As Alimia says, most people have no idea what this means, so you must sell the benefits, too.

Sell the benefits. The key that's often missed in selling is not converting the product knowledge we mentioned above into *benefits* the customer can understand. The most important question you must answer is the one the customer almost never asks out loud, *What's in it for me?*

Customers don't care that it's a two-speed, seven-cycle washer until they realize what those features can do to help them get their clothes cleaner or make their washing chores easier. While it may be interesting to learn that a lawn mower has a five-horsepower motor, that fact won't mean much to customers unless they can relate it to being able to cut the grass faster. In other words, communicate the *benefits* of the features your products offer.

To bring home the importance of selling benefits and features, Clinton Appliance and Furniture owner Dwight Horne has a selling strategy that works for his store in Clinton, North Carolina. Each week he and every member of his sales staff have an assignment. They select one product and learn ten to fifteen of its features—and the accompanying benefits.

They dig out catalogues and product brochures and write down their answers. (They all agree they retain the information better if they write it down.) Then Horne compares all the answers to his own and selects the best ten, which are then typed and used as resources for all the salespeople. "It's a great learning and training exercise," Horne says.

Sell the advantages. What every salesperson must next communicate to the customer is the answer to the unspoken question the customer is asking at this point, *Why should I buy from this person?* Unconsciously, your customer may be comparing the products, features, and relationships you offer to those he can get somewhere else. Make sure he's making the right comparisons.

At this writing, some Michigan stores felt that Wal-Mart was misleading customers in some of its advertisements. According to *USA Today* (March 18, 1994), Wal-Mart agreed to sign a deal with Michigan's attorney general, Frank Kelley, to stop running the allegedly misleading advertisements. Kelley said Wal-Mart's ads weren't comparing apples to apples, and the newspaper cited several examples, including an ad where Wal-Mart claimed its price was lower than the competition's, but Wal-Mart's offer was for a smaller-size product than what the competition had for sale.

Are your customers comparing apples to apples? When Lee Sherman realized his Hahn Appliance customers were not making equal comparisons with regard to products, he launched an effective advertising campaign to correct that situation. The slogan was "Hahn Appliance. Compare Apples to Apples."

The question we hear over and over is, *Do you knock the competition?* While the answer to that will depend on your comfort level, we think it's much better to emphasize what you can do for the customer, rather than what your competitor cannot do.

4. Overcome the Objections

As one sales professional puts it, "Objections are your friends." The idea is to encourage prospects to express their objections (not just think them) so you can uncover concerns and buying motives, address them, and make the sale.

In these days of "match any price" discounting, price is probably the objection you encounter most often. The ideal situation is to build a level of trust and rapport with a customer and communicate the benefits so well that price will not be the main issue. That's the ideal.

Whatever the objection, listen attentively and handle it quickly. Don't argue, and don't offend. Remind the customer of the benefits and advantages of doing business with you. Stress the extra value that your company offers, such as free delivery, in-store financing, money-back guarantees, your excellent service department, and fair policies. Present your own value package and lead the customer to the decision that your offer is better.

While your big-box competitors may be selling only a *product*, you can distinguish yourself by selling a *package of values* that includes not just the product but many additional services *and* a long-term commitment to your satisfaction.

5. Close and Supplement

In a recent study by Chonko, Cabellero, and Lumpkin, the researchers found that salespeople attempt to close the sale less than a third of the time. Most salespeople would rather wait passively for the customer to *volunteer* to buy.

While experts have identified many ways to close a sale, the basic tactics are:

Always be closing. A professional salesperson begins the sales process with the end in mind: Everything moves toward the end result, the sale. The key is to help prospects decide how—not whether—they will buy.

Ask for the sale. Zig Ziglar tells the story about a huge insurance policy that Henry Ford purchased many years ago. Upon learning about it, one of Ford's insurance-selling friends was quite upset that Ford hadn't bought the policy from him. When the friend asked why, Ford responded, "You didn't ask me."

Always ask for the sale.

Some effective closing questions that are used by many successful salespeople are:

- Can you see how this would meet your needs (or solve your problem)? Be specific. You already know what benefits the customer is looking for. Address them: "It will save you money" or it will "Make your life more fun."
- Since I haven't heard any objections, I'm assuming you agree with me, right?
- Are you ready for us to talk about the final details?
- Shall we go ahead and get started with your order?

Now that your customer has made the commitment to buy, you think the sale is over, right? Wrong. Once the customer has decided to buy, reinforce the buying decision immediately, but don't babble with excitement. Doing so will only make the customer question his or her judgment in buying from you. It's a good idea to summarize the transaction and give the customer an idea about what the next step is.

After that initial buying decision is made, don't make one of the biggest mistakes that salespeople make: failure to suggest additional products. Remember our example above about the building supply store? The same rule applies to virtually every type of retail business.

In a clothing store, if your customer selects a suit, he may also need a shirt, tie, and maybe a belt. If a woman buys a dress in a clothing store, she might appreciate seeing a necklace or earrings that would accessorize the dress. If you have just sold a tennis racket, wouldn't your customer be likely to need some tennis balls or perhaps a new tennis shirt?

We suggest that you train your sales staff to keep making subtle suggestions for additional products the customer might need until it's clear the customer is satisfied. One company we know reminds employees to do this by posting signs near the cash register that read "HI SAM." The words are an acronym for "Have I Sold Additional Merchandise?"

A word of caution: Don't overdo this. Being too pushy at this point may inhibit future business.

In seminars that we conduct, one of the exercises we have the audience do is to make a list of all the additional items that someone who is purchasing a can of house paint might need. How many items could you list? The record so far is forty-eight in three minutes. Ask your salespeople to do the same exercise with products you sell and then encourage them to suggest those items to your customers.

Statements such as, "Is that all?" or "Will there be anything else?" are "sales killers" because it's too easy to give a no answer to those questions.

6. Follow up and Make Them Customers for Life

So you've made the sale and suggested additional items the customer bought. Are you through yet? Not quite. If you want to turn those buyers into lifetime customers, now's another opportunity to do it.

What happens *after* the sale is crucial not only to keep your current customers, but also to generate new business. Never take customers for granted. Never. Try these six tactics:

1. Contact your customers after the sale to show your appreciation for their business and ask for their contin-

ued business. A thank you, whether written or verbal, is always a nice touch and always appreciated.

2. Send a "customer satisfaction" survey. Get answers to those critical questions: *How are we doing?* and *How can we improve?*

3. Prove that you're dependable by making sure that any services after the sale (delivery, warranty work) were handled satisfactorily.

4. Handle any complaints promptly.

5. Add the names of your customers to your mailing list and keep in regular contact with them. At specified intervals—every six months or so—suggest other related products or services they might be interested in.

6. Ask for referrals. One way to build sales is to find other customers like the ones you currently have. Your current customers are an excellent source of future customers.

Visualize Success

While selling can be gratifying—in terms of personal satisfaction and financial gain—it can also be very difficult when the customer says no. Rejection just comes with the territory.

If you or your salespeople tend to feel a little defeated after hearing too many noes, consider some of these pearls:

> Someday I hope to enjoy enough of what the world calls success so that someone will ask me, "What's the secret of it?" I shall say simply this: "I get up when I fall down."
>
> —Paul Harvey

> Results? Why man, I have gotten a lot of results. I know 50,000 things that won't work.
>
> —Thomas Edison

> If at first you don't succeed, you're running about average.

> If at first you don't succeed, redefine success.

Putting that kind of perspective on the situation can be helpful. Another tactic that the successful selling professionals use is borrowed from the athletes: They *visualize* success. Watch a snow skier before a big race, and you might see her standing on the top of the mountain, eyes closed, swaying back and forth. She's visualizing all the turns and gates on the mountain and "practicing" the moves she'll have to make to master them.

Successful athletes also spend their time erasing negative experiences from their minds and replacing them with winning images. While many people know that Babe Ruth hit more than 700 home runs, most people don't realize that he struck out more than 1,300 times. He certainly didn't step up to bat expecting to strike out. He was there to win and that's what he expected to do.

Psychologists say that it's much more effective to move toward a positive, rather than moving away from a negative. As Robert Schuller said: "The me I see is the me I'll be." For instance, if you want to lose weight, put a picture on your refrigerator of a thin, attractive person instead of a fat, ugly one! And smart football players don't say, "Don't miss the ball," they say, "Catch it and run with it."

It will be easier to visualize your success and achieve desirable results if you remember that selling is a people-serving-people process. The process should include the following:

- Training your staff to care about serving customers
- Learning to listen to customers in order to zero in on their needs
- Practicing courtesy in every situation
- Learning about your products and services so you can point out the benefits and advantages
- Suggesting additional items that will save your customers time and additional expense
- Making every customer feel welcome and appreciated
- Following up sales with a thank you and a satisfaction survey

Eight

Managing Information

I keep six honest serving-men
  (They taught me all I knew);
Their names are What and Why and When
  And How and Where and Who.

—Rudyard Kipling

John Wooden, former coach of ten national champion UCLA basketball teams, has said, "It's what you learn after you know it all that counts." The more you know about your business, the more likely you are to survive and prosper. Every successful company we know gathers and analyzes management information regularly.

We will cover three types of information in this chapter:

1. Financial information
2. Customer information
3. Productivity and efficiency information

You Can't Manage Numbers You Don't Have

Sound financial management is based on facts, not feelings. When you have good numbers (facts) you will be able to plan, organize, and control what has to be done. Financial management will help you trim expenses, eliminate waste, grow your profits, and save on income taxes.

When we started our first business, our initial financial system was simple. It consisted of a medium-size cardboard box and a checkbook. We deposited all invoices, receipts, bills, and other paperwork in the box. We paid our bills out of the checkbook.

During the first several months everything went smoothly. Then near the end of the first year the box got full about the same time our checking account hit empty. We knew we had a problem but didn't know what it was. Attorney and corporate executive Owen D. Young described us well. He said, "It is not the crook in modern business we fear but the honest man who does not know what he is doing."

Records Are Vital

Records are the groundwork you need to successfully build your business. You must have good records to create accurate financial statements. You must have accurate, timely financial statements to make good decisions. It follows then that good records are vital to good decision making.

However, there are several other valid reasons for keeping accurate records in addition to making good business decisions. These include:

- The Internal Revenue Service requires you to keep records for tax purposes.
- Accurate, up-to-date records are a prerequisite for borrowing money from a financial institution.
- You can use your records to uncover waste and internal shrinkage (theft).
- Records provide the basis for measuring effectiveness and efficiency.
- Accurate records aid in tracking seasonal trends.

First you should determine if your record-keeping system will provide all of the information you need, when you need it. This information is critical because you cannot manage numbers you don't have.

Back to Basics

The late Vince Lombardi was a professional football coach whose teams always excelled in mastering the basic functions of the game. Once after a humiliating loss to the Chicago Bears, Lombardi called a Monday morning meeting for his team, the Green Bay Packers. He told them quietly that they needed to get refocused on the basics. He then held up a football and said, "Gentlemen, this is a *football*."

Even if you are a veteran business owner, please bear with us as we review a few basics. Like a good football play, your records must be *simple, timely, accurate, relevant,* and *consistent.*

There are at least seven basic sets of records or journals that you should maintain. Some businesses may require additional information for management or reporting purposes, but usually this information is enough to start with.

1. *A sales journal.* The sales journal is a record of revenue coming into your business. You can divide revenue into several categories such as product lines, services, suppliers, and geographic areas.

2. *An expense journal.* The expense journal is a running record of all expenses incurred in the normal process of doing business. We suggest that you pay all bills by check and let your checkbook register act as a backup for this journal. Organize expenses into common groups such as wages, payroll expenses, utilities, advertising, rent, supplies, and repairs.

3. *An accounts receivable schedule.* Accounts receivable are monies you haven't collected for products or services already delivered. Your accounts receivable schedule should record each credit sale by customer name, date, the product sold or service rendered, and the dollar amount. You can maintain this list for current accounts (those unpaid for thirty days or less) and past due accounts (those unpaid for thirty days or more). We will discuss managing your accounts receivable later in this chapter.

4. *An accounts payable schedule.* This schedule is a list of suppliers and others to whom your business owes money. It is a running record that tracks to whom, for what, how much, and when the money is due.

5. *A payroll journal.* Monthly, quarterly, and yearly payroll reports are required by many state agencies and the federal

government. The payroll journal is a single source to record all applicable information regarding your employees' earnings. This journal allows you to record all regular and overtime pay, social security taxes, federal income taxes, Medicare taxes, state income taxes (where applicable), earned income credits, federal unemployment taxes, and state unemployment taxes (where applicable).

6. *A fixed asset schedule.* The IRS recognizes that the tangible assets of a business—buildings, equipment, vehicles, furniture, fixtures, etc.—may wear out or decline in value—that is, depreciate—over time. They allow business owners to calculate the decrease in value, or depreciation, and to deduct it from their earnings.

To ensure that all deductions are taken properly you need to keep records of when assets are purchased, the type of asset (buildings, vehicles, equipment, etc.), and the original purchase price. Calculating the amount of depreciation you can deduct from your net income can be complex, and we recommend that you involve a professional in the process.

7. *An owner's journal.* The owner's journal is a record of money that the owner(s) of a sole proprietorship or some partnerships have put into or taken out of the business.

"Pouring" Your Financial Foundation

Once you have recorded all of the financial transactions for a period in the proper journals and schedules, it is time to bring these ingredients together. Like sand, gravel, water, and cement are mixed together to make concrete, your records can be combined to form financial statements.

These statements, when properly formed, become the foundation of your financial decision making. Nearly every decision you make for your business will have financial impact. For example, if you wish to try a new, aggressive promotion strategy, you'll need to know if you have the cash to support it. If you want to expand with borrowed capital, you'll need to prove to the lender that you can repay the debt.

There are three financial statements every business should generate on a regular, timely basis. These statements are:

1. The profit and loss, or income, statement
2. The balance sheet
3. The cash flow statement

Your financial statements work together as a unit. All three are required to create a complete financial picture of your business.

The Profit and Loss, or Income, Statement

The profit and loss statement is more commonly called an income statement and that is how we will refer to it throughout the remainder of this chapter. The income statement is a composite or summary of a company's sales and expenses over a specific period of time. It should be prepared at least monthly. The income statement is established according to a system of ground rules known as Generally Accepted Account-

Exhibit 9. A typical income statement for a small retail store.

Bubba's Hardware

Income Statement for Month Ended January 31, 1994

Net Sales		$48,000
Cost of Goods Sold		36,000
Gross Profit		$12,000
Operating Expenses:		
Wages	$5,400	
Rent	800	
Payroll expense	650	
Advertising	600	
Insurance	450	
Interest	300	
Supplies	200	
Miscellaneous	470	
Total Expenses		$ 8,870
Total Net Income		$ 3,130

ing Principles (GAAP). These rules apply to all businesses, large or small. Income statements follow the general format shown in Exhibit 9.

The Balance Sheet

The balance sheet provides a record of the financial health of your company as of a certain date. It is a snapshot of your business at that point in time.

The balance sheet shows the book value of your business and contains two main sections. The first is a record of assets, which includes anything the business owns that has monetary value. The second is a statement of liabilities and owner's equity.

On the balance sheet, total assets must equal the combined totals of the liabilities and owner's equity. Expressed as an equation: Assets = Liabilities + Owner's equity. The assets—items the business owns—are listed in two main categories: current assets and long-term, or fixed, assets.

Current assets are those that can be readily converted into dollars through your normal business cycle. These include cash, accounts receivable, and inventory.

Long-term, or fixed, assets are not readily converted to cash and have usefulness to the business over longer periods of time. Long-term assets include items such as buildings, land, vehicles, equipment, and furniture.

The liabilities—what the business owes—are also listed in two main groups: current liabilities and long-term liabilities.

Current liabilities are the short-term financial obligations of your business that are payable within one year. Examples would include accounts payable, taxes, current portion of long-term debt, and short-term loans.

Long-term liabilities are all debts not due for payment within one year. These would include the noncurrent portion of all loans on your land and buildings, equipment loans, and mortgages.

The difference between the total assets (the value of what the business owns) and the total liabilities (what the business owes) is known as the "owner's equity" or the "net worth" of the business. Sometimes the level of debt exceeds the value of the assets, and the owner has a negative equity position or a minus net worth.

Exhibit 10 is a sample balance sheet. Note that the assets are grouped at the top of the balance sheet and the liabilities and owner's equity are listed on the bottom half. The categories and format of the balance sheet also follow GAAP.

The Cash Flow Statement

The final statement is the cash flow statement. As the name suggests, this record tracks the flow of cash in and out of your business. A sample cash flow statement is shown in Exhibit 11.

Note that Carrie's Cleaners (Exhibit 11) had a negative cash flow for the month of June. This may be a seasonal problem that is easily explained. However, if the situation were to continue, Carrie could operate for only another nine months before running out of cash.

Though negative cash flow for any given month is not usually a major problem, the trend is the important factor to monitor. If this month's negative cash flow continued into other periods, it certainly would be cause for concern.

Most financial consultants agree that cash flow projection is an essential planning tool for a growing business. We believe that, because you're reading this book, you want your business to grow and prosper; therefore, we recommend that you use a projected cash flow statement to increase your odds of success.

A Monthly Analysis

We often counsel small businesses who generate their financial statements at the end of the year. When tax time approaches they believe it's time to gather up their records and see how much they owe.

When you get management information only once each year, you can make corrections only once each year. This presents a real challenge to effective financial management.

Exhibit 10. A typical balance sheet for a small retail store.

Betty's Bath Boutique

Balance Sheet, December 31, 1994

Current Assets:		
Cash	$ 500	
Accounts receivable	1,500	
Inventory	24,000	
Total Current Assets		$ 26,000
Fixed Assets:		
Building	$54,000	
Furniture and equipment	10,000	
Vehicles	10,000	
Total Fixed Assets		$74,000
TOTAL ASSETS		$100,000
Current Liabilities:		
Accounts payable	$12,000	
Notes payable	16,000	
Current portion long-term debt	4,800	
Total Current Liabilities		$ 32,800
Long-Term Liabilities:		
Mortgage payable (building)	$25,000	
Notes payable (vehicle)	3,500	
Total Long-Term Liabilities		$ 28,500
Owner's Equity:		
Betty Brown, Owner	$38,700	
Total Equity		$38,700
TOTAL LIABILITIES and OWNER'S EQUITY		$100,000

Exhibit 11. A typical cash flow statement for a small retail store.

Carrie's Cleaners

Cash Flow Statement for June 1994

Beginning Cash Balance:		$2,000
Cash receipts (sales)	$4,000	
Accounts receivable collection	1,200	
Total Cash Receipts		$5,200
Total Cash Available		$7,200
Cash Disbursements (Paid Out):		
Salaries	$2,000	
Payroll expense	240	
Delivery expense	500	
Supplies	360	
Rent	600	
Repairs and maintenance	200	
Owner's withdrawal	1,500	
Total Cash Disbursements		$5,400
Cash Flow		($ 200)
Ending Cash Balance		$1,800

Today, in business, you've got to be aware of what's going on around you and be ready to react quickly.

We recommend that you get all three financial statements at least once each month. This allows you to make adjustments (management decisions) every thirty days.

Many independent businesses find that once they are organized and have their journals in place, the actual monthly summary takes only a few hours to complete. Until you've gone through all the steps a few times it may take longer.

You may feel that, even having the information, you still don't know more than you did before. Take heart and don't give up. You will gradually begin to see some patterns develop.

You will see why trends are forming in the early stages and how to make adjustments in your business to slow the decline or accelerate improvements.

In Chapter Nine, we will introduce some financial management tools you can use. The prerequisite for using the tools is having accurate and timely income statements, balance sheets, and cash flow statements.

The CASE Method

A simple, straightforward approach to financial analysis is to use a method we developed with David Shipman, a business analyst, consultant, and former commercial lender. Shipman came up with the CASE acronym to describe the method, which comprises these elements:

Compile the information.
Assess the financial impact.
Solve and implement.
Evaluate and review.

Here's how the CASE method works:

• *Compile the information.* We recommend that you collect at least three years of financial statements—income statements and balance sheets—and place them side by side. If you don't have three years of financial data, use what you have. Once you begin the analysis process you can always add new information as it becomes available.

• *Assess the financial impact.* The purpose of compiling financial data is to let you see several numbers at one time. You can compare specific items like sales, gross profit, and net income in either dollar amounts or percentages. You can compare your information to previous years of your own business or to other businesses in your industry.

Through this process you can identify problem areas and potential financial pitfalls. You may find strong performance areas or numbers in steady decline. The impact and significance of your assessment may be great or minimal. The advantage is you know what is going on before it becomes an insurmountable problem.

Once the assessment is completed, you can use management tools to zero in on specific problem areas. These tools include danger signal tests, common size analysis, trend analysis, financial ratios, budget and forecasting, and variance comparison. We'll explain these tools and explore their usefulness in Chapter Nine.

- *Solve and implement.* After you use the tools to pinpoint problem areas, you can list possible solutions. Try to find as many ways as you can to solve the problem. You want a lot of ideas.

After you generate a list of several potential solutions, try to hone in on the best one. Eliminate ideas that cost too much, consume too much time, or require too much manpower. Take the best two or three solutions and develop them further for evaluation. Usually one solution will surface as the most practical.

The next step is to implement the solution. The greatest solution won't solve the problem if it isn't put into practice. Define the solution in writing. List what needs to be done, by whom, and when. Remember, it pays to be flexible. Expect to make a few revisions or adjustments to any plan.

- *Evaluate and review.* Once the best solution is implemented, it is important to follow up by evaluating your progress. Give the solution adequate time to work; then check on the progress. Review the results and make changes if necessary.

Twelve Pieces of the Financial Puzzle

While working with struggling businesses that wanted to prosper and grow, we've found twelve pieces of financial information that are critical to success. Please understand that these twelve elements, which we call "puzzle pieces," are not all you have to know to survive and prosper; they simply serve as a starting point. You are already somewhat familiar with the first five puzzle pieces, because they come right off the income statement.

The puzzle pieces, explained below, will help you in thinking about critical elements of financial management. When you are comfortable with all twelve elements, you can move on to the more sophisticated management and analysis tools.

1. *Sales.* Your sales, the first major item on your income statement, reflect the dollar volume of business your company has done over a period of time. This number reflects the level of exchange—usually money for products or services.

Many businesses track this number daily, weekly, monthly, and yearly. The sales amount should be exclusive of sales tax collections and any returned merchandise. It can reflect the volume of services provided as well as products sold.

2. *Cost of Goods Sold.* The next major item on your income statement is the cost of goods sold, also commonly referred to as the cost of sales. This is not the amount of inventory you bought during the period, but rather the actual cost—including freight and handling—of the inventory that was sold. To obtain an accurate cost of goods sold, begin with an inventory level for the period. Add your purchases for the period to the beginning inventory to arrive at the total amount of goods available for sale. Subtract the ending inventory to get an accurate cost of goods sold. See Exhibit 12 for an example.

3. *Gross profit.* The difference between your sales and the cost of goods sold is your gross profit. This puzzle piece tells you how much money is left from your revenue to pay for operating expenses during the period.

4. *Operating expenses.* The operating expenses, sometimes referred to as fixed expenses or overhead, are those incurred by being in business. These expenses are required to operate the business, regardless of the level of sales or activity. Operating expenses include the costs of such items as rent, insurance, administrative personnel, advertising, and supplies.

Every one of the new breed pays close attention to these

Exhibit 12. Calculating cost of goods sold.

Paula's Pet Palace

Cost of Goods Sold for September 1994

Beginning inventory (August 30, 1994):	$12,400
Purchases made in September 1994:	+16,600
Total goods available for sale in September:	$29,000
Ending inventory (September 30, 1994):	−13,000
Total cost of goods sold (September 1994)	$16,000

expenses. Just as a high level of body fat is bad for an athlete, high operating expenses are unhealthy for small businesses.

5. *Net income.* Net income is what's left of sales after all expenses—cost of goods sold and operating costs—are taken out. Net income is taxable income, not your take-home pay. This is a number that every business owner wants to increase.

6. *Inventory.* For most retail businesses, inventory plays an important role in financial management decisions. It's a "must know" number to manage. We pointed out earlier that you need monthly income statements and that in order to have accurate cost of goods sold information you need beginning and ending inventories for each month. This means that your cost of goods sold is only as accurate each month as your inventory count. Inventory control and monitoring may be the best reasons to move into high technology.

There are two primary methods of monitoring inventory. The first is the periodic method, in which goods are physically counted periodically to establish the inventory level. The second method is the perpetual type, in which the inventory level is continuously maintained by adding in purchases when they occur and subtracting units as they are sold. The primary advantage of the perpetual method is that the current level of inventory is always known. Exhibit 13 lists common inventory management goals. Exhibit 14 offers tips on eliminating obsolete inventory.

Exhibit 13. Common inventory management goals.

Goals in managing inventory will vary from business to business. Here are some that apply to most businesses:

- When sales are *increasing,* grow your inventory at a slower percentage rate than sales.
- When sales are *decreasing,* reduce your inventory by a percentage greater than your sales decline.
- Decrease your inventory as a percentage of sales.
- Eliminate out-of-stock conditions.
- Decrease differences between actual counts and accounting records.
- Increase annual inventory turns.

Exhibit 14. Eliminating obsolete inventory.

Inventory can grow stale. Rather than sitting on it or throwing it away, try these five tips:

1. *Trade it or barter with it.* Work with your suppliers to exchange your stale or dead inventory for other inventory that is saleable. Some companies specialize in bartering inventories, and you may be able to trade with another business.
2. *Add value with it.* Package overstocked items with other goods to increase the value perception and close rate. We packaged inexpensive grass trimmers with lawn mowers. "Buy the mower, get the trimmer free." This tactic helped close lawn mower sales.
3. *Hold a special discount sale.* Any dollars recovered from stale inventory can be put back to work for you.
4. *Return it to the source.* Talk to your suppliers. If they won't give you a 100 percent return rate, try to negotiate whatever you can.
5. *Give it away.* Find a charity that will take your unwanted inventory and give you a tax deduction in return. Work the public relations angle too. The media may find your generosity newsworthy.

7. *Inventory turnover.* This puzzle piece lets you know how fast your merchandise is moving. There are two methods that may be appropriate to use to determine this ratio. In method 1, the stock to sales ratio, the average inventory (determined

by taking the beginning inventory plus the ending inventory and dividing by 2) is divided into net sales to determine the number of turns.

In method 2, the stock to cost of goods sold ratio, the average inventory is divided into the cost of goods sold to determine the number of turns. To see how the numbers vary, look at the example in Exhibit 15.

8. *Accounts receivable management.* Many small businesses extend unsecured credit to their customers as a method of boosting sales. We have worked with hundreds of "cash poor" businesses and we often find that the reason for the lack of cash is poor accounts receivable management.

No one likes to tell customers no when they ask for additional credit or more time to pay. In addition, no one wants to be a hardnose and demand immediate payment even if the payment is past due. The result is often a significant drain on your cash flow as slow-paying customers use you as their bank or credit card company.

Exhibit 15. Two methods for determining inventory turnover.

Acme Hardware

Sales	$1,000,000
Cost of goods sold	750,000
Average inventory	125,000

Method 1: Stock to Sales Ratio

$$\frac{\text{Sales}}{\text{Average inventory}} = \text{turns} \qquad \frac{\$1,000,000}{\$125,000} = 8.0 \text{ turns}$$

Method 2: Stock to Cost of Goods Sold Ratio

$$\frac{\text{Cost of goods sold}}{\text{Average inventory}} = \text{turns} \qquad \frac{\$750,000}{\$125,000} = 6.0 \text{ turns}$$

Faster turnovers with either method are usually considered as positive. As a rule of thumb, shoot for six to seven turns until you get your industry's data. Then you may want to aim higher.

We suggest the following ten steps to manage your accounts receivable process.

1. Consider positioning yourself—as the new breed has—to accept all major credit cards. Then stick to a *cash, check, or credit cards only* policy.
2. If you decide to accept open accounts, establish a written credit policy and provide a copy to your customers.
3. Be selective in giving credit. You must have a method of determining who is creditworthy and who is not. Remember, not all customers who accept your credit terms will pay you.
4. Get a *signed* application from the customer that verifies that he understands your credit policies and agrees to abide by them.
5. Do a credit check before you issue credit. Update each active credit file with a new credit report yearly.
6. Monitor your accounts receivable closely. An aging statement allows you to categorize your accounts as current (less than thirty days old), thirty to sixty days, sixty-one to ninety days, and over ninety days.
7. Make an effort to collect all accounts over thirty days old. Try a "second notice" billing, a personal letter, a phone call, or a personal visit. The important thing is to do something. Don't let past-due accounts grow older.
8. Build late-payment charges into your credit policy. Credit card companies charge for using money; banks do too—why shouldn't you?
9. To speed up your collectible period, bill more often. Instead of waiting until the end of the month to send out bills, send them out every other Friday.
10. Offer discounts for early payment if your margins will stand the decrease.

9. *Accounts payable management.* Frequently, accounts receivable problems are the root cause of accounts payable problems. If you aren't being paid for merchandise you've sold, it

will be hard for you to pay your suppliers. Therefore, the best defense against payable problems is taking the offense in credit collections.

However, not all accounts payable problems are caused by slow-paying customers. Here is a list of other potential causes and solutions:

1. Overly aggressive buying practices. Don't get carried away when you go to market. It's easy to buy more than you need, especially when attractive discount or payment terms are offered. The solution is to know your *open-to-buy numbers* and stick with them.
2. Underestimating the amount of payables due this month. The solution is to keep an accounts payable schedule so you can check one record to see what's due.
3. Gradual buildup of inventory. Over time, building inventory can cause cash shortages. The solution is to monitor inventory levels closely and to slow buying levels to match sales.
4. Inappropriate use of working capital. Don't put your short-term operating money into long-term assets. Arrange financing for fixed assets over an extended payback period.

Here are several advantages of accounts payable management:

1. You have improved relations with suppliers and manufacturers.
2. You are able to take advantage of discount terms offered for early payment.
3. You avoid interest and penalties added to late or partial payments.
4. Suppliers are often more willing to negotiate merchandise returns, discounts, terms, and trades with businesses who always pay on time.
5. Suppliers and manufacturers are more likely to offer special deals to their most creditworthy customers.
6. Your ability to borrow from your local lender is en-

hanced when you can demonstrate excellent trade credit history.

10. *Cash position.* The cash position is a calculation of how much cash you must generate to pay typical monthly expenses. It is a method of working backwards from known expense levels to arrive at the level of daily sales required. Exhibit 16 shows a five-step method for calculating it for your business.

11. *Liability (debt) position.* The liability position of a business is a balance sheet check to determine whether the business is acquiring debt or paying it off. To determine your position, use the total assets of the business as your base value. For example, assume that ABCX Company's balance sheet shows $100,000 in total assets, $70,000 in total liabilities, and $30,000 in owner's equity. The amount of liabilities is 70 percent of total assets.

Generally speaking, we'd like to see this percentage trending downward. This would indicate that business assets are growing at a faster rate than debt or that the company is retiring debt as compared to assets.

We would recommend that you compare your percentage to your industry average. If your percentage is significantly higher than your industry's average, you may be overleveraged and need to reduce debt. If you are significantly below your industry's average, you may be underutilizing your assets and borrowing power.

12. *Owner's equity position.* The owner's equity position is the inverse of the liability position we discussed in puzzle piece 11. If the debt-to-assets percentage is 70 percent, as in the previous example, then the owner's equity position is 30 percent. If the debt percentage increases, the owner's equity decreases. If the business reduces debt, the ownership percentage increases.

Once again there is no specific right or wrong ratio here, but generally we would prefer more ownership and less debt. A conservative, risk-averse owner would prefer high equity levels, a high-roller type wouldn't be concerned about more debt.

Exhibit 16. Calculating cash position.

1. Using last year's income statement, list the sales, gross profit, and operating expenses, as shown below.

ABCX Company	
Sales 1994	$1,000,000
Gross profit	250,000
Total annual operating expenses	200,000

2. Divide your sales by your gross profit.

$$(\$1,000,000 \div 250,000 = 4.0)$$

This calculation reveals that you must produce $4 in sales to cover $1 in expenses. If your numbers come out to 2.71, it means you need $2.71 to cover $1 in expenses.

3. Determine the actual number of days your company is open for business. Our example, ABCX Company, closes on Sundays and six national holidays. It is open 307 days each year.

4. Divide your total annual operating expenses by the number of days you are open for business.

$$(\$200,000 \div 307 = \$651.47)$$

This tells us that ABCX's expenses average $651.47 for each day it is open for business.

5. We can now calculate the amount of cash sales and receivables collection—actual cash coming into your business—it will take to cover all expenses. Multiply your answer from step 4 by the factor calculated in step 2.

$$(\$651.47 \times 4.0 = \$2,605.88)$$

We now know that ABCX Company must generate $2,605.88 in sales every day to generate enough gross profit to cover daily operating expenses. This figure represents the company's minimum cash position.

Exhibit 17. Some new breed liability equity ratios.

Company	Liability Position	Equity Position	Source Year
Target	76%	24%	FY93
Kmart	60%	40%	FY93
Best Buy	58%	42%	FY93
Wal-Mart	57%	43%	FY93
Circuit City	54%	46%	FY93
Toys "R" Us	46%	54%	FY93
Home Depot	41%	59%	FY93

Exhibit 17 shows the ratios of some of the new breed. You'll notice that these companies differ in the amount of leverage they are willing to accept.

Customer Information

Just as you can't manage numbers you don't have, it is difficult to serve customers you don't know. We aren't suggesting that your business can never satisfy needs and wants of customers unknown to you. Rather, we're saying that the better you know your customers, the more likely you are to anticipate their needs and wants and position your business to exceed their expectations.

While many small businesses struggle with the financial elements outlined earlier in this chapter, there is even a more barren wasteland that is devoid of facts and short of details. It is the land of *What do you know about the people who walk through your front door?*

Here are eighteen areas where you need specific customer information to compete with the megastores.

1. How many customers (potential buyers) walk through your front doors every day? every month? every year?
2. How many customers make purchases every day? every month? every year?

3. How much does your average customer spend with you each visit? each month? each year?
4. How would you define your customer using demographic characteristics (such as age, income, marital status, gender, household size, educational level, and employment)?
5. Identify three national or regional trends that affect your ability to serve customers in a *positive* manner.
6. Identify three trends that affect your business in a *negative* manner.
7. List five words your customers would use to describe your business image to others.
8. List ten specific benefits you offer your customers that Wal-Mart and other new breed stores can't.
9. How many of the benefits you listed in answering question 8 could your customers identify?
10. If your customers knew these benefits, how would they rank them in order of importance?
11. What are the ten most popular products or services your customers buy from you?
12. What percentage of your customers are repeat customers (regularly shop your trade area) as opposed to one-time shoppers (visitors, tourists)?
13. What percentage of your customers live within 5 miles of your store? 10 miles? 25 miles?
14. What percentage of your customers do you know well enough to call them by their full names? (Reading "Bob" on the patch of a mechanic's shirt doesn't count.)
15. What would your present customers like to buy from you that you aren't selling now?
16. What items do people leave your community to purchase most frequently? (This is known as "retail or service leakage.")
17. What hours would your customers like you to be open?
18. How could you create a mailing list of your top 100 customers? Top 200?

You will be able to use the customer information gathering tools in Chapter Three to answer some of the questions above. Your goal should be to gather information from primary sources—via questionnaires, focus groups, and one-on-one interviews—and secondary sources—your own customer records, census data, trade publications, and other published information.

It is not imperative that you know everything today. However, you will need to start the process right away. Ignorance may be bliss, but in business, bliss can cause failure. Knowledge of your customers will help you serve them more effectively.

Productivity and Efficiency Information

In economics, *productivity* is defined as "being engaged in the creation of economic value." This concept is a critical component of successful small businesses: They all add value to the products and services they provide to their customers.

The efficiency factors are intertwined with value and productivity. Value is "perceived by the customer." It is the "balance of price versus quality and quantity." When we bring these factors together, they allow us to produce real value with minimal effort, expense, and waste.

This information becomes useful to you after you have put all of the pieces of your financial puzzle together and gathered a significant amount of customer data. Your financial information is a prerequisite to good decision making, and customer information is a higher initial priority than productivity and efficiency factors.

However, once you move beyond the basic levels of information management, you'll find that you are spending more time on productivity and efficiency analysis and less time generating financial statements and customer data. As you improve your management skills and reach for greater efficiency and productivity, don't forget the basic premises presented earlier in this chapter. They are: You can't manage numbers you don't have, and you can't serve customers you don't know.

By managing productivity and efficiency (P&E) factors, you will use many components of information you are gathering now and will expand your need to gather and analyze additional data. For example, if you wish to determine how well your investment dollars are performing, you can use the return on investment tool in Chapter Nine. This ratio, or relationship, uses information from your income statement and balance sheet to quantify your return. This number can be compared to those of other businesses to see how efficiently you're using your money. In addition, you can compare your return to other forms of investment to see how productive your capital is.

Many P&E factors do not use financial statement or customer information. Instead, they require additional knowledge of your business operation. For example, a propane retailer may consider the number of gallons of propane delivered per truck as a measure of P&E. A photo processor may wish to consider the average rolls of film processed per employee per hour. An appliance dealer may wish to measure the closing effectiveness of the sales staff. These factors can be critical to business success, and you must make provisions for tracking information that may be germane for only your business or industry.

The final category of P&E information may use some information from traditional sources and other nontraditional sources. For example, a drug store or hardware store may wish to measure sales volume per employee. They would combine sales information from the income statement (a traditional source) with payroll records (nontraditional). Or, a clothing retailer may wish to monitor sales per square foot of selling space before and after redecorating. Once again, the analysis would require sales data (traditional) and facilities information from lease or real estate records or physical measurement (nontraditional).

There are three questions you should answer before gathering P&E information. They are:

1. Will having this information allow us to serve our customers more effectively?
2. Will having this information motivate our staff to be more productive and efficient?
3. Will this knowledge allow us to be more profitable or increase the value we pass on to our customers?

Now you're ready to try some of the tools in the next chapter. We suggest that you read the entire chapter before trying to determine your next steps.

Nine

Tools for Gathering, Analyzing, and Using Management Information

'Tis not knowing much, but what is useful, that makes a wise man.

—Thomas Fuller

What can your financial statements tell you about your business? How can you find out what your customers really think about your products and services? Is your business operating efficiently? Is your business strong or are you vulnerable to the megamerchants?

This chapter includes several management tools to evaluate what is going on in and around your business, and what it means. We suggest that you read through the entire chapter before utilizing any of the tools.

We'll start with a short analysis we use as consultants to determine how a business is doing. We call it the "Danger Signal Test." (See Exhibit 18.) This is not a sophisticated tool, but a quick check of your vital signs using financial information and management's views to determine if your company is experiencing early warning signs of distress.

The Common-Size Analysis Tool

A good way to analyze income statements and balance sheets is to use the common-size tool. Common-sizing is a technique

Exhibit 18. Danger signal test.

For each category, circle the number with the statement that best describes the current condition of your business. (For example, if your business is experiencing increasing growth in sales, you would circle the 0. If your sales took a slight dip this year for the first time, you would circle the 2.)

Sales (Revenue)

0   Increasing with steady growth.
1   Fairly stable with no significant growth or decline.
2   Slight decline current year only.
3   Definite downward trend spanning two years or more.
4   Significant decline, major drops in revenue.

Cash on Hand

0   Increasing balance and flow.
1   Steady balance or slight decline.
2   Decreasing balance, tightening cash position.
3   Cash shortages, managing float.
4   Cash deficit; bank is covering insufficient checks.

Accounts Receivable Condition

0   Increasing at a rate lower than sales.
1   Increasing at a rate equal to or slightly greater than sales.
2   Some accounts slipping to thirty days past due.
3   Increasingly slow pay—thirty to sixty days past due.
4   Critical—affecting payables—sixty days past due.

Accounts Payable

0   All current—all discounts taken.
1   All current—missed some discounts.
2   Cannot pay on time—fifteen days or more past due.
3   Creditors calling—thirty days or more behind.
4   Some or all vendors demanding cash on delivery.

Gross Profit and Gross Profit Margin

0   Increasing profit ($), margin (%) equal or increasing.
1   Stable profits, margin holding steady.
2   Slight decline in dollars and percentages.

Exhibit 18. (continued)

3 Losing dollars and percentages, but covering overhead.
4 Major decline—profit will not cover overhead.

Inventory Turnover

0 Increasing turns on inventory.
1 No increase, steady rate.
2 Slight slowing in turnover rate.
3 Increasingly slower trend over last two years.
4 Dramatic drop in turnover rate, dead inventory increasing.

Operating Expenses

0 Decreasing in dollars and as a percentage of sales.
1 Steady as a percentage of sales, some growth in dollars.
2 Slight growth as a percentage of sales.
3 Moderate overall increase as a percentage of sales, some categories up significantly.
4 Large increase as a percentage of sales.

Debt

0 Decreasing as a percentage of total assets.
1 No change as a percentage of assets.
2 Slight growth compared to assets.
3 Growing debt, declining assets.
4 Lenders limiting or denying additional borrowing.

Banking Relations

0 Lender informed, anxious to extend credit.
1 Lender informed, willing to talk about credit.
2 Lender informed, showing signs of concern.
3 Lender requesting financial information due to decline in financial condition.
4 Lender positioning itself to recover assets.

Management Team

0 Productive, efficient—teamwork evident.
1 Pressed for time, but making progress toward goals.
2 Time crunch, some stress, short fuses.
3 Crisis management mode, can't stay ahead of fires.
4 Avoiding decisions, denying problems.

Exhibit 18. (continued)

Staff Relations

    0 Productive, efficient—teamwork evident.
    1 Some complaints, but everyone working hard.
    2 Obvious morale problems, bickering, work slowing.
    3 Increased absenteeism, lower morale, key employees becoming disgruntled.
    4 High absenteeism, losing key people.

Customer Relations

    0 Customer counts increasing, positive word of mouth.
    1 Customer counts steady, neutral feedback.
    2 Customer counts decreasing slightly, increasing complaints and returns.
    3 Moderate drop in customer counts, and declining sales per customer.
    4 Significant drops in customer counts, growing numbers of unhappy customers.

Total the numbers you selected for each question. Compare your total to the rating scale below:

    0–6   No immediate danger, all systems go.
    7–12   Slight danger, monitor higher value areas.
    13–24   Moderate danger, take preventive action in higher danger number areas.
    25–36   Imminent danger, sure signs of trouble—failure a strong possibility if immediate action isn't taken to turn around.
    36+   Deep trouble—failure certain without immediate intervention and outside help.

Please note that this test is not a complete or thorough analysis of your business. Rather, it should be used to make a cursory evaluation of your situation and to isolate potential problem areas.

that converts the dollar amounts on your financial statements to percentages. You use one element from the statement as a base value and compare all other elements to it.

Common-Sizing the Income Statement

The sales amount is the base value used in common-sizing the income statement. See Exhibit 19. All elements on the income statement are divided by sales to calculate common-size percentages. For example, if the business generated $100,000 in sales for November and the cost of goods sold was $68,000, the common-size cost of goods sold would be 68 percent (68,000 ÷ 100,000). The advantage of this tool is that you can compare all income statement categories regardless of whether the business is growing or declining.

Notice in Exhibit 19 that all sales amounts, the base value, are 100 percent when common-sized. Divide any number in the year by the sales amount to get the common-size percentage.

Though all numbers changed from year to year, we can see in 1994 that the cost of goods sold increased 5 percent compared to 1993. This jump is not obvious when looking at dollar amounts only, because sales also increased dramatically for the same period. However, common-sizing allows you to

Exhibit 19. Common-sized income statements

	1993	1994	1995
Sales	$100,000 (100%)	$111,500 (100%)	$ 98,000 (100%)
Cost of goods sold	$ 68,000 (68%)	$ 81,395 (73%)	$ 65,660 (67%)
Gross profit	$ 32,000 (32%)	$ 30,105 (27%)	$ 32,340 (33%)
Operating expenses	$ 22,000 (22%)	$ 25,645 (23%)	$ 22,540 (23%)
Net income	$ 10,000 (10%)	$ 4,460 (4%)	$ 9,800 (10%)

see and correct the problem as the owner did in 1995. You can use this tool to isolate problem areas and make adjustments quickly.

Common-Sizing the Balance Sheet

The total assets amount is the base value used to common-size a balance sheet. See Exhibit 20. Total assets are always 100 percent, and every number on the balance sheet is compared to it. The common-size percentages are calculated by dividing the numbers by total assets.

Exhibit 20 shows three years of simplified balance sheets reflecting a stable, growing company. The only apparent glitch was in 1994 when current liabilities jumped 3 percent over the previous year. The owner spotted the jump through common-sizing and was able to bring the category back into line in 1995.

You may be curious about the jumps in owner's equity. Generally speaking, increases in the percentages of owner's

Exhibit 20. Common-sized balance sheets.

	1993	1994	1995
Current assets	$ 30,000 (30%)	$ 33,000 (30%)	$ 34,000 (30%)
Fixed assets	$ 70,000 (70%)	$ 77,000 (70%)	$ 80,000 (70%)
Total assets	$100,000 (100%)	$110,000 (100%)	$115,000 (100%)
Current liabilities	$ 15,000 (15%)	$ 19,800 (18%)	$ 17,250 (15%)
Long-term liabilities	$ 50,000 (50%)	$ 48,000 (44%)	$ 46,000 (40%)
Owner's equity	$ 35,000 (35%)	$ 42,200 (38%)	$ 51,750 (45%)
Total liabilities and equity	$100,000 (100%)	$110,000 (100%)	$115,000 (100%)

equity—the amount of the business value free of debt—is considered positive and desirable.

The Trend Analysis Tool

Trend analysis is a financial management tool that uses information from the income statement, balance sheet, and cash flow statement. You use this procedure to spread—lay out side by side in columnar form—your numbers, and by doing so spot trends. For example, you might discover by spreading five years' income statements that while sales have increased every year, the gross margin has decreased both as a percentage of sales and in dollar volume. You can use a trend analysis to examine historical financial statements and to project future business conditions based on historical trends. It works on both dollar volumes and common-size percentages.

Using Trend Analysis on Income Statements

This tool can be used to compare day-to-day, week-to-week, month-to-month, and year-to-year trends. While all categories can be examined, usually only the major components of the income statement are spread initially.

For example, you may wish to examine income statements from the past five years. In examining sales, cost of goods sold, gross profit, operating expenses, and net income categories, you discover that your operating expenses are increasing both in dollar volume and as a percentage of sales. You then need to spread every expense category (wages, payroll expense, insurance, supplies, repairs, vehicle expense, etc.) to determine the reason or reasons these expenses are growing disproportionately.

Using Trend Analysis on Balance Sheets and Cash Flow Statements

Balance sheets are most often compared on a year-to-year basis, though you can compare them as often as they are prepared. However, since significant changes occur on a more moderate pace on the balance sheet, it isn't as meaningful to do so. Using this tool on the cash flow statement is somewhat limited because usually cash flow statements are not common-sized. Therefore, you can spread and trend only dollar amounts. It can be used and is often effective in spotting and predicting cash flow trends, but other tools in this chapter may be more useful.

Ratio Analysis Tools

Ratios are comparisons of one number to another. We use ratios every day. We express the ratio of distance traveled compared to fuel used as miles per gallon. We discuss the cost of our home in relation to its size as dollars per square foot. These are useful everyday ratios.

It seems natural that businesses use ratios to compare numbers as well. However, most independent businesses still aren't using ratios to help them compete with the megamerchants.

There are nearly twenty common ratios used by various industries. We offer eight as a starting point in this book.

Balance Sheet Ratios

These ratios measure liquidity, solvency, and leverage. Start with these three to see how your business is doing compared to your industry:

1. *Current ratio.* This ratio measures your current assets compared to your current liabilities. This ratio answers the question, Does your business have enough current assets to pay off all of your current debts? Divide your total current assets by your total current liabilities to calculate this ratio.

$$\text{Current ratio} = \frac{\text{Total current assets}}{\text{Total current liabilities}}$$

A larger ratio is preferred because it indicates your ability to pay all current bills with money to spare. The generally accepted standard is 2:1. Check with your trade association to find your industry's norms. A low ratio means that your business may not be able to pay all bills as quickly as it should. In addition, you may be missing out on cash discount terms and alienating suppliers. A high ratio means that you have a lot of cash that might be better off put to work in other areas of the business.

2. *Quick ratio.* This ratio, sometimes called the acid-test ratio, is a measure of your ability to pay all current debt if inventories are excluded from your current assets. Divide the total of your cash, cash equivalents (stock, securities, etc.), and receivables by total current liabilities.

$$\text{Quick ratio} = \frac{\text{Cash} + \text{Cash equivalents} + \text{Accounts receivable}}{\text{Total current liabilities}}$$

Once again, a larger ratio is preferred. Generally, a ratio of 1:1 is acceptable. Compare your number to your industry to see how you're doing.

A low ratio means that your business may not be able to pay bills in a timely fashion, thereby missing discounts or making suppliers unhappy. A high ratio means that you have more cash reserve than you may need to meet current obligations. Consider moving some of your cash into areas where it can earn more.

3. *Debt to net worth ratio.* This ratio compares all of the liabilities (debt) of your business to the amount of the business you own. Divide total liabilities by your net worth.

$$\text{Debt to net worth ratio} = \frac{\text{Total liabilities}}{\text{Net worth}}$$

Generally, the higher this ratio, the more risk your lender or creditors associate with your business. You gain increased flexibility as you lower this ratio.

A low ratio means increased financial security and greater

borrowing power. A high ratio indicates less financial security and limited ability to acquire outside funds.

Income Statement Ratios

There are two main ratios derived from the income statement. They are the gross profit margin ratio and the net profit margin ratio. Both of these ratios are critical to improving the amount of money generated on your bottom line.

1. *Gross profit margin ratio.* This ratio is the percentage of sales left after subtracting the cost of goods sold from your sales. It indicates the percentage of sales left to pay operating expenses. Divide gross profit by net sales.

$$\text{Gross profit margin ratio} = \frac{\text{Gross profit}}{\text{Net sales}}$$

Which is more desirable, a higher or lower margin? Interpretation of this number has grown significantly more complex with the advent of the new breed of discounters and category killers. For decades the typical retailer attempted to increase this ratio by keeping the cost of goods sold between 50 and 60 percent of sales. This left 40 to 50 percent as profit to pay operating expenses and generate income for the owner(s).

The new breed departed from this traditional approach and pushed gross profit margins below 20 percent of sales. By controlling operating expenses (overhead), the aggressive new breed was able to deliver profit to the shareholders and hold margins thin at the same time.

If you are struggling with this dilemma, we suggest that you study Chapter Ten carefully. You'll get help in pricing and improving your value perceptions.

2. *Net profit margin ratio.* Also referred to as the return on sales, this ratio is the percentage of sales dollars left after subtracting the cost of goods sold and all operating expenses except income taxes.

$$\text{Net profit margin ratio} = \frac{\text{Net profit before tax}}{\text{Net sales}}$$

Ideally, this number will be as high as possible. This ratio measures the effectiveness of managing sales and expenses; and in general, the higher the net income percentage, the better.

A low ratio means that business expenses are too high or that sales are too low to support the overhead level. A high ratio means that the business is earning well and that expenses are being controlled effectively.

Management Ratios

Some ratios require both income statement and balance sheet information to calculate. We refer to those ratios as management ratios:

1. *Inventory turnover ratio.* This ratio is an indication of how well you are managing your inventory. Generally, the more you turn your inventory, the more profit you generate. The two equations below reflect our mention in Chapter Eight that there are two methods of calculating this ratio. We suggest that you contact your industry trade association to see which method is more generally in use.

$$\text{Inventory turnover ratio} = \frac{\text{Net sales}}{\text{Average inventory (at cost)}}$$

Alternative method:

$$\text{Inventory turnover ratio} = \frac{\text{Cost of goods sold}}{\text{Average inventory (at cost)}}$$

A low number of turns means you may be overinventoried or perhaps carrying too many slow-moving items. A high number of turns usually indicates effective use of inventory dollars and that your inventory is generally what your customers are looking for.

2. *Accounts receivable turnover ratio.* This ratio measures how well you're collecting credit accounts. If you offer thirty-

day credit terms, ideally you would collect your receivables twelve times per year.

$$\text{Accounts receivable turnover} = \frac{\text{Net sales}}{\text{Accounts receivable balance}}$$

Generally, the more times you collect your receivables, the better. A low ratio may mean you have a lax collection policy or have some slow-paying (potentially bad credit) accounts. A high turnover ratio may mean you have effective credit policies or that your accounts are all fast-paying.

3. *Return on investment ratio.* The final ratio may be the most important overall. The return on investment ratio measures the amount of return or profit you are earning on the dollars you've invested in your business.

$$\text{Return on investment} = \frac{\text{Net profit before tax}}{\text{Net worth}}$$

Since this ratio tells you if the effort you put into your business is worth anything, you want as high a percentage as possible here. Generally, a return on investment of 10 to 15 percent is required to ensure future growth.

A low percentage means that you might have been better off investing in savings bonds or Treasury bills. A high percentage can mean that you are utilizing creditors for much of your operating funds or that you are running the business efficiently.

Ratio analysis tools can help you spot trends, compare your business operations to others in your industry, and establish goals to aim for. Ratios can be an early warning system for your business. No problem is more easily solved then when it is a small one.

You may come to think of these ratio tools as your best friends. They are simple to use, easy to understand, and provide information you can't get effectively any other way.

These tools will never replace good management. However, they *can* make you a better manager. You will have to be a better manager to stay ahead of your new breed competitors.

Budget and Forecasting Tools

Perhaps no tools are more underutilized by small-business owners than budgets and pro forma (forecasted) income statements, balance sheets, and cash flow statements. These tools are the tools of planning. It's time to repeat the maxim that "Business owners don't plan to fail; they just fail to plan." The budget is both a plan and a statement of financial goals.

Budgeting is a process of analyzing many factors that affect your business operation. The factors include historical information (your past financial statements), present conditions and current information (what's going on now) and future expectations (what's likely to happen).

Some of these factors are beyond the control of your business. For example, economic trends, industry trends, government regulations, and competitive factors. Other elements include those you now have—or did have—control over. These are factors such as past financial performance, your banking relations, vendor relationships, and personnel resources.

The Master Budget

Your master budget or master plan should contain your pro forma financial statements. A good place to start is to project future performance on the basis of historical results. Assume that your sales have grown steadily at an annual rate of 3 percent for the past four years. You can logically assume, if no major shake-ups occur, that the trend is likely to continue.

On the other hand, if sales have increased steadily but a new, aggressive competitor is coming to town, you might be wise to forecast a dip in sales until you can counter the competitive force.

After you establish your sales projections, move on through the other elements of your income statement. If you are a retailer, a higher sales level will bring the need to purchase more to sell. This may improve your ability to buy in volume and thereby decrease the per unit cost. Either way, factor in the cost of goods sold and project gross profit dollars.

The next step is to analyze operating expenses. Will they hold steady in spite of the increase in sales—with the inherent increase in activity—or will you need to add part- or full-time help?

After new income is calculated, start your pro forma balance sheet. How will income statement activities affect your assets and liabilities? Will you need to borrow to increase inventory? Will you need to add a delivery vehicle? Will you need short-term capital to keep suppliers paid in timely fashion in order to take discounts? This will have an effect on your income statement as well.

Next, forecast your cash needs. We've seen businesses exceed sales goals, maintain expense budgets, and still run out of cash. Growth can outstrip your ability to produce cash. Use your projected income statement and balance sheet to help you predict cash requirements.

Finally, consider these facts as you lay out your master budget:

1. Profit is essential. Your business will survive in the long term if you are profitable.
2. Growth is not the same as success. Don't focus on growing a large business. Focus on satisfying your customers at a profit. Growth may come, but if it doesn't you're still successful.
3. You don't have to be big to be good. Pound for pound the wolverine is a champion. Be quick rather than big.
4. Your master budget is not set in concrete. It is a plan, and should give you flexibility. When you see an opportunity, be flexible enough to take advantage of it.
5. You can't plan forever. There are two points here: You must take action after you plan, and forever is too far away to plan for. Most planners agree that forecasting beyond three years produces marginal returns.

The prerequisites of good budgeting are:

1. An understanding of your industry, current trends, and environment
2. Historical financial statements as a basis to build on
3. Some specific, achievable, measurable goals
4. An enthusiastic owner, dedicated to success, willing to plant seeds today for a future harvest

The Variance Comparison Tool

This tool allows you to examine your business by comparing actual results with:

1. Forecasted (budgeted) amounts
2. Previous results
3. Results of other businesses in your industry

The variance comparison differs from trend analysis in that you need only two numbers to make the analysis.

This tool also works well with the budgeting and forecasting tools. For example, in Exhibit 21 ABCX Company uses this tool to see how well its operation is performing compared to budget.

Note that in Exhibit 21 even though the cost of goods sold was higher than budget, this was not considered unfavorable because the increase mirrored the growth in sales. Both operating expenses (higher than budgeted) and net income (lower than budgeted) are considered as unfavorable variances.

Variance analysis can also be used to find differences in common-size comparison to industry averages statements. We show an example in Exhibit 22.

In Exhibit 22, ABCX's cost of goods is slightly higher than the industry average, causing the gross profit to be lower. Both of these factors are considered as unfavorable. However, ABCX's operating expenses are lower than the industry, resulting in favorable profits.

Exhibit 21. Sample variance comparison.

ABCX Budget Variance Comparison
Income Statement, January 1994

	Budgeted	Actual	$ Variance Favorable/ (Unfavorable)	% Variance Favorable/ (Unfavorable)
Sales	$10,000	$10,100	$100	1%
Cost of goods sold	$ 7,000	$ 7,070	$ 70	1%
Gross profit	$ 3,000	$ 3,030	$ 30	1%
Operating expenses	$ 2,500	$ 2,700	($200)	(8%)
Net income	$ 500	$ 330	($170)	(34%)

Exhibit 22. Sample industry-oriented variance comparison.

Budget Variance Comparison
Common-Sized Income Statement 1995

	Industry Average	ABCX Company	Variance Favorable/ (Unfavorable)
Sales	100%	100%	N/A
Cost of goods sold	65%	66%	(1%)
Gross profit	35%	34%	(1%)
Operating expenses	31%	29%	2%
Net income	4%	5%	1%

The main purpose of variance analysis is to pinpoint areas that need your attention. In Exhibit 21, the operating expenses are the cause of the unfavorable variance from the budget. You would want to check both the accuracy of the budgeted amount and the reason for overspending.

In Exhibit 22, you would focus your attention on why the

cost of goods sold was higher than the industry norm. It could be faulty purchasing practices such as not taking discounts, not buying from the best source, or not buying in proper quantities. It could be faulty pricing strategies such as not adding on enough markup, offering unnecessary discounts, or shrinkage and theft. It could also be that the competition has caused the market to be softer than the industry norm or a combination of several of these factors.

The important element is that you know where to begin your search for the root of the variance or problem.

Sources of Financial Information

To effectively use the financial tools we've outlined in this chapter you may require other information. We are including this brief list as a starting point for your search.

- Your own trade association and trade publications. [*Check with other businesses in your industry or search the* Encyclopedia of Associations *at your local library.*]
- Accounting Corporation of America, 1929 First Avenue, San Diego, CA 92101. [*This organization publishes the* Parameter of Small Businesses, *which classifies operating ratios by industry group.*]
- Dun & Bradstreet, Inc., Business Information Systems, 99 Church Street, New York, NY 10007. [*This firm publishes annual key business ratios.*]
- National Cash Register Co., Marketing Services Department, Dayton, OH 45409. [*This firm publishes* Expenses in Retail Businesses, *a guide of comparison for business owners.*]
- Robert Morris Associates, Philadelphia National Bank Building, Philadelphia, PA 19107. [*Publishes ratio studies for more than 200 lines of businesses.*]
- The Small Business Administration. Call 1-800-827-5722 to obtain a free listing of publications.
- Your local Small Business Development Center. [*These college- or university-based centers offer free confidential coun-*

seling, training, and resources.] Call 1-800-827-5722 to locate the center nearest you.

Other Useful Tools

The Customer Batting Average

The customer batting average (CBA) is one of our favorite tools because it helps you analyze information that you can use to grow your business in three ways, as shown on page 186. To use this tool, you must record three numbers for the period you wish to analyze. First, you must know your total customer traffic. This is a count of everyone who comes into your business or with whom you make contact. The second number

Exhibit 23. A form for tracking customer batting average information.

Clinton Appliance and Furniture

Weekly Sales and Close Percentage

Salesman _____ Week of _____ to _____

Day	Customers helped	Customers Sold (closed)	
Monday	10	(Name, Amount)	
		Bill James	$435.58
		Mary Smith	$284.30
		Roger Allen	$719.41
		R. D. Lathum	$118.19
		LaVerne Artz	$948.00
		Nancy Love	$449.68
		Francis Larkey	$299.47

Total customers helped: 10
Total number of sales: 7
Total sales volume: $3,254.63
Percent closed: 70%
Average dollars per sale: $464.95

---

is the number of buyers. The third number is the amount of sales dollars collected.

Dwight Horne, owner of Clinton Appliance and Furniture in Clinton, North Carolina, developed a form his sales staff uses to track CBA information. He agreed to share it with us so you could use it to design one that will work for you. Exhibit 23 is an abbreviated version of Horne's form.

Horne uses a similar form—one sheet covers an entire week—to improve the CBA and to identify potential weak areas that need management attention. We hope you use a form similar to this one to capture information for your business.

We conducted a research survey of the top retail businesses in one of America's "small" cities. This research revealed that only 4 percent of those surveyed tracked the information needed to calculate their customer batting average. After we discussed the tool, 100 percent of the respondents agreed that having the information would be beneficial to their business.

In Exhibit 24, we detail the information needed to determine your customer batting average and calculate other related factors.

Using the information in Exhibit 24, we can calculate Bob's customer batting average. Divide the number of buyers (336) by the total potential customers (420) to get a batting average of .800 (or 80 percent). We now know that eight of ten people who walk through Bob's front door purchase something.

This number may be high or low depending on the indus-

Exhibit 24. Determining your customer batting average.

Bob's Hardware, Week of September 11–16, 1994

Number of walk-ins for week	420
Number of buyers (transactions)	336
Total sales for week	$4,704
Customer batting average	.800
Average dollars per sale	$14.00
Average dollars per customer (including nonbuyers)	$11.20

try and the season. Since a hardware store is a destination store—that is, a store where you usually go with a definite need in mind—we feel this number may be a little low.

This tool also helps us develop other information. For example, we now know the average buying customer spends $14 (total sales divided by number of sales transactions). We also know that every customer who walks through the door is worth $11.20 in sales (total sales divided by total traffic).

We can use this information along with our customer profile to evaluate other parts of our business. Traffic counts can help evaluate the effectiveness of your advertising. The customer batting average can help evaluate the effectiveness of your sales staff or find weaknesses in your product or service. Most importantly, it gives everyone in your business something to shoot for. Your goal should be to improve all of these numbers.

Using the CBA to Grow Your Business

There are three ways to improve your business using the information from the customer batting average tool. You can:

1. *Increase walk-in traffic.* This is a promotion tactic that should focus on getting the right message to the target market. Remember, each walk-in is worth $11.20.
2. *Increase the customer batting average itself.* Turning walk-ins into buyers will involve several tactics. It is critical to discover why the customer didn't buy. Merchandising, pricing, customer service, personal selling, and inventory control will provide the starting points.
3. *Increase the amount of the average sale.* To improve in this area, you will need to build merchandising, suggestive (add-on) selling, product knowledge, and selling-up skills. You may also have to adjust your inventory selection and frequency of ordering.

All in all, CBA is a solid tool to help you learn more about your customers and to serve them better.

One-Shot Productivity and Efficiency Tools

Here is a list of other tools you can use to measure and improve your store's effectiveness.

1. *Sales per square foot.* Divide total net sales by the number of square feet used by the business.
2. *Sales per square foot by department.* Divide total net sales for the department by the number of square feet used by the department.
3. *Sales per employee.* Divide total net sales by the total number of employees. Add part-time employees together to get full-time equivalents (FTEs).
4. *Sales per hour.* Divide total net sales by the number of "open for business" hours.
5. *Gross profit per square foot.* Divide total gross profit by the total of square feet used by the business.
6. *Gross profit per square foot by department.* Divide total gross profit earned by the department by the number of square feet used by the department.
7. *Gross profit per employee.* Divide the total gross profit by the total number of employees (FTEs).
8. *Gross profit per hour.* Divide the total gross profit by the number of hours you are open for business.
9. *Net income per square foot.* Divide total net income by the number of square feet used by the business.
10. *Net income per employee.* Divide the total net income by the total number of employees (FTEs).
11. *Service revenue billed per service employee.* Divide total net service revenue by the total number of service employees (FTEs).
12. *Service hours billed per service employee.* Divide total service hours billed by the total number of service employees (FTEs).

Ten

Purchasing and Pricing for Profit

It's not the number of skins you sell; it's how much profit you make.

—Early caveman-era hide trader

One of our favorite "profit stories" is about Bob and Joe, two young men who decided to go into the watermelon selling business. They jumped into the old pickup early one summer and drove down south to get a big load of vine-ripened "black diamonds."

They negotiated a price with a farmer who wanted 9 cents each for the melons. Bob finally got him *down* to ten for a dollar. They picked a heaping load and headed home. The next day they set up shop under a big shade tree on a busy corner in town. They hand-lettered a large sign that said FRESH WATERMELONS—10¢ EACH.

In no time at all, they sold every single melon. They were grinning from ear to ear as they counted their money. The grins faded a little when they realized that after deducting gas and lunch money they had less than when they started.

These young men were nobody's fools. They studied the situation and finally hit upon a solution. The obvious answer was to get a *bigger truck!*

Bob and Joe aren't the only ones to experience the "bigger truck syndrome." It frequently happens when small businesses focus on increasing sales without examining all factors that contribute to profitability.

This chapter deals with two critical components of profitability: purchasing and pricing. Good management of these two functions will help you compete with any competitor, even the new breed. You'll be able to build your profits, and profits are necessary if you're going to stay in business very long.

Samuel Gompers, the first president of the American Federation of Labor, said, "The worst crime against working people is a company which fails to operate at a profit."

Gompers's goals for the union were to bring higher wages and better working conditions to all members. However, he realized that no company—large or small—can stay in business, pay good wages, and offer benefits without profit. In our free-enterprise system, profit is the engine that pulls the entire economic train. You must have profit to grow and prosper in the arena with the megamerchants.

Increase Your Purchasing Power

We believe that buying smart puts money in your pocket before you sell anything. When you buy it right, you can sell it right. By improving your purchasing techniques, you can correct many profitability problems.

If you are feeling pressure from companies like Wal-Mart, the category killers, or other off-price competitors, you'll want to use some or all of the proven purchasing strategies in this section. They will help you reduce your cost of goods sold, lower inventory levels (or increase inventory turns), and enhance your value image with lower prices.

Taking Away the Advantage of Clout

One of the most talked-about advantages that the new breed of megamerchants has is their tremendous purchasing power. As the nation's largest retailer, Wal-Mart bought more than $50 billion in various product lines in fiscal 1994. A company with that kind of clout does tend to get the attention of even the largest manufacturers.

However, the law regarding terms of sale in buyer-vendor

relations is written to favor small businesses. The Robinson-Patman Act was enacted by Congress in 1936 to protect small independent grocers who were facing a new breed of competitor known as *supermarkets*. Right after the Great Depression, supermarket chains were formed to streamline food distribution and increase efficiency in the industry. These chains eliminated traditional costs and bought in large quantities. This allowed them to sell for a profit at prices lower than smaller businesses were paying for similar merchandise. Sound familiar? History does seem to be repeating itself with the new breed today.

The Robinson-Patman Act does hold some hope for small-business owners. Essentially, the law says that manufacturers must sell the same quantities of the same goods at the same price. They cannot discriminate regardless of the buyer. The question then becomes, *Who can buy in the same quantities as the megamerchants?*

The Benefits of Joining Buying Groups

Who can match the buying power of Kmart, Home Depot, or Best Buy? Buying groups can—and do every day. Buying groups are organizations that coordinate or pool the buying needs of many small businesses into larger orders with major manufacturers or suppliers. The result is purchasing power—big-dollar buying clout. Buying groups are forming all over the country to help small businesses lower their cost of goods sold.

Some of the groups are organized as cooperatives, others as collectives, and a few as for-profit associations. Some of the groups are large and sophisticated, like Cotter and Company of Chicago, which has nearly 7,000 member hardware stores around the country. Other groups are small, local, and as simple as a group of four or five merchants pooling orders. Regardless of size and sophistication, these groups are springing up in almost every retail market segment.

Murray Provine is the president of the 2,500-member Key America buying groups, whose members sell major appliances, consumer electronics, and home furnishings. "Our groups were organized with the customer in mind," says Provine in describing some of the major advantages that buying groups offer their members. "We find that our members' customers prefer to buy from local dealers with personal service before and after the sale."

Provine knows that every customer is interested in price too. "Our buying clout now exceeds $2 billion," he says. "When you combine the purchasing power of thousands with local, personal service, you get an independent dealer who can compete with anyone."

North Carolina Key group member Dwight Horne is a believer. "If you would have told me ten years ago that I'd be paying $5,000 per year to belong to a buying group, I'd have said you're crazy," Horne admits. "But, I can tell you now that it's the best money I ever spent." Horne says he gets more than double his membership fees back in year-end rebates alone. "But that's not the biggest advantage. I'm buying right—that's the key. For example, I'm getting my best-selling console television for $90 less than I was before joining the Key group. When you're buying right, you can sell against anybody."

Some buying groups offer benefits in addition to lower prices. Some groups provide merchandising, sales, and service training, financial counseling, and computer bulletin boards so members can trade inventory and marketing support.

The Texas Marketing Guild, a furniture buying and marketing organization, offers members full-color flyers at a fraction of the usual cost. Group member John Warrick, a Plainview, Texas, furniture store owner, credits the flyers for helping his store attract new customers. "Since we started using the flyers and mailing to a carefully targeted list, our sales are up 40 percent, and our profits are up more than that," Warrick says.

Warrick does warn other owners to look carefully at buying organizations before joining one. He points out that not all groups are created with the retailers' interests utmost in their minds. "We looked at several different options before deciding to join two groups," he says. "Our Guild is a unique organization in that there are no monthly fees. We all have to work in the guild as a condition of membership, and every member is required to serve on a committee. Some work on the flyers, others negotiate with manufacturers, and some select new lines. We all benefit from the collective wisdom of others."

Some retailers who don't belong to buying groups themselves are receiving the benefits through suppliers who do. Casey's, the Winslow, Arizona, hardware and builder's supply store we profiled earlier, doesn't belong to a buying group. However, it does get great prices and support services from one of its vendors, the Amarillo Hardware Company, which is a member of the Distribution America buying group. Casey's president, Robert Gondek, says, "We rely on Amarillo Hardware's buying power to help us hold our prices in line. We're like partners; if they're buying right, we're buying right."

C. B. Streeter, vice president of marketing and sales for Amarillo Hardware, says, "There are thirty-eight distributors in our wholesale buying group. Combined, we have over $2 billion in purchasing power. More importantly, we can help each of our retailers customize their buying programs so that they are buying the right amount, at the right price, at the right time." Streeter says other traditional wholesalers are also using buying groups to enhance their purchasing power.

If you feel a buying group might offer you opportunities to enhance your purchasing power, we suggest that you start your search for one with your trade association. If they are unaware of any groups, visit with other businesses in your industry and contact the editors of the trade publications that you subscribe to. Keep your eyes open when you visit retail buying markets and industry trade shows. Many buying groups market their services there. Look at your library for listings of associations.

Find the Right Suppliers

Buying groups may not fit your situation or be able to fulfill all of your purchasing needs. In many industries traditional wholesalers or distributors may offer all the purchasing power you need. Many of these traditional middlemen have become lean and tough in order to pass along savings to their retailer customers.

Unfortunately, not all have reacted to the new breed of megastore competition and some are still trying to conduct business as usual. These suppliers are creating unnecessary overhead and are making it very hard for the retailer to cover all costs and still be in the ballpark pricewise.

You may need to evaluate your vendors to determine if they are the best source for your business. Ask the following questions:

1. Does this vendor's pricing structure allow me to cover all elements of cost and produce an acceptable profit, or do I find my competitive position slipping along with my gross margins?
2. Does this vendor place heavy emphasis on getting my order right the first time, or am I always on the phone to resolve variances between what I ordered and what I got?
3. Does this vendor bill regularly and accurately, or do bills show up at random times with errors?
4. Does this vendor usually have what I need in stock, or am I often paralyzed by out-of-stock items and frequent back orders?
5. Does this vendor ship back orders automatically, or do I have to remember to reorder?
6. Does this vendor ship back-ordered items after the season for the item is past?
7. Does this vendor offer discount terms, and does my volume often match the minimum to qualify for them?
8. Does this vendor offer seasonal dating terms on applicable merchandise?
9. Does this vendor offer regular, timely delivery as a part of the basic price—or at an additional cost?
10. Does this vendor have liberal return programs so I can match the new breed's "no hassle" return policy?
11. Does this vendor offer *value added services* such as prepricing, overnight shipping, or year-end order summaries?
12. Does this vendor offer help in merchandising, sales training, promotions, or store layout?

13. Does this vendor offer co-op advertising support?
14. Is this vendor large enough to support my growth?
15. Is this vendor local enough to understand my market?

Work With Your Vendors

When you're satisfied you've found a good buying source, build a working relationship with that vendor. Just as you need constant feedback from your customers, your suppliers need to hear from you.

It is always appropriate to call a vendor to discuss general topics such as industry trends, market conditions, and competitive strategies. However, you certainly should communicate directly and quickly under certain circumstances. We'd suggest a quick call if:

1. You won't be able to pay your bill on time.
2. Your vendor's order-filling accuracy starts to slip.
3. You learn that you're getting a new megastore competitor. (The vendor may have information that can help or may be able to put you in contact with someone who is familiar with how your competitor operates.)
4. A competitor really hammers you on price-sensitive items. Follow up by mailing a copy of your competitor's ads or flyers.
5. The number of out-of-stocks and back orders starts to increase.
6. You hear rumors about special deals or packages from manufacturers.
7. The level of people service slips (that is, sales, order taking, delivery, accounting/billing, etc.).
8. The level of returns on any one item or product line increases significantly.

Stay Alert for Better Buying Opportunities

Even if your vendor relations are in great shape and your competitive situation is sound, stay alert for new opportunities in your line of business.

Never take your suppliers for granted. Be aware of the

comings and goings of wholesalers and distributors. Listen to every new opportunity; get the details even if it doesn't fit your plans right now.

Build Your Pricing Skills

Several years ago we sat in on a pricing seminar at a national farm implement show. The moderator asked panel members to describe their pricing strategies.

Two dealers who ran large, apparently profitable dealerships had the most to say on the topic. The first, an old-timer, said he never sold a tractor or farm implement if he didn't make his 28 percent gross margin. The other, an aggressive younger man, avowed that he had *never* lost a sale on price—margin be damned. Ironically, neither of these dealers are in the implement business today.

When you lower prices across the board to meet the competition, you place your business at risk. If, on the other hand, you never lower prices, you'll start to lose credibility and eventually customers too. It seems like a lose-lose proposition.

Effective pricing is the key to managing profits. The days of taking a standard markup on everything are gone. Nor can you just cut prices to match the competition without regard for your costs.

Arriving at a Selling Price

How small businesses arrive at a selling price is an interesting study. Many retailers use a constant multiplier for every product or service to arrive at a final selling price. For example, a 1.429 multiplier will yield a gross profit of 30 percent. (This assumes that the multiplier is applied to the product cost and the product is sold at full retail price.) Retailers have used this method for many decades.

Service businesses more typically will price their services based on their perception of their own value. We have counseled dozens of service providers over the past six years. Many of them have questions about how to price their services.

Others admit that while they may have a "standard price" for each job or a "standard rate" per hour, they often cut their standard price to get a job or adjust the number of hours billed because they know the customer will react negatively to a higher charge.

Both strategies (standard retail multipliers and service seat-of-the-pants) make it easy for the giants to convince consumers of the value of their products. They use loss leaders and constantly reinforce the value perception with hard-hitting advertising.

Price your goods or services to sell without losing sight of profit. This would be an easy part of your job if market conditions never varied, and if the new breed always played by the rules. However, conditions do vary and discounters don't play by established rules, so pricing for profit becomes an area of your business that requires constant attention.

The Elements of Price

There are five elements of price to consider as you establish your pricing structure:

1. The cost of sales
2. The cost of operations
3. A reasonable return on the capital you've invested
4. Your personal income needs
5. Your need for capital for renewal, continuation, and growth

Most businesses we've counseled cover the cost of sales, operating expenses, and income for the owner, but very few consider a return on their investment or make any attempt to set aside capital for growth or renewal. However, your equipment will wear out, your fixtures will require updating, and your facilities will need to be either remodeled or replaced over time. Anticipate these costs and include them in your long-term pricing structure. They are part of the cost of doing business.

True profits for your business come only after you cover

all costs, pay yourself well, generate a reasonable return on your investment, and make provisions for continuance of the business.

The Value Perception

Although profit is essential and covering all costs critical, your business will not survive unless your customers feel that you give them value. The purpose of this section is to help you position your business as a better value provider in the minds of your customers.

Your customers' perception of value rests on the delicate balance of price versus quality and quantity. We illustrate this balance in Exhibit 25. Imagine a seesaw with price sitting on one end and quality and quantity on the other. When the price goes down or the quality-quantity goes up, the customer perceives more value. When the price goes up and the quality or quantity goes down, the customer sees less value and is less likely to buy or be satisfied.

Remember what your customers believe about your business is more important than what you believe. (We're only talking about value perception here.) If your customers believe your prices are too high, it doesn't matter if they're not. If in the customer's mind he will get a better deal elsewhere, he'll go elsewhere. Once you get your prices in line you may have to rebuild your "value" image in the mind of your customer.

You and your staff are also a part of your customer's perception of value. Your knowledge, your experience, and your personal touch all add to the value of your products or services. Everyone loves to do business with people he knows and trusts.

Your "worth" adds to the value perception of your business. However, if you are never around, or don't work the floor as much as you used to, don't be surprised if your customers don't come around as much either.

In the beginning, the mass merchandisers focused on the price end of the value perception seesaw. They frequently promoted off-brand merchandise with very low prices.

As their sales exploded in the 1970s, they began to carry

Exhibit 25. Value perception indicator.

Higher Satisfaction Level Higher Quality or Larger Quantity	Lower Satisfaction Level Higher Price
▪ Very satisfied ▪ More positive word-of-mouth advertising ▪ Easy to show benefits	▪ Less likely to buy ▪ Buys are needs-driven ▪ Will buy less

Quality—Quantity   Price

WILL BUY   WILL BUY

▪ Less satisfied ▪ Potential negative word-of mouth ▪ Tough to show benefits	▪ More likely to buy ▪ More likely to buy more ▪ Buy more frequently
Lower Quality or Small Quantity Lower Value Perception	Lower Price Higher Value Perception

more quality brand names. Today, you can find most major brands on their shelves.

Wal-Mart focuses heavily on both the quality and price elements. Its current advertising slogan is: "Always the low prices, always." Kmart uses similar psychology, because all advertising is aimed at building value perception in the customer's mind. Kmart's current low-price slogan is: "Everyday Low Price Anytime and Every Time." McDonald's restaurants package sandwiches, fries, and drinks and call these combinations "value meals."

You Don't Have to Beat Wal-Mart's Price

Nearly every time we conduct one of our *Coexisting With Wal-Mart©* workshops, at least one retailer complains about Wal-

Mart's prices, saying that Wal-Mart sells some products for less than the retailer can buy them for. When we hear that complaint, we know that the company is not buying as well as it could be.

You don't have to beat the discounter's price; you only need to be close. Remember, customers don't always buy the lowest price; they buy what they believe to be the best value. However, if your customers see a big difference in your price on the same items compared to the discounter, you lose not only the sale but your value perception as well.

Lower Your Prices to Increase Your Value Perception

Without question, one of the quickest ways to change your value perception is to lower your prices and advertise like crazy. You'll generate some sales and gain some customers. However, we don't want you to get more sales and then go broke. That can happen if you lower prices to a point where your selling price no longer covers all of your costs.

Our intention in writing this book is to help you become more profitable, regardless of your sales level. The best way we've found to build your value perception and maintain profit margins is to use a variable pricing strategy.

The Flex-Pro© Variable Pricing System

The Flex-Pro Variable Pricing System is a seven-step strategy for maintaining desired profit margins for your business without losing the perception of value in your customer's mind. The seven steps are as follows:

1. *Know your competitors' prices for any item you sell.* For example, let's assume you're selling a four-roll package of brand-name toilet tissue. A quick survey of the competition shows the same brand at Wal-Mart for 97 cents, Kmart for 99 cents, and a local supermarket for $1.49. Wal-Mart and Kmart have established your competitive target at under a dollar.

Your customers, who are not vitally interested in your success, take time to notice these prices. Since you are vitally interested, stay on your toes and make sure you know your competitors' prices.

2. *Compare your prices to your competitors' prices.* In the example in step 1, Wal-Mart is the price leader at 97 cents for the toilet tissue. If you're selling the same tissue at $1.29, your price is 32 cents higher, for a percentage difference of nearly 33 percent.

If you allow this price differential to go on, you may lose some perception of value. Your 33-percent-higher price level may cause customers to believe you're higher on everything.

Compare prices often. Your customers are comparing every time they shop. We recommend a monthly general check in addition to reading weekly flyers and monitoring radio and television ads.

3. *Determine price sensitivity.* Items that are sensitive to competitive pricing are known as *visible* items. Visible items include products and services that are utilized by a wide variety of customers, items that are disposable or consumable, or items that are fast moving. Visible items are frequently promoted and often used as *loss leaders* or *come-ons.* Most big-ticket items—cars, major appliances, furniture, etc.—will be price-shopped and are therefore visible or price sensitive.

In Exhibit 26, we show a tool you can use quickly to determine a product's price sensitivity. We'll use the toilet tissue from the previous examples to do a sample sensitivity evaluation.

4. *Know what overall gross profit margins you need to cover all costs.* Maintaining margin is a challenge for most businesses. In the sample income statement in Exhibit 27, we show a business that is operating with a gross profit margin of 40 percent. Stated another way, this business generates 40 cents on every dollar of sales to pay for all other costs.

It is important that you recognize all costs in determining the overall margin you need. In the above income statement there are three types of cost. The first is *cost of sales,* the second is the *fixed, or operating, expenses,* and the third is the *desired profit, or net income.* For the purpose of this discussion, we include profit (net income) as a cost you must cover. (Don't

Exhibit 26. A sample sensitivity evaluation.

Brand-Name Four-Roll Package Bathroom Tissue		
Characteristics	*Yes*	*No*
▪ Used by a wide range of customers	X	
▪ Disposable/consumable	X	
▪ Fast moving/high inventory turn	X	
▪ Advertised and promoted heavily	X	
▪ High-dollar-value item		X
▪ Limited selling season		X
▪ Frequently used as a loss leader item	X	
Total	5	

Determination = Very sensitive

Rating scale (Score 1 point for each yes answer.)
  0 = Not price sensitive   1 = Slightly sensitive
  2 = Somewhat sensitive   3 = Moderately sensitive
  4 = Sensitive   5+ = Very sensitive

Exhibit 27. Sample income statement.

	Common-Sized (as a % of sales)	
1. Sales	$100,000	100%
2. Cost of sales	60,000	60%
3. Gross profit	40,000	40%
4. Operating expenses	30,000	30%
5. Net income before taxes	$ 10,000	10%

forget the other two costs we discussed earlier—return on your investment and long-term capital.)

Your goal is to generate enough gross profit to cover your operating expenses and produce the net income percentage you desire. To follow through on step 4, we need to maintain a gross profit of 40 percent in our example. Many businesses use a standard markup percentage to achieve their overall margin. In our simplified example an item which costs 60 cents would sell for $1. Thirty cents would be used to pay for operating expenses yielding 10 cents, or 10 percent net income.

This all sounds wonderfully simple until you realize that the chains are going to keep their prices very low on highly visible items. *And*, if you are going to keep your perception of value with your customers, you will have to break away from your old "mark everything up 40 percent" philosophy.

Your competitors know exactly what margins they want to maintain. One of the key benefits the new breed gets from the heavy investment they've made in technology is the ability to monitor daily margins. They can adjust the price mix immediately if margins start to slip. This is an important reason for you to have accurate financial statements every month.

5. *Decrease margins on price-sensitive (visible) items that your competitors carry.* Your objective in this step is to lower your prices on visible items so that they are close to your competition—*even* if it means cutting them to near cost. (We'll show you how to get the margin back in step 6.) We suggest that you bring your prices down to within 5 to 10 percent of the market leader. You may even wish to advertise a few specials that are lower than your competitor's.

Note: You will not have to lower prices on all of your inventory, just the most price-sensitive items and those items that are exactly the same as your competitor's (i.e., same brand, same size, same product number, etc.). For many retail stores the crossover items and price-sensitive items may be only 10 percent or less of the inventory count. However, even if it is 20 percent of your inventory on which you need to reduce prices, you still have the other 80 percent of your inventory on which to increase prices to get your profit margin back up.

Any discussion of lowering prices as a defense against low-price competition would be incomplete without the mention of price points. Certain "price points" are sensitive. For example, even though it means giving up 5 cents of profit, a price of 99 cents may generate more sales and profit than a price of $1.04. Accordingly, a price of $9.99 seems to be much lower than a price of $10.49 even though it is only 50 cents less. Once you are in a range between price points, there seems to be little resistance to higher prices. For example, if an item is priced at $12.39, increasing the price to $12.99 appears to have little effect on sales volume.

6. *Increase margins on items that are not price sensitive (blind).* This is your opportunity to get back the margin you gave up on price-sensitive items in step 5. Increase prices on all items that are not price sensitive and items that are not carried by your competitors.

The main objective of step 6 is to equalize or improve the overall profit margin in your business. At the same time you are lowering prices in step 5, you need to adjust prices on the *blind* items in this step.

The easiest way may be to simply increase your markup on all inventory that is not identified as price sensitive. For example, assume that you reduced your overall profit margin to 37 percent when you lowered prices on your visible, cross-over inventory. You will need to regain 3 percent to be even with where you were prior to reducing prices on price-sensitive items.

You may find that it will take an additional markup of 4 or 5 percent on your blind inventory to regain the 3 percent you gave up overall. Monitor this process closely to see what changes occur.

By using this technique, merchants often find that they can actually improve their gross profit margin while still keeping that all-important value perception.

7. *Continue the process.* To be a survivor you should continue using these steps from now on. You'll need to compare prices, monitor margins, and adjust pricing. The Flex-Pro Variable Pricing System is an ongoing process, not a one-time quick fix. You'll need to continually react to the marketplace. By keeping an eye on everyone's prices and monitoring your margins you can position yourself to reap maximum profits.

Price-Sensitive Items

We are often asked in our workshops for a list of the most price-sensitive items. To our knowledge no complete, documented list exists. However, with the help of a team of student researchers at West Texas A&M University in Canyon, Texas, we analyzed the printed flyers that Wal-Mart, Kmart, and Target distributed in the Amarillo, Texas, area during 1993.

Our findings are tabulated in Exhibits 28 and 29. We think you may find the results interesting.

Exhibit 28. Most often advertised items in the flyers of Wal-Mart, Kmart, and Target.

1. Nintendo/games	26. Portable stereos
2. Cameras	27. Boys' shirts
3. Ladies' jewelry	28. Over-the-counter drugs
4. Ladies' panties	29. Ladies' shorts
5. Ladies' shoes	30. Microwave ovens
6. Ladies' shirts/blouses	31. House paint
7. Upright vacuums	32. Household batteries
8. Bath towels/washcloths	33. Film/camera
9. Televisions	34. Ladies' sweaters
10. Ladies' jeans/slacks	35. Girls' shorts
11. Men's shirts	36. Telephone answering machines
12. Ladies' bras	37. Juice
13. Sheet sets	38. Pantyhose
14. Cordless phones	39. Pillows
15. VCR tapes	40. Men's shorts
16. Candy/candy bars	41. Deodorants
17. Exercise equipment	42. Comforter sets
18. Laundry soap	43. Storage boxes
19. Carpet/rugs	44. Tires
20. Shampoo	45. Bicycles
21. Ladies' watches	46. Ladies' purses
22. Men's briefs	47. Dinnerware
23. Cookware	48. Dolls
24. Infants' wear	49. Toilet tissue
25. VCRs	50. Motor oil

Exhibit 29. The top twenty flyer items advertised by the Big Three.

Target	Kmart	Wal-Mart
1. Nintendo/games	Exercise equipment	Women's jewelry
2. Cameras	Ladies' jewelry	Bath towels
3. Ladies' blouses	Cameras	Nintendo/games
4. Cordless phones	Girls' pants sets	Ladies' shoes
5. Ladies' jeans	Automotive/service	Infants' wear
6. Ladies panties	Tires	Ladies' panties
7. Televisions	Vacuum cleaners	Ladies' bras
8. Shampoo	OTC drugs	Sheet sets
9. VCR tapes	Men's shirts	Sheet sets
10. Laundry soap	Ladies' shirts	Men's shirts
11. Ladies' shoes	Guns	Cameras
12. Candy/candy bars	Televisions	Ladies' T-shirts
13. Answer machines	Ladies' panties	Ladies' pajamas
14. Portable stereos	Ladies' shoes	Candy/candy bars
15. Juice	Towels/washcloths	Men's shoes
16. Chips/snacks	Razors/kits	Men's slacks
17. Ladies' bras	Floor coverings	Microwaves
18. Deodorants	Pillows	Toys
19. Eye care products	House paint	Ladies' watches
20. Phones	Pantyhose	Exercise equipment

A Final Thought

Remember that good pricing begins with good buying. If you aren't buying right, even the variable pricing strategy may not keep you competitive with the new breed. Investigate buying groups who serve your industry. Keep your eyes open for potential suppliers who can better meet your needs and offer better prices and buying terms.

By all means, use a blended or variable pricing system to maintain a positive value perception in the mind of your customers. Start increasing your purchasing power even if the megamerchants haven't yet moved in next door. You're always ahead of the game if you are buying and pricing correctly.

Eleven

Profiles of Survivors, Successes, and Superstars

My formula for success? Rise early, work late, strike oil.
—Jean Paul Getty

Ah, for the days when the pace was slow, Main Streets were booming, customers were plentiful, and the superstores hadn't started their march across the land.

Those days are gone and you're still around, which is a pretty good indication that you have one of the major ingredients for success: perseverance.

John Newbern said, "People can be divided into three groups: those who make things happen, those who watch things happen, and those who wonder what happened."

If you're not already in that first group that *makes* things happen, resolve right now to get into it. Even with the huge competition from the price-driven megastores, there are opportunities for success and there's money to be made. All across the country, right across the street from the superstores, small independent retail and service businesses are prospering. Ask yourself the question, *Why can't it be me?*

In the pages that follow, we introduce you to some of the people who *are* making things happen. To find these people, we talked to trade association executives, managers of buying groups, magazine and newspaper editors, chamber of commerce directors, and many others. Many of the men and women we profile have been recognized by their communities and their associations for their outstanding achievements.

By focusing completely on satisfying their customers and by sharpening their skills in all the other areas we talk about throughout this book, they are managing not only to survive but also to thrive in the land of the retail giants.

You can, too.

Breed & Co.
Hardware, Housewares, Lawn & Garden
Austin and San Marcus, Texas

The day we visited Breed & Co. in the Texas Hill country town of Austin, we could have filmed a commercial. Stopping customers as they left the store, we asked them for their opinions of the store. The resulting testimonials weren't just good, they were *fantastic!*

With such rave reviews, it's no wonder that visitors to Austin will have a tour list that includes the University of Texas, LBJ Library, Barton Springs, and . . . Breed & Co.

Located in an old Austin neighborhood, this unique, upscale store is a combination of three businesses: hardware, housewares, and lawn and garden. Their heftiest competition is in the hardware and lawn and garden areas, where they spar with Home Depot and Builders Square, who have combined space of 320,000 square feet. Are the owners worried? Not particularly. They've found their niche.

When Truman and Ann Breed bought the store twenty-four years ago, it was an old-line hardware store that specialized in unusual, hard-to-find hardware items. The Breeds kept their pledge to the previous owner to continue the tradition.

They carry more than 45,000 SKUs, and the word is out that if you can't find it at Breed & Co., you won't find it in Austin. It's not unusual for customers to come in with a long list of bizarre parts they need, and leave with all of them neatly wrapped. If Breed & Co. doesn't have what you're looking for, they'll get it for you and notify you when it's in.

In addition to the unique items they stock, Breed carries the standard assortment of the hardware trade and keeps a close eye on the competition. "We have a list of about 120 items of so-called 'price sensitive' items and regularly check our prices against Home Depot and Builders Square," Breed says. "We don't want to be embarrassed." (He credits his buying co-op with helping him keep prices low.)

Though 50 percent of their business is still hardware, the Breeds have greatly expanded their offerings, thanks to Truman's wife, Ann, who became active in the business after raising their two sons, Greg and Jeff. Both work in the business. (Jeff runs the San Marcus branch.)

Ann put her artistic talents to work in selecting new products for an expanding garden and gift department. Truman admits he questioned some of her initial buying decisions, but when her selections "flew out the front door," he realized she wasn't just creative, she had an instinct for what would sell.

Now, just down the aisle from the "heavy metal items" such as hammers and bolts, customers will find Italian pottery, Waterford crystal, gourmet coffee and candies, coffee makers, gifts, and garden plants and furniture. A new bridal registry is winning praises from brides-to-be. Its success figures prominently in expansion plans for Breed & Co.

As they contemplate adding space or another location, the Breeds can both remember the sleepless nights that accompanied their previous decision to expand.

The year they built their current building—a two-story, 12,000-square-foot building—Builders Square moved to town. Truman says, "About that same time, someone pulled the curtain on the building boom in Austin and construction stopped." People thought they were crazy to be building in such an uncertain economic climate, and Truman nervously projected a deficit of 20 percent.

But instead, their revenues have steadily climbed, and they've never had a down year, posting annual gains of about 12 percent. The Breeds believe that part of their success stems from their fierce dedication to continually improving the store and the merchandise. Ann elaborates, "You go into some stores and they just look 'tired.' We constantly update our store and are always on the lookout for new things on the market."

Their niche includes not just products, but also an ambiance

so superlative that as Breed says, "A day doesn't pass—honestly—
that I don't have a customer come up and tell me that they've had
a fantastic buying experience."

Their goal is to greet customers as soon as they walk in the
door and, as Ann says, "I don't care who you are or what you
look like, when you walk in here, we'll treat you with courtesy and
dignity—whether you have a ring on your hand or in your nose."

Their service policies have become almost legendary. The
company philosophy is to service what it sells, not just look for
the "fast turn." And if the customer needs a new faucet, an
employee will show how to install it. Ann adds, "And if you're
very old, we'll go out to your house and do it for you."

They've even been known to light floor furnaces and change
light bulbs for regular customers. Do they charge for such services?
"Heavens, no," Ann quickly responds. "They're our *neighbors.*"

Such warm, friendly attitudes aren't reserved just for customers. "We have a very strong family feeling here among all our
employees," says Truman. "We do a lot of hugging and thanking
people for what they do."

Employees are kept completely informed of the progress of
various departments and all financial records are entirely open to
scrutiny by the company's fifty-seven employees. They initiate
their own competition to generate the highest revenues per department. Competitive salaries, team meetings, profit-sharing plans,
and insurance benefits help keep employees happy.

The employees aren't the only ones who are happy. Both
Truman and Ann Breed truly love what they're doing. Even though
Truman is on the floor eight hours every day, on Sundays—the
only day the store is closed—Truman often comes in just to walk
up and down the aisles. "I look at the hammers and everything we
have and just get a very warm feeling," he says. "This is fun!"

And judging from comments we heard from people throughout the store, it's obviously fun for customers and employees, too.

Jim Myers Drug
Pharmacy, Home Health Care, Medical Equipment
Tuscaloosa, Alabama

Tell Jim Myers that times are tough in the pharmacy business
and he just might laugh at the understatement. In addition to stiff

competition from such heavyweights as Wal-Mart, Kmart, chain drugstores, and grocery store pharmacies, he also has to contend with other independents and mail-order pharmacies. Undaunted by the challenge, he says confidently, "We consider ourselves *their* competition."

He backs up the statement with an impressive list of statistics. Statewide, he has the highest volume in pharmacy sales per square foot—$3,300 per square foot compared to a chain store average of about $270 per square foot. Sales in 1993 increased 32 percent over the previous year.

They fill an average of 425 prescriptions a day, and on some days that figure has soared to 900. Myers and his staff of forty employees have generated the bulk of this volume from one of his two locations that has only 1,300 square feet.

It's no surprise that with records like those, Myers has attracted the attention of not just clients but also national organizations and the national media. Myers won the award in 1992 for Alabama Small Business of the year, was a 1993 runner-up for the prestigious Blue Chip Enterprise award, and has been featured in national magazines as well as the local press.

Myers is no newcomer to the hard work that it takes to win such a reputation. While working in a small pharmacy in Mississippi as a stock clerk when he was just thirteen years old, Myers decided to make pharmacy his lifetime work. To pay for pharmacy school, he worked the midnight-to-morning shift at an all-night drugstore. The only time he had left for studying was the 45-minute streetcar ride he took twice a day.

In spite of the hardship, he finished pharmacy school in three years and had to get a dispensation to take his state boards because he was then only twenty years old.

That work ethic has carried him through forty years of pharmacy work and gives him the drive he needs to build his business. "We go after business aggressively," he says, and adds another clue to his success: "We try to be first in whatever we do."

He was first to offer free blood sugar and blood pressure screenings, first with free fleet delivery of prescriptions and hospital equipment, first to offer free respiratory screenings, and first to provide at-home nursing intravenous services. The list goes on. Other services include twenty-four-hour emergency services, a drive-through window service, and a telecommunications program that allows the hearing-impaired to call in prescriptions.

While education—for both clients and employees—has long been a part of the pharmacy's mission, Myers has expanded that aspect of his business even more since moving into a new 8,000-square-foot two-story building in March of 1994.

At the new pharmacy, clients can go to the "education center" to counsel with a pharmacist about their medications, watch a videotape about medical conditions such as diabetes, and generally become better-informed consumers. "We take time to educate, not just dispense medication," says Myers, and he cites the high number of patients who come in with pill bottles and have no idea what they're taking and just say, "I need the pink ones."

Myers also hosts several diabetes seminars each year. When they first started the seminars, they had about twenty people attend. Now, the seminars draw more than five times that number, and Myers sees this as an important part of their educational and marketing program. Noting an increasing number of clients with sleep disorders, a new seminar topic on the subject is titled, "Sleepless in Tuscaloosa."

The seminars are organized by a marketing coordinator who also oversees other aspects of their promotions program, including newspaper, television, direct mail, health fairs, and radio.

Amid the uncertainties in the health care field, Myers is always looking for opportunities. He and his employees seek out new ideas and monitor new trends by constantly listening to their customers and scanning more than ten periodicals. Because whatever the future holds, Myers pharmacies want to be there *first*.

Berlin G. Myers Lumber Corp.
Lumber and Building Materials Center
Summerville, South Carolina

Twenty-five miles inland from Charleston is the beautiful historic town of Summerville. It's home to lovely old buildings, towering pine trees, gardens filled with fragrant flowers, and people like the Myers family who speak in a nice, slow, southern drawl and still say "ma'am" when speaking to ladies.

It's also home to Berlin Myers Lumber Corp. (BMLC), a company that has attracted national attention for the quality of its products, the service to its customers, and its reputation as the "cleanest lumberyard in America."

Under the watchful eyes of Berlin Myers, Sr.—who founded the company in 1939—and his two sons, Berlin Myers, Jr., and his brother, James—the company is thriving against the stiffest competition it has had in its fifty-five-year history. A new Lowe's supercenter opened recently right down the street. Home Depot, HQ (a division of Hechinger's), and a number of regional chain stores and other independents are within a few miles. As Myers, Jr., says, "It's a very, very competitive market."

But far from being nervous about the competition, Myers seems to delight in it. "They're only as much a threat as I allow them to be," he says. His only regret is that he's not closer to Lowe's. "They're able to spend literally millions of dollars in advertising," he explains, "and obviously attract a great number of people that I can't attract."

BMLC is working hard to attract some of those customers with an aggressive advertising program that encompasses radio, television, print, and "whatever comes along." Myers says, "You can't be all things to all people, and we'd love to be in a position to service those people who leave there [Lowe's] unsatisfied. Hopefully when they leave that store, they will think about where they can go without having to drive another ten to fifteen minutes."

The Myerses didn't wait for the superstore to open to try to get people thinking about BMLC. Instead, the Myerses rented space on a billboard in the field where the superstore was under construction and boldly invited customers to come to BMLC. "However, they had us take it down," Myers admits. He added, "We want to pick at them a little bit, but we don't want to make them mad."

After the superstore opened, Myers took note that the competition's advertisements promised a lot but always contained asterisks that directed would-be customers to the exceptions in fine print. With a feistiness that belies his mild manner, Myers countered with a "There are No Asterisks at Berlin Myers" campaign.

The Myerses and their thirty-one employees are constantly looking for ways to differentiate themselves from the competition and pay close attention to the advertised specials of the discounters. "We're always looking for an opportunity to raise our prices," Myers says with a laugh. "We don't want anyone to think that we're a low end dealer."

Instead, BMLC limits its product lines to very high-end products, which it displays with lots of flair in an attractive, spotless 100,000-square-foot facility. Unique hand-painted signs direct homeowners and contractors to beautiful displays of gothic windows, stained-glass doors, moldings, and decorative products. A full-scale deck BMLC built *inside* generated a lot of attention.

The Myerses know the importance of community involvement and are active in community events. They also constantly seek new ideas through their affiliations with the Carolinas/Tennessee Lumber Association and buying co-ops. "I think anybody who doesn't change is doomed to disappear from the face of the earth," says Myers. "I don't think anyone can do business the way they were doing yesterday and survive."

But even at BMLC, some things never change. Customers can still expect to get a lot of attention from well-trained, knowledgeable employees—some who have been there forty-five years. They'll also still be greeted at the door by a salesperson who will take their order and load it for them. If they want, they'll also get free delivery and specialized services from an on-site millwork shop. But what they won't get at Berlin Myers Lumber Company are *asterisks*.

Ebaugh's Gifts
Gifts, Collectibles, Cards, and Baby Clothes
McPherson, Kansas

In many ways, the story of Ebaugh's echoes the tales of what life in America used to be. McPherson, Kansas, is a town where people often forget to lock their doors, where store owners can still call 90 percent of their customers by name. And don't bother getting out identification when you write a check—they trust you.

But while many retail merchants along Main Streets are failing, Ebaugh's owner Debbie Kramer has posted strong annual growth of about 15 percent over the past few years.

Kramer's success hasn't gone unnoticed. In 1991, she earned a state award for Outstanding Woman-Owned Retail Business of the Year and is president of the chamber of commerce. "I put back into the community because the community's been good to me," she says.

Her store sits in the first block of Main Street. Like many old-time Main Street merchants, the "wonderful people" who had owned the store for twenty-five years had, due to health reasons, lost some of their fire. They were not going to new markets, not looking for new products, and "They just wanted to continue to make it on what they knew," Kramer says. And Wal-Mart was just down the street.

When she bought the store in 1988, Kramer knew she wanted to slide into the transition gradually. "I didn't want to lose any of the customers that they had had in the past by making a big change," she says, "yet I wanted to develop my own store and pull in my-age friends as well as some younger people."

She aggressively sought new products at markets across the country and kept an eye out for what Wal-Mart was carrying. "Any time I purchase a product that is new in my store, I always ask my reps if this is sold to the mass merchandisers," she says.

You'll find gifts of all sorts, kitchen items, collectibles like Cherished Teddies and Precious Moments, greeting cards, a bridal registry, and bridal accessories. You can also order a gift basket, have a picture framed, or shop for a baby or toddler in the Babyland department at the back of the store.

And whether your purchase is 20 cents or $200, Ebaugh's will gift-wrap it for free and deliver! Kramer thought long and hard about the policy of the previous owners to limit these services to gifts over $10. But what she found was that "the same person who may want me to wrap and deliver a $5 gift this week may come in next week and spend $70 on herself and not ask to have a thing done. So I just feel like it all comes around."

Such services are just a few of the things that draw customers to the store. "We all try very hard for customer service, and we're a very friendly store. We do our best to go out of the way," says

Kramer. "It's the little things that our store can offer that the mass merchandisers can't that keep us successful and growing."

Little things like tracking which items in the collectible lines each customer has so there's no risk of duplicates, or taking orders over the phone to "pick something out," or notifying bosses a few days before Secretary's Day and asking them if they want to purchase baskets again this year.

"We're always looking for ways to make things easier on our customers," she explains, and adds, "If there's been any change over the years it's that people want to shop as easily as possible and with as little effort, and in as fast a time as possible."

Her accommodating attitude had helped attract customers from Wichita, 60 miles away. A catalogue program has also increased traffic by drawing customers from out of town. She sends the holiday catalogues, produced by her buying group (Palmer Marketing) to current customers and selected zip codes in other cities.

Ebaugh's also hosts an invitation-only pre-Christmas open house at the first part of November, complete with wine and cheese. "The first year we did it, it was great," says Kramer, "and last year our numbers doubled."

Kramer loves what she's doing, and the atmosphere is one that many retailers would envy. She says, "This is a fun business. You have only happy occasions, dealing with birthdays, anniversaries . . . people are usually in a good mood when they're here, and that makes it a fun atmosphere to work in in the first place."

Fisher's Office Products
Office Supplies, Furniture, Equipment, and Service
Boise, Idaho

When in 1986 Gary Mahn and his wife, Kathy, bought an old-line mom-and-pop office supply store that had been in business for fifty years, the business had twelve employees and in its best year had had revenues of $900,000.

Now, eight years later, the store has revenues in excess of $7 million and more than seventy employees. But it hasn't been an easy road.

Shortly after the couple bought the store, the office supply discounters began a parade into town that forced the Mahns to reevaluate their high margins and service policies. They didn't shy away from the challenge. "It's really true that competition brings out the best in us and makes us get better," says Gary Mahn. The challenge, he says, was "Get creative or die."

Mahn says many similar businesses weren't up to the challenge, and in the past five years roughly half of the independent office supply dealers in the country have closed their doors or been absorbed by larger companies.

The Mahns chose instead to get creative. Against impressive competition—Office Depot, Costco, OfficeMax, and Boise Cascade—the Mahns made four decisions: They joined the Basicnet buying group (one of the largest in the country), invested heavily in a sophisticated industry-specific computer system, moved into a 15,000 square foot distribution center, and moved their retail operations into a historical building in downtown Boise. The renovation they oversaw in the retail location won national design awards.

The Mahns also aggressively seek new ideas. "If you stick your head in the sand, don't attend trade shows, you'll never learn new things," says Mahn. Another factor in their success was to pick their "niche market." Fisher's chose to focus on the larger businesses—those with fifty or more employees—which the Mahns identified as a segment that wanted and deserved competitive prices but also appreciated the service that Fisher's could provide.

The commercial end of the business functions out of the central distribution center with state-of-the-art freight-moving equipment. Commercial customers can directly access Fisher's computer system to place orders and check prices.

At their downtown retail location, they have a large, upscale gift and card department and a showroom for office furniture and machines. Mahn says that becoming an exclusive dealer of a major brand of copiers has helped propel profits. They also landed a major contract to provide office products for the state of Idaho when the state decided to bring its business into the private sector.

At the cornerstone of all operations is *service*. A team of salespeople regularly call on customer accounts, giving them extra attention along with the little "perks" that have made Fisher's famous.

Mahn explains, "Each order is accompanied by a couple of Tootsie Rolls, which is a little bonus for our customers. It's not a big deal, but customers love it. If we don't give a customer a Tootsie Roll, sometimes they call and ask where they are!"

Linked with that idea is their monthly newsletter, aptly named the *Tootsie Roll Report,* which goes to selected customers and employees. The newsy, friendly, four-page flyer profiles a customer- and a team-member-of-the-month and highlights company and community events. As Mahn says, "It shows our customers that we're human beings."

The company uses flyers and catalogues extensively with much success. With a customized jingle, Gary Mahn's voice on Fisher's radio ads has become very recognizable. For special events such as Christmas and Valentine's Day, Fisher's invites guests to noontime open houses and provides lunch for customers while they browse. "It's been very popular," says Mahn.

Mahn believes that his community involvement has been critical to the success of the company. His dedication to the preservation of the downtown business district helped pave the way for the Downtown Boise Association, one of the many associations in which he's active.

For his community spirit and his company's success, he earned an award for the 1994 Boise Area Chamber of Commerce Small Businessman of the Year. In 1993, Fisher's was designated as a Blue Chip Enterprise in a national program sponsored by Connecticut Mutual Life Insurance Co., the U.S. Chamber of Commerce, and *Nation's Business.*

He's quick to share the accolades with team members and says simply, "Team members make the difference in any business. We motivate them by giving them plenty of responsibility and authority, by profit sharing, and by numerous pats on the back." Free Tootsie Rolls can't hurt, either.

CompuSystems
Computer Systems and Supplies
Washington, Missouri

While the computer trade associations are telling dealers that specialization is the only way to survive against the megamerchants, Joe Wolf is proving them wrong in his 2,300-square-foot store in Washington, Missouri, just a few miles west of St. Louis.

And while many other computer merchants are rushing to follow the standard advice, Wolf steers clear of the pack. Instead, he has firmly established his niche as a full-service computer dealer. "Anything to do with home or business computers, we'll do it," he explained. And enough customers are taking him up on the offer that he has been able to post healthy 25 percent annual sales increases.

With a Wal-Mart Supercenter at his back door and Best Buy, Circuit City, and CompUSA all nearby, other dealers might feel a little threatened. But instead of cringing from the competition, Wolf invites customers to bring in competitive advertisements. "When customers walk in, we can compare line by line the competition's advertised products with what we sell. We're not a high-pressure organization. We tell people that the best thing they can do is to go out and learn as much about it as they can."

Wolf loves the competition's thirty-day money-back guarantee because "we have a lot of people who, within that thirty days, realize that they made a mistake, take their system back, and then buy it from us," he says.

Wolf and his staff of twelve highly skilled employees work hard to prevent buying mistakes at CompuSystems. They spend a lot of time with customers evaluating their needs and will even go to customers' locations to see what they have. "We take *time* with our customers," Wolf says.

According to Wolf, another buying mistake computer customers make at the discounters is buying equipment that isn't expandable or upgradable. "They build in obsolescence into their machines," Wolf explains. In contrast, the systems that Wolf sells using "industry standard architecture" are his own PC Plus label, which can be expanded as the customer's needs grow. He contends, "If you stay with us, you have a constant upgrade path." Wolf also sells name-brand computers as well as a full line of computer software and supplies.

Wolf believes the service his store offers customers is unmatched by the discounters. If a customer has a problem with a computer and has to take it back to one of the chain stores, Wolf says the chances are the person who helped them doesn't know any more than the customer did. "At our store," he says, "it's not just, 'come in, pick up a box, and we'll see you later.' "

In sharp contrast to that type of service, CompuSystems offers toll-free technical support *forever.* "If customers have a question," Wolf says, "we'll do our best to answer it."

Customers look closely at price when purchasing high-ticket items like computers, but Wolf says he's able to keep his prices competitive by being in the ASCII group, a computer buying group. Before joining the group, he devoted much of his time to purchasing. "Now if I compare the prices I was getting before joining the group," he says, "which took me literally hours each day to negotiate, ASCII has already negotiated that price or a little bit better."

Though Wolf only spends about 1.5 percent of his revenues on advertising, he feels they get a lot of bang for their bucks. He utilizes newspaper, radio, and cable television to carry his message. Occasionally, he'll sponsor an entire radio program and then get the host to do commercials for the company.

A monthly newsletter that they produce in-house has generated a lot of positive feedback. "We don't run the hard sell in the newsletter," he quickly adds. He says it is mainly informational about new products and tips on how to utilize the computer better. An on-line bulletin board allows customers to access information (and computer files) twenty-four hours a day, 365 days a year. They've also developed their own electronic catalogue so customers can check—and compare—prices easily, then hopefully order the products from CompuSystems.

Perhaps one of the most unusual approaches he has taken is to send faxes through his automated fax system—run by computer, of course. Once a year, Wolf hires temporary employees to canvass about 500 businesses in their trade area, asking them if they would mind receiving one-page promotional faxes from time to time. About 95 percent of the business owners express an interest, and out of those, Wolf says, "nearly 100 percent get to be our customers to some degree."

Wolf began building his customer base even before he opened his store in 1986. While he worked in data processing for a major corporation, many friends asked him for advice about what type of computer equipment to buy. He talked to them for a long time about their needs and their budgets and then found the best computer for their money. Pretty soon, he was working twelve hours a day between his two jobs and was $50,000 behind in orders. He decided to devote full time to the computer business.

Since opening the store, he has seen a steady increase in revenues and expects that sales in 1994 will jump 30 percent over 1993 revenues. What's his secret? His answer is quick and emphatic. "I'm not a person who believes there is any secret out there. It doesn't matter whether you're selling computers or you're selling anything else. It's the same equation for all businesses: Get good people, find a product you believe in, and back it up with great service, and make your prices competitive." So now the "secret" is out. Sounds pretty simple to us.

Hahn Appliance Center
Major Appliances
Tulsa, Oklahoma

If you needed to buy a new appliance in Tulsa, Oklahoma, you might not go to Hahn Appliance Center first. But once you entered the attractive, friendly, impressive showroom at Hahn's you probably wouldn't be inclined to go anywhere else.

Hahn's owner, Lee Sherman, has worked hard to make it a place where customers feel comfortable. A receptionist would greet you as soon as you entered the store because, as Sherman says, "I don't want someone to be in our store more than fifteen seconds without being greeted."

You might be impressed to see working appliances displayed in attractive homelike surroundings. If you were in the market for a washing machine, they'd hook one up so you could watch how it agitated. Would a quiet dishwasher be more important to you than one that merely cleans last night's spaghetti off the dishes? They would have several plugged in and working so you could compare noise levels.

An impressive inventory includes hundreds of models of refrigerators, stoves, washers, dryers, dishwashers, and microwaves. Hahn's also offers product knowledge and service that is unmatched by his price-driven competitors Best Buy, Circuit City, and Sam's.

Knowledge and service are big factors in the value package that Hahn's offers customers. Their "gold label price" includes delivery, hookup, a second-year warranty, and a thirty-day no-lemon guarantee. If you don't want some of those services, Hahn's will gladly deduct them from the price.

Once customers hear about all the extras that the gold label price includes, many of them tell Sherman, "Wow, you're cheaper than the other guys and they guaranteed their prices are the cheapest." Sherman responds with a smile, "Obviously they're not, but if it would make you feel better, I'll raise mine."

Sherman learned the business from the bottom up. Before buying the store in 1983, he worked as an appliance wholesale factory rep for twelve years. While putting in sixty- to eighty-hour weeks, he tried to infuse his tireless energy into his dealers.

"I said, 'Let's have a sale, let's redo the floor, let's hook this washer and dryer up,' " says Sherman, "and they'd tell me it was too much trouble."

According to Sherman, that attitude—and the bust of Tulsa's oil boom—helped put twenty-two independent retailers out of business between 1983 and 1992 and was a big factor in allowing the discount stores to come in and "eat those people alive."

Sherman dug in and has thrived. Store revenues have more than doubled since he became full owner in 1990. Sherman attributes the success to the fact that "I really had a focus on my business and the type of customer I have and how to appeal to that customer."

He carved out a special niche in the built-in market because when the crunch hit, new construction came to a halt while remodeling increased. In marked contrast to the treatment they received at other stores, customers found that Sherman was happy to help with remodeling projects. "I thought if there was an area where people were going to get run out of one store, shoot, I'll take care of them," says Sherman. Today, Hahn's is recognized as the headquarters for built-ins.

Taking care of customers is what the store is all about. Hahn's well-trained employees are paid higher than the industry average because, as Sherman says, "I have better people." His training program includes monthly all-staff sessions which conclude with dinner out for everyone, Sherman's treat.

All employees are required to rotate positions for a day so they have a sense of being in another person's shoes. Says Sherman, "This heightens their awareness of the hardship they put on their coworkers when they don't do their jobs right."

Several "private letter" sales are part of his yearly marketing calendar, and the sales, which are open to a select mailing list, generate $45,000 to $60,000 in revenues during a six-hour period. In addition to direct mail, he also uses billboards, radio, television, and newspaper advertising. Integrated into the plan are his special events, which his wife and active partner, Sally, helps organize.

Sherman serves on the board of his buying group, Key Southwest, and constantly seeks out new ideas at Key meetings, and NARDA shows. When he goes out of town, he visits dealers to see what ideas they're using that he can adapt. Sherman also credits strong community affiliations with helping him keep on top of changing market conditions.

Even after more than twenty years in the business, Sherman is still excited about what lies around the corner. "I still see a lot of things out there that I could do better, that I haven't even tried yet," he says, "and that's what keeps me excited."

Direct Tire Sales
Tires and Auto Service
Watertown, Massachusetts

No one who's set foot into Direct Tire Sales could be too surprised at the great publicity the company has been getting lately. Its dedication to customers has become almost legendary, catching the attention of not just customers but also publications like *Fortune* magazine, *Inc.* magazine, and *USA Today*. Owner Barry Steinberg was also named National Tire Dealer of the Year and New Englander of the Year along with a variety of other awards.

Understandably pleased with the accolades, Steinberg explains, "Like a sports team, we're just clicking." From his single outlet on one of the busiest streets in the Boston area, Steinberg and his thirty-eight employees produced sales of over $6 million in 1993, an increase of about 3 percent over the previous year. Not bad, considering the fierce competition, flat market, and a recession in New England.

Though his biggest competition is National Tire Wholesalers (NTW), the field is full of other players like Sam's, Firestone, Sears, Costco, and Pace. "There are more players in the market," Steinberg says, "and when that happens, it creates price wars."

He's winning the war by refusing to fight. "We let the public know that we *are* more expensive. I won't compete in the low price arena," he says, "and they can't compete in the service arena." Up front about his target customer, he says, "I don't want a *consumer* who will drive all over town to save a few cents on a can of tuna fish. I want a *customer* we can keep for life."

Considering his team of qualified, friendly employees and a large menu of services, he'll likely get his wish. Steinberg hires carefully, after three interviews at different times a day (to test for consistent energy levels), and trains continually. "We build an environment where customers and employees alike feel that it's the right place to be."

That attitude, a pay scale that is 15 to 25 percent higher than average, and the company's attitude toward teamwork help keep Direct Tire's employee turnover rate at a minimum. But when the need arises, it's not hard to find a new employee. "We have a reputation for being a good place to work, and people come to us," Steinberg says.

So do the customers. Arriving at the store, customers are greeted by sharply dressed employees who personify the company's image: polite, knowledgeable, honest, and clean-cut. Customers who have a few minutes to wait while their car is being expertly fixed by certified mechanics can check out the latest magazines in a spotlessly clean customer lounge. There they'll find complimentary gourmet coffee (with real cream), herbal teas, soft drinks, and pastries from the bakery across the street.

For customers with no time to wait, Direct Tire will provide one of the company's fifteen free loaner cars or cheerfully call a taxi. "Everyone deserves to be pampered," says Steinberg.

The ideas for the loaner cars and for a profitable tire storage program originated in employee meetings, where the perpetual question is, *How can we do it better?*

Legendary service generates valuable word-of-mouth advertising, which Steinberg supplements with radio advertising. Though his specific radio techniques are "somewhat proprietary," he offers these clues: Try to become a fabric of the radio station, and make sure the radio people are customers. He writes the ads, customized for the audiences of each station, and they all begin with the recognizable voice, "Hi, this is Barry Steinberg of Direct Tire." Regardless of the ad, the theme is the same: service and people.

Steinberg developed and trademarked a slogan, "We'll Fix It So It Brakes," and used the slogan on billboards on the Massachusetts Turnpike. Direct Tire monitors how customers hear about the company, and many of them still answer, "I saw your billboard." Oddly enough, they haven't had the billboard in almost five years!

A more recent tactic that also brings in the customers is the "Toyo Tire Indestructible Tire Warranty." Explains Steinberg, "We took a brand of tire that was proprietary to me, gave it an extended warranty and all the 'bells and whistles' and advertised it like crazy." As long as you buy the tires from Direct Tire and have them aligned once a year, Steinberg will replace the tires free if anything goes wrong with them for as long as you own the car. As a result, Direct Tire's business exploded by about 30 percent.

Community involvement is very important to Steinberg and his wife, Penny, and they work hard on philanthropic projects to build a better future for the community.

What's in store for the future of Steinberg and Direct Tire? In spite of frequent suggestions, he's not interested now in franchising, but he adds with a laugh, "Maybe I'll write a book!" And, considering the number of visitors he's had who want to study his success, maybe he should.

Page One
Books, Music, Computer Software
Albuquerque, New Mexico

Page One bookstore in Albuquerque, New Mexico, has been a model for other bookstores for most of its thirteen-year history.

After Yvette and Steve Stout bought the business in 1981, they studied their options and realized their choices were to "lead, follow, or get out of the way." They chose leadership and haven't looked back since. Instead, they have been looking *forward* from the very first days when they started out in their small, 2,000-square-foot newsstand.

In the mid-1980s, they developed a product mix that has since been copied by independents and chain stores across the country. They were among the first in the nation to add CD music and computer software to the traditional mix of books, magazines, and tapes. "I used to say that we had a product mix that no one else in the country has. Now our unique product mix is being modeled by the chains," says Steve Stout.

After expanding the original store several times, the Stouts decided to build a new store across the street. Confident they had a successful product mix, they turned their attention to how to allocate space in the new store.

"We have always been literally among the first to use computer systems to track inventory and purchasing, and we decided to utilize a computer model to determine space requirements for the new store," says Stout. In March of 1993, the Stouts and their 100 employees moved into a bright, airy, attractive 25,000-square-foot store and converted the original store into Page One Too, a used book store.

Though its sales figures are confidential, Stout is pleased with the company's growth rate and says, "We've always been ahead of the book industry as a whole. Any problems we've had at Page One have been due to rapid growth." Displaying a characteristic sense of humor, he adds, "Either that or poor management."

Albuquerque, a city of 400,000 people, has its share of independents and chain stores. By Stout's calculations, there are more than twenty book stores in the city including such book industry giants as Bookstar and the first Hastings multimedia supercenter. A new Borders store is set to open in mid-1994.

Stout isn't afraid of the competition. He says, "I never even think about them. I'm always embarrassed that I don't go in and check out what they're doing."

Maybe the reason is the competition is busy checking out what he and Yvette are doing. "The chains have always visited our store, making fact-finding trips to Albuquerque like they do all over the country," says Stout.

When they come, what they find is a state-of-the-art book store staffed by friendly employees and filled with a product mix that includes about 200,000 titles. By category, the store sells about 50 percent books, 15 percent computer software, 25 percent music, and 10 percent gifts, novelties, and newspapers.

Stout doesn't enter the price wars with the chain stores, except in the area of hardcover fiction books, which are all sold at a 25 percent discount, a tradition they have had since the newsstand days. "We are trying to hold firm on not discounting anything else because we think that is just an insidious circle," says Stout.

Another war the Stouts don't fight with the chain stores is the *titles war*. "I don't think it's important how many titles are on the shelves," says Stout, "I think it's more important who you buy your books from. We think in terms of what books we have out there that are hard for people to find."

As a result of that philosophy, Page One takes a lot of pride in stocking offerings from many of the small presses across the country, which, Stout admits, is not a particularly unique approach. "There is a movement by the independents to feature the small presses," he says. "Small presses often don't give chain stores unfair business advantages so independents tend to have a lot of loyalty to small presses."

Stout is quick to point up the fact that they support the small presses more for philosophical reasons than for financial ones. "You can't justify the expense of dealing with the small presses based only on customer visits," he says.

To those people balking at such disregard for the bottom line, he responds, "Yvette and I have never done business strictly to make money. We have never made a decision based on money . . . because our mission is to give Albuquerque a chance to read what they want to read, to be entertained if they want to be entertained."

Whichever they choose, customers can sample before they buy. Page One invites customers to lounge in any of their seating areas (that can accommodate 100 people) and browse through books and magazines before they purchase them.

At any of the store's ten listening areas, customers can preview any musical selection. The store also has ten stations where customers may preview computer software on topics that range from accounting packages, to games, to word processing programs. "We've always wanted people to listen to music and try out software before they buy," explains Stout. "We thought that we ended up with a lot happier customers and fewer returns."

Having happy customers is a top priority at Page One, and they have strategically placed their customer-service section in the center of the store. Stout says, "We've always thought that customer service was so important that we wanted the customer to walk in the door and be able to look ahead and say, 'That's where I can get help.' Employees try to greet all customers as soon as they walk into the store."

Like many other bookstores, Page One has an on-site coffee house, which can serve fifty customers their choice of drinks, pastries, salads, sandwiches, or desserts. Stout believes having the coffee bar, which is subleased to a restauranteur, has been part of a total package of offerings. As Stout explains, "A bookstore is so much more than a coffee house in terms of excitement and activity."

The Stouts build on that excitement and activity by hosting about 100 special events a year, ranging from author signings to poetry readings, musical performances, and software demonstrations. Stout laments the fact that New Mexico isn't a big enough market to draw some of the big name authors or performers, but says that makes customers even more appreciative of the celebrities that *do* come to town.

While other book sellers are rushing to find the magic formula that will help them become leaders in the battles with the retail giants, Stout offers this advice:

- Find a business partner who is smart in ways that you're not.
- Don't listen to your accountant.
- Don't listen to your attorney.
- Don't be too preoccupied with the bottom line.

Judging from their success, maybe it's pretty good advice.

Baum's & Hanover Linen
Women's Apparel (Baum's)
Linens, Domestics, and Gifts (Hanover)
Morris, Illinois

While Jim Baum was on a deep-sea fishing expedition, an old fisherman gave him the best piece of advice he's ever gotten: "Son, don't watch the pitching boat. Instead, keep your eye on the horizon."

"That's part of the difficulty with retailing today," says Baum, who's president of Baum's, a women's apparel store, and Hanover Linen. "If I've got a computer system going haywire, my shipments aren't arriving on time, and I have a leaky toilet, it's real hard to be thinking about what Wal-Mart is doing, or the category killers, or the superstores."

Baum's has weathered many tough storms during its 120-year history in Morris, Illinois, a 10,000-person community just 65 miles southwest of Chicago. And despite the latest wave of competitors who are drawing customers away from their downtown location, owners Jim and Carol Baum have no plans to jump ship, as some of their counterparts are doing. "I feel like we ought to get Willie Nelson to put on a Retail Aid concert," he quips.

A sense of humor and a strong family legacy of retail experience have propelled Baum's success. "We did not stand around and wring our hands when Wal-Mart came to town," he says. "We continued to do what we thought we were doing best."

In both Baum's and the Hanover Linen Store (across the street), customer service has been sharpened. Baum praises the excellent group of employees who "intuitively work very hard to please the customers."

Both stores have also narrowed their focus. "We're trying to carry more and more of less and less," he says. For Baum's, that means defining his niche to older women who wear larger dress sizes. At Hanover, Baum has changed the product mix, adding small furniture, matching bedding accessories, pictures, and mirrors.

To counteract the customer exodus from downtown, the

Baums have spent more of their advertising dollars outside of Morris trying to portray Baum's as a destination store.

Baum is constantly looking for ways to improve. "I think it's pretty clear that in today's environment, you have to be different," he says. As he often does, Baum is seeking input from his staff of twenty-four employees. "I'm sending them all a questionnaire asking them to give one suggestion of how we ought to be more different than we are now."

Baum also actively seeks ideas from a variety of other sources. He confesses, "I've probably never had an innovative idea in my life, but I think I have very good instincts about what to copy and I know a good idea when I see one." He adds, "But you can't see one unless you're out there looking."

And he's always looking. Active in several associations, Baum was recognized by the National Retail Federation (NRF) as the 1993 Small Store Retailer of the Year. In 1994, he was elected chairman of the NRF Small Stores Board and vice chairman of the NRF Board and also serves on the Illinois Retail Merchants Association.

It was at one of these association meetings that he got the idea for his "50 Plus Club," which has become a very successful relationship builder and marketing tool. Directed to customers over fifty, members get special discounts, birthday presents, and rebates on purchases over a certain amount. Baum opens about six "50 Plus" accounts for every regular charge account.

Another special promotion that has worked well is the "Gift for the Giver" program. Customers get a card during early November which is punched for every purchase they make in the store. When they've finished their Christmas shopping, Baum gives the customer a gift, pegged at about 3 to 4 percent of the amount of the purchases. "We've given candy, boxes of private-label jellies and jams, or gift boxes from our Crabtree and Evelyn selection," says Baum. "Then we tell them, on Christmas day, to open their little gift from Baum's."

Giving is part of what the Baums are all about. So is keeping their eyes on the horizon.

Mr. CB's
Beach and Boating Activewear, Bait and Tackle, Boat Rentals
Siesta Key, Florida

Just about a half-mile from Sarasota, Florida, on the island of Siesta Key sits a beautiful Cape Cod style building right on the water. Rent a boat, buy some tackle, get the latest tips on where (and what) the fish are biting, and swap fish stories with the owner.

You might just be surprised at who the owner is. Mr. CB's owner, Aledia Hunt Tush, is not a burly sea captain but a petite, energetic Virginia native whose love of the water and the state of Florida lured her (pardon the pun) into buying the shop in 1976 while visiting relatives.

The original store sold mainly bait and tackle with added offerings of boat and bike rentals. In the eighteen years she's owned the store, Tush has constantly updated her products and services—as well as the facilities—and now has a diversified assortment of all the original offerings plus a complete line of fishing tackle, fly fishing products, snorkeling supplies, water skis, marine and sun products, and rod and reel rentals. A full line of beach and boating activewear—which employees refer to as their "boatique"—has proven to be a big hit and has attracted a whole different set of customers.

Changes and expansions weren't just restricted to products and services. Tush has constantly revamped and remodeled, and today's attractive, well-merchandised store is vastly different from the shack that it originally was.

As a measure of her success, Tush's shop earned the distinction in 1993 of being voted the area's best bait and tackle shop. Two years earlier, it was selected as the 1991 Small Business of the Year by the Sarasota Chamber of Commerce.

With many of her products, she faces stiff competition from Wal-Mart, Kmart, and other independents, as well as flea markets that buy close-outs and discontinued items and then sell them at hugely discounted prices.

Tush and her employees keep a close watch on all their competitors. To counter the stiff price competition, she has honed her buying strategies. She matches prices on very visible items that are staples of the business, but "I try not to buy the same things that the Wal-Marts and Kmarts buy," she says, "and then I don't have to sell head-to-head against them." She also offers several services and products that the discounters can't—boat rentals, live bait, rod and reel repairs.

Tush is no stranger to hard work, and the shop is open every day but Christmas. She also works hard at pleasing customers. The key, she says, "is to listen to your customers and listen to what they want"—and then give it to them.

One way she's found to build rapport with her customers and provide the information they want is to sponsor seminars. While she's quick to point out that they aren't big moneymakers, she says, "They build traffic and build the respect that customers have for you."

Hosted by one or more of the eight captains who work out of the shop, the seminars offer fishing tips and maps that will help customers land "the big ones." On a tip employees picked up reading a trade publication, the store offers hands-on training the day after the class, when the captains take participants on excursions to put into practice skills learned in the seminar.

It was no accident that an employee offered this suggestion. Employees read and discuss articles they read in publications as part of staff meetings they hold informally to kick around ideas and make decisions. It's important to include employees, says Tush, "because if they're not behind what we're doing, they're not going to be as supportive as they could be."

Having quality employees, she believes, is a key factor in overcoming competition from the chain stores. "Independents can make a difference because they have employees with time and expertise to help the customer."

Mr. CB's operates on the team concept in employee relationships. Though turnover in her store is minimal, when Tush needs to hire a new employee, she strives to offset any weaknesses she perceives in her current team. Then, "The first thing they have to understand is the customer is number one, and the second thing is that they have to work together as a group."

Tush's dedication to teamwork isn't confined to employees. She also works hard to develop and nurture good relationships with manufacturers and representatives. "If you can build that rapport with them, they'll help you," she says. "If deals are available or if there's a way of finding lower prices, they'll work with me a little bit closer if I've become one of their loyal customers. That's a big help when you're up against the Kmarts and Wal-Marts."

Dumminger Photography
Specialty Camera, Minilab, and Portrait Studio
Fremont, Ohio

Ken Dumminger keeps a file of letters that have been written to Dumminger Photography over the years. From crisply printed business letters to those scrawled by a child's uncoordinated young fingers, they all bear the same message: "Thanks for all you do for us."

The file is thick because he believes strongly in supporting his community through service, leadership, and contributions. His efforts earned him not only the respect of his community but also the county's annual award for "Corporate Citizen of the Year."

His dedication to his town—just 35 miles east of Toledo—is matched by his desire to form good relationships with its citizens. "We know our customers' families and have dealt with their joys and sorrows. I love people and that's what keeps me going," he says. And it shows.

That attitude and his love of photography, which has spanned almost thirty years, have helped him survive the competition from Wal-Mart, a Super Kmart, and formidable regional chains. His store offers retail camera and equipment products, a minilab, and a portrait studio. But though his store processed more than a million photographs in 1993, in recent years he has posted only modest sales increases of 5 to 7 percent.

Like other independents, Dumminger feels the crunch of his competition and the recession, which have forced people to reevaluate their buying habits. "People will bicker over the price while forgetting that the price also includes the intangibles like service and quality," he says.

Acknowledging that the mass merchandisers can "beat me to death on price," he says, "they can't beat our service," and that's where he and his staff of five knowledgeable employees focus their efforts. "We spend hours communicating with our customers and helping them become better photographers."

They advise customers on not only the right camera to buy, but also how to use the camera to document life's exciting moments. "We've become the outreach arm of family histories," says Dumminger.

To combat the stiff price competition of the retail giants, Dumminger prices his "price-sensitive items" at or near chain stores prices and avoids mentioning prices in his ads. "I promote a product or service and why a customer needs it," he says "and I'm always trying to sell the 'sizzle,' " which he defines as the excitement and the emotion of photography.

He believes if he does a good job of selling the sizzle and instilling a love of photography, he'll increase his customer base and guarantee a future market for his products and services. He strives to do that by utilizing some creative promotion strategies.

Some samples: He donates a camera, film, and processing to every new mother who delivers a baby over Mother's Day weekend. He encourages Sandusky County citizens to document their community by sponsoring an annual photo contest. (Winning photographs are also used in advertising campaigns for the county parks district and the convention and visitor's bureau.) Following Operation Desert Storm, he processed film free for returning soldiers.

With each roll of film processed at Christmastime, Dumminger gave customers a coupon for a free 5-by-7 picture with Santa. Customers frequently ordered additional copies, and many purchased photo greeting cards. To foster repeat business, he has a "shutter club" frequent buyer program. For each seven rolls of film processed, the eighth one is free.

As Dumminger will quickly point out, another big ingredient in his store's success is an employment team that often wins accolades from customers. "Give them an environment where they can learn, make mistakes, grow, excel, and prosper," he says. "They in turn will put their energy and wisdom back into your company. And above all, make sure everyone is having fun."

From the sound of things, that's just what they're doing.

Twelve

The Kaizen Strategy

He who stops being better stops being good.

—Oliver Cromwell

The Japanese word *kaizen* (ky'zen) means "continuous improvement involving everyone." In essence, the kaizen philosophy is a quality improvement process that every small business can adopt. Its premise is simple and straightforward: Everything can be improved and it's everyone's job to see that it is. Each employee, owner, vendor, and service provider adds to the quality process.

In the late Sam Walton's autobiography, *Made in America*, David Glass, Wal-Mart's CEO, talked about his friend and boss. Glass said that Walton "gets up every day bound and determined to improve something." If continuing improvement was important to the man who founded the nation's largest retail company, it has to be important to us.

Kaizen *must* spread throughout every small business. Why? Because the new breed of big-box merchants, megastores, category killers, and lean independents have issued a challenge: *Get better or perish*. Your survival and future prosperity will depend on your ability to implement ongoing changes that improve every aspect of your business.

You have probably noticed by now that the overriding themes of this book are *change, improve*, and *succeed*. This chapter incorporates all of the other survival strategies into one common focus: improvement.

We encourage you to look for kaizen ideas when you visit competitors' stores. You can learn from others, and as Oliver Goldsmith said, "People seldom improve when they have no model but themselves to copy after."

234

You will find some overlap with material discussed in detail in other chapters. We do not apologize for the duplication. It is intended. We want you to read this chapter again and again. Use it as a thought starter for developing your own kaizen strategy. We hope you will implement many of the tactics we give you, but you'll need to go beyond our thoughts and add your own. Share sections of this chapter at your next staff meeting. Your associates may have some great ideas on how you can improve your customer service or information tracking.

Do it now. Start today. Don't just read this chapter and go on as usual. Instead, when you read a kaizen tactic that you know will work in your business, put it to work *now*. There is a Chinese proverb that says, "A journey of a thousand miles begins with a single step." Take that step now.

Several of the suggestions have to do with measuring a variety of areas of your business. Those who use the kaizen process tell us this: "You cannot improve what you cannot measure."

When you talk to successful owners who are building thriving businesses and opening second and third locations, you'll find they deal with facts over feelings. Yes, they admit that they often are forced to make decisions without complete information, but that isn't the way they like to operate. Implementing the kaizen process will require some additional fact gathering. Embrace the opportunity and accept the challenge of change. Your future depends on the decisions you make today.

Run every decision you make through a filter that asks, How will this help our customers? or Will this make us more efficient and productive?

Kaizen Tactics
273 Powerful Suggestions
For Improving Your Business

For your convenience, we have listed these improvement tactics in specific categories. You may wish to start by reviewing the kaizen tactics in your weakest areas.

Kaizen and Your Customers

1. Read *Swim with the Sharks* by Harvey Mackay. Pay special attention to Lesson 3 on page 21 of that book.
2. Develop your own customer profile using the tools in Chapter Nine of our book.
3. Count potential customers every day. If people are walking into your business in increasing numbers, your promotion strategies are working.
4. Compute your customer batting average (total walk-in traffic divided by the number who make purchases).
5. Set goals to improve your customer batting average.
6. Compute the dollar volume of your average sale (total sales divided by the number of purchases).
7. Train your staff in the art of *suggestive*, or *add-on*, *selling* and set goals to increase the average sale.
8. Talk to your customers every day. Ask them how you're doing in terms of meeting their needs. Spend some time selling.
9. Talk to your twenty-five largest (highest-volume) customers every month.
10. Contact any former customer as soon as you learn he is a *former* customer. Find out why he stopped doing business with you. Correct the problem when you find out what it is.
11. Learn your customers' names. Remember, all business is *personal*. If you have two employees and you and your employees learn just one customer's name each day, you'll gain more than 1,000 new names every year!
12. Call your customers by their names.
13. Greet customers as soon as they enter your business. Make eye contact and smile.
14. Inspire your employees to provide great customer service by leading them by example. Your customer *attitude* is a powerful motivator for your team.
15. Teach your team to build your business with courteous, professional telephone techniques. Don't spend

$1,000 on Yellow Pages advertising and then blow it when the phone rings.

16. Conduct a customer survey to find areas that need improving. (See Chapter Three or contact your local Small Business Institute, Small Business Development Center, or college or university may be able to help.)

17. Find out when your competitors are open for business.

18. Find out when your customers want to shop. (Ask them!)

19. Ensure that your open-for-business hours provide plenty of hours for your customers' convenient shopping.

20. Keep your promises. If you say you open at 9:00 A.M., open at 9:00 A.M., not at 9:03, 9:06, or 9:17.

21. Make certain every employee attends at least one customer service training program every year. Contact your chamber of commerce or Small Business Development Center to see when the next one is scheduled.

22. Calculate the dollar value of every potential customer and post it for all employees to see. Keep them focused on the importance of the customer.

23. Thank every customer for his or her business. You need customers; they don't need you.

24. If you sell big-ticket items—$100 or more—follow up after every sale. Call each of these customers or drop them a thank-you note. It shows that you care, that you want them to be fully satisfied, and that you appreciate their business.

25. If you sell little-ticket items, follow up with your regular repeat customers. Let them know you value their business.

26. Take every opportunity to subtly point out to your customers the benefits of doing business with you.

27. Solicit customer suggestions.

28. Give customers public recognition for useful ideas. A plaque, special mention in your newsletter, or a picture in your print ads is a nice way to say thanks.

29. Set aside a bonus kitty for your employees who are delivering whatever-it-takes customer service. For example, set aside $100 per month for $5 *above-and-beyond awards*.
30. Give verbal praise and financial reward to any employee who generates such outstanding service that your customers inform you about it.
31. Considering new products? Ask your ten best customers what they think about them. They will be flattered you've asked and may tell others that you have the items, if you decide to carry them.
32. When you have walk-in customers who *just want to look around*, ask for their opinion on a new product. Make sure it's at the back of the store so they have to walk by a lot of your inventory. You may not make a direct sale, but the customer will feel involved and will see some of what you have to sell.
33. Are some of your customers businesses? Offer them free *advertising* space in your newsletter. It's a great way to thank folks who do business with you.
34. Put your home phone number on your business card. One CEO we know told us that he seldom gets more than a call or two per month, but many new accounts—customers—have been impressed because the top executive is accessible.

Kaizen Your Costs (Eliminate Waste)

35. Take time to do every job right the first time. (If there isn't time to do it right, where will you find the time to do it over?)
36. Remember that everything is negotiable.
37. Strive to reduce overhead costs as a percentage of sales.
38. When you look at expenses to reduce, analyze your largest expense categories first. A small reduction percentagewise in a large category may be worth more than a 20 or 30 percent reduction in a small one.
39. Strive to reduce your costs of goods sold. Better buying means easier selling.

40. Check every expense category on your income statement against businesses of similar size in your industry.
41. Set goals to bring your expenses to a position of "better than your industry average."
42. Don't ignore small expense categories. A dollar saved is a dollar earned. Costs that are eliminated drop dollar for dollar to your bottom line.
43. Install energy saving light bulbs and fixtures.
44. Put timers on your thermostats.
45. Change furnace and air conditioner filters regularly.
46. Insulate for heating and cooling savings. Energy savings paid for the insulation in one of our stores in two years and saved thousands over the next ten years.
47. Put timers on your lights.
48. Ask your utility suppliers for other money-saving tips.
49. Don't buy long-distance service from the first company to make a pitch for your business. Get all the details. We thought we had a great 800 service at $5 per month and 23 cents per minute until we got an offer of $0 per month and 16 cents per minute.
50. Eliminate fancy add-on telephone services. Eliminate the *nice;* keep the *needed.*
51. Use the phone book instead of directory assistance at 50 cents per call. Let your fingers walk for themselves. Don't use the automatic dialing service provided by directory assistance. It's too expensive.
52. If you're traveling, try to eliminate calls billed to your room. You'll often pay more than double the going rate.
53. Check your phone service provider to see if a call-waiting option is less expensive than adding a new line. (Or you may be able to eliminate an existing line.)
54. Plan your calls. Use a checklist to cover the major points; then get off the phone. Not only do you

reduce your phone bill but you also gain an even more valuable commodity—time.

55. Check the cost of faxing versus mailing. Go with the least expensive. Encourage customers to fax *you*.

56. Eliminate overnight deliveries whenever possible. Use the fax; mail the follow-up.

57. Use two-day delivery services at 25 percent of the cost of overnight. (A little planning can save a lot.)

58. Combine mailings. High-volume mailers often mail several pieces to the same company every day. Put them together when you can.

59. Buy lighter-weight mailers and envelopes. Use light-weight paper. You can often eliminate a second stamp—a savings of more than 40 percent.

60. Clean up your direct-mail lists. One of our clients found nearly a 10 percent duplication and error rate in a list they used regularly.

61. Cull the list for every mailing. Not all customers on your list may be targets for a particular offer.

62. Check to see if there's a "presort" company in your area that combines mailings from small businesses and splits the savings.

63. Eliminate the fax cover sheet. Instead, use the small transmittal notices in the margins of your first page.

64. Transmit faxes and other telephone data when the rates are lowest—usually after 11:00 P.M.

65. Check the costs of printing versus copying. In quantity, printing may be less expensive.

66. Make two-sided copies. You can save postage, paper, and trees.

67. When printing, check prices from time to time. A recent price check (three phone calls) saved nearly $30 on 1,000 forms.

68. Watch the cost of service contracts. Renew for one year at a time and eliminate most of them. Your copier may be the exception where a service contract is cost-effective.

69. Store office supplies together. Avoid duplication by keeping a list in the storage area of what's on hand.

70. Buy supplies like gift wrap and ribbon in the off-season. One retailer who did a strong Christmas business told us he saved nearly $1,000—or more than 50 percent—by buying his gift wrap, ribbon, and tags at the end of the selling season.

71. Print high-quality, color letterhead to use for customers, prospects and clients. Use an inexpensive black-and-white version for other purposes.

72. Reward employees who make money-saving suggestions. Encourage thrifty ideas. In 46 B.C. Cicero wrote, "Men do not realize how great an income thrift is."

73. Use a graphic artist instead of an ad agency to help you design a logo, letterhead, or brochures.

74. When taking your artist-designed work to a printer, try to negotiate for the 10 to 15 percent rebate commission an ad agency would get from the printer as well.

75. Save your time and money by letting a travel agent find the best rates for travel.

76. Clean your own windows—often.

77. Do your own janitorial work (or offer to let your employees earn a little extra).

78. Try to find a retired maintenance person to handle minor electrical, plumbing, and carpentry repairs. It's a win-win situation.

79. Don't buy "new" when "used" will do. This works for property, fixtures, equipment, and furniture. When we opened our first store, everything but our inventory was used. We saved thousands.

80. Buy used vehicles. Be patient. Let several dealers know what you're looking for and wait. Check national repair records before selecting a model or brand.

81. Maintain your company vehicles regularly. This can extend the useful life by as much as 100 percent. Keep them clean and instruct your drivers to drive courteously. Your image is at stake.

82. Use colorful signs on your vehicles and get more mileage out of your advertising.

83. Lower the cost of outside accounting and legal services by doing more of your work in-house.

84. Write your own contracts and have your attorney look them over.

85. Organize your own accounting information in an orderly manner and save on the professional's time.

86. Review all professional and insurance costs annually. Make certain all charges are correct and fair.

87. Reduce insurance costs by eliminating unnecessary coverage. Use caution here: The key word is *unnecessary*.

88. Raise insurance deductibles to lower rates. You should never insure for losses you can afford to take.

89. Have your insurance coverage rebid every two or three years. Companies and rates change. Don't get into the rut of automatic renewal.

90. Manage your workers' compensation costs with careful monitoring and safety programs. Make sure all job classifications are accurate. Incorrect risk assessments can double or triple rates.

91. Save money by refinancing debt. As we write this, interest rates are very low. Refinancing can lower payments and free up operating cash or shorten repayment times.

92. Work with your banker to consolidate installment notes, credit cards, and credit lines to lower rate packages.

93. Monitor service charges and fees from your financial institution. Ask why you're being charged. It may be a mistake. Shop around; if others offer free services, negotiate. Move accounts as a last resort. (See Kaizen Your Banking Relationship, below.)

94. Don't let checking account balances sit idle. Get an interest-bearing account.

95. Negotiate credit card processing fees. If the volume has increased you may be able to get a lower rate. Consider electronic processing options.

96. Monitor credit card usage in your business. Can you afford to eliminate low-usage, high-cost cards?

97. Cut payroll costs by reducing pay period frequency. Going to every other week or to monthly payroll periods can free up administrative hours for more-important work. Phase in the changes.
98. Consult with a tax professional to reduce taxes or keep your tax payments working longer for you. The rules are complex, but an expert can almost always save you money—legally and ethically.
99. Use outside contractors instead of employees when the costs are lower. Consider the cost of benefits, FICA, withholding, etc.
100. Let your employees pick up some of the increasing health care costs. Some small-business owners are paying a flat fee—$100, $150, $200—per month and letting the employee pick up the balance. This has a twofold benefit: (1) It gives the employees—who otherwise often take it for granted—a better sense of the value of the benefit, and (2) it allows you to cap your costs.
101. Consider adding part-time help instead of paying overtime.
102. Cut benefit costs with flexible spending accounts for your employees. These IRS "Section 125" plans allow you to set aside employee wages tax-free for benefits such as child care, nonreimbursed health costs, and other nontaxable benefits. Your business can save more than 7 cents in reduced taxes on each dollar put into the plan.
103. Check with your trade association, chamber of commerce, or with the National Federation of Independent Businesses to see if group insurance policies are available to lower costs.
104. Consider employee leasing options.
105. Take every trade discount you're entitled to.
106. Make fewer purchases of larger volume to capture volume discounts or free freight offers. Work on a just-in-time basis.
107. Consider joining a barter exchange. Try to trade your

products or services for others you buy regularly. You save the difference between cost and retail.

108. Trade cost-saving ideas with other businesses like yours. We know a business owner who jotted down her ten best cost-saving ideas and sent the list to ten other small-business owners. Within a month, she had received more than thirty additional ideas she could use.

109. Don't forget to add all capital purchases to your fixed-asset list so you can take the depreciation deduction.

110. Read the expense-deduction part of the IRS's *Small Business Tax Guide* (publication 334). Don't miss deducting any expenses.

111. Use your employees in slow seasons to do work you would otherwise have to pay others for. We know a Tennessee appliance dealer who used his sales and service employees to completely remodel the interior of his store. It was a pleasant break from the routine, ensured job security, and saved the owner thousands of dollars.

112. Consider luxury expenses like leased luxury cars, Rolex watches, and first-class travel carefully. Harvey Mackay, best-selling author and the president of the $200 million Mackay Envelope Corporation, advises business owners to buy cheap cars and put their money to work.

113. Recycle for savings. Use the back of unused copies for printing rough drafts.

114. Reuse laser printer cartridges and save as much as 50 percent of the cost of new ones.

115. Reink printer ribbons.

116. Reuse floppy disks.

117. Reverse file folders and use them again.

118. Use refillable pens and pencils.

119. Recycle aluminum cans, cardboard, and paper. Donate to nonprofit organizations for publicity if there are no direct cost benefits.

120. Reuse mailers and shipping containers when your image isn't at stake.

121. Invest in a sign-making machine or graphic software to reduce outside printing and design costs for signage. Hand-lettered signs may cause you to lose sales and if poorly done may lower your value image.
122. Cut out nonperforming advertising. Better yet, move this money into promotions that work.
123. Measure the performance of your advertising. Use different traffic builders for print as opposed to electronic ads. When customers ask for the special, you'll know the source.
124. Every contract should be renegotiated when it comes due. Got a lease? Shop around, use comparable space (dollars per square foot, etc.) to improve your negotiating position.
125. Using an advertising agency? Push for a lower commission.
126. Using a janitorial or lawn-care service? Trim the costs or find alternatives. One owner chopped 50 percent off lawn-care services by hiring an employee's son who needed summer work.
127. Right-size your labor force. (Yes, we even deal with sacred cows here.) Inefficient or unproductive employees can drain your profits. One employer we know replaced two undermotivated full-time workers with two "hungry" part-timers, saving forty hours of labor per week.
128. Trim promotion costs by training everyone to promote your business. When you deliver your products or services, have delivery personnel pass out business cards and flyers to neighboring businesses.
129. Avoid the cost of collection companies by making your own collection calls to delinquent accounts. Calls are many more times effective than letters. After you call, follow up in writing as a reminder.

Kaizen Your Associates

130. Empower your employees with kaizen understanding. Discuss this chapter with them. Show them the importance of continuing improvement.

131. Create a kaizen incentive or reward program. Pay for every valid improvement strategy your employees submit to you in writing. Offer plaques, money, time off, or some other reward.

132. Discuss the financial condition of your business with your employees. Help them understand their stake in its success. When they feel they are a part of your business, their contributions will increase.

133. Create written job descriptions for every type of employee you need. List special personality traits and skills required for each job.

134. Next, review your present employees. Are current staff members well matched for the jobs they have? Can you improve some of the matches? If some employees aren't good matches for anything, they might be happier working for another company.

135. Evaluate everyone in your company every year. Let them know how they are doing on a formal basis. Don't forget to praise good behavior whenever you see it.

136. Recognize good work from your associates, whether fresh new faces or an old veteran. Look for unique ways to reward those who are not in the most visible part of your business, such as your stock clerks or bookkeeper (as opposed to your sales staff).

137. Always recognize an associate's personal best. Any new "high" deserves public acknowledgment.

138. Don't neglect your most talented workers to devote more time to less talented staff members. *All* employees need your time, encouragement, and leadership.

139. Let your more talented workers mentor (tutor) employees who need improvement.

140. Surround yourself with people more talented than yourself. Steel magnate Andrew Carnegie has this epitaph on his tombstone: "Here lies a man who knew how to enlist in his service better men than himself."

141. Delegate a few new tasks every month. Your employees will appreciate the added confidence and respon-

      sibility, and you will have more time to devote to other tasks.

142. Make a checklist (who, what, when, etc.) so you can monitor delegated tasks.
143. Take time every day to listen to your staff.
144. Take time every day to talk to your staff.
145. Involve key employees in major decisions.
146. Give all employees their own business cards.
147. Praise publicly.
148. Criticize privately.
149. Remember that employees won't earn you very much until they are well trained.
150. Cross-train key employees.
151. Remember, people satisfy customers.
152. Employees make many first impressions for your business. Encourage them to dress conservatively so as to offend *no* customers. Invest in vests or smocks to create a more uniform appearance.
153. Set a good example by dressing professionally yourself.
154. Be specific in explaining how you expect your employees to dress for work.
155. Compliment associates who dress appropriately.
156. Provide opportunities for personal growth.
157. Pay for training when employees pass or complete the courses.
158. Encourage skill building, whether or not it's job related.
159. Teach by example the career benefits of telling the truth, keeping your word, taking responsibility for your actions, planning and prioritizing every day, and keeping the workplace organized.
160. Focus on finding solutions, not detailing the problems.

Kaizen Your Banking Relationship

161. Pull a copy of your personal and business credit report every year. Correct mistakes *before* you visit your banker.

162. Let your banker know how you're doing, even when you don't need to borrow money.
163. Take copies of your financial statements to your banker at least once per year. If you've had a great quarter, share those statements too.
164. Arrange for working capital—lines of credit—before you need it. You can negotiate better terms when you're not in dire need.
165. Get approval for more than you need.
166. Never borrow more on your credit line than you need.
167. When you need to arrange long-term borrowing, be well prepared.
168. Anticipate the banker's three basic questions: (1) How much do you need? (2) What do you need it for? (3) How will you pay it back?
169. Take projected financial statements to show your repayment ability based on anticipated profits. Don't forget to include a cash flow statement. Bankers love cash flow; you should too.
170. Be prepared to answer questions about your projections.
171. Remember that banks are like rental car companies. Car companies rent you a car, charge for every day you use it, and expect to get the car back. Banks rent money, charge interest, and expect repayment of principal.
172. Remember, all bank terms are negotiable.
173. Educate your banker. Share relevant trade articles on your industry. Get him or her a copy of any good publicity your business receives.
174. Get to know several people at your bank, people with varying levels of responsibility. In that way, if your main contact leaves, you won't be a complete unknown.
175. Introduce your key employees to your banker.
176. Invite your banker to visit your business.
177. Invite your banker to do business with you.
178. Introduce potential customers to your banker.

179. Recommend your bank to employees and associates.
180. Evaluate your business using the six Cs of credit. See Tactics 181 through 186, below.
181. *Character.* Your personal integrity. Your personal history. Perhaps the most important determinant.
182. *Capacity.* Your company's financial strength, track record, and repayment ability.
183. *Confidence.* Your attitude and belief in your own ability. This should come across not as cocky, but assured.
184. *Capital.* Your debt to equity ratio. Your ability to secure other equity sources.
185. *Conditions.* The area economy and the condition of your industry.
186. *Collateral.* Your backup repayment sources.
187. Remember, *risk* is responsible for *rate.*

Kaizen Your Technology

188. Consider purchasing a computer to help you track financial information, customer data, and other business facts.
189. Learn some of the trade jargon so you'll know how computer systems are sized and sold.
190. Check your trade publications for hardware and software recommendations.
191. Analyze your needs before you visit a computer dealer.
192. Be certain that what you buy is upgradable and compatible.
193. Make certain the system you buy has fax/modem (communication) capabilities.
194. Talk to others who are running similar systems before you buy anything.
195. Investigate the cost of point-of-purchase scanning systems. Bar-code readers are coming down in price.
196. Look into marketing databases which might help you identify potential customers.
197. Evaluate commercial on-line services such as America

Online, CompuServe, Prodigy, and others that may contain valuable business-building information.

198. Gather information on software packages that will help you monitor and manage inventory.
199. Generate customized and personalized mailing lists for current and potential customers.
200. Learn to use the "mail-merge" function of your word processing software to make monthly mailings less time-consuming.
201. Evaluate custom label-making packages. They can save hours of time and give professional-looking results.
202. Consider interfacing electronically with your vendors and suppliers.
203. Study invoicing and billing software packages that may help you speed up accounts receivable collection.
204. Get information on professional sign-lettering machines. Some systems let you print standard formats for just pennies per sign.
205. Evaluate desktop publishing software that can help you create classy brochures, newsletters, and signs.
206. Investigate shareware (low-cost software packages) offerings to see if any might help you.
207. Get an 800 phone number.
208. Invest in a fax machine.
209. If your business needs a professional image, pay a little more and buy a laser printer.
210. Check out customer management software.

Kaizen Your Pricing

211. Remember, to sell it right, you've got to buy it right.
212. Locate a buying group that serves your industry. Get the details and then talk to members.
213. Make a list of ten items that your competitors are selling better than you can. Call your suppliers to see what they can do.
214. Locate at least three new buying sources this year.

215. Put a variable pricing system into practice today. See Chapter Ten.
216. Keep price-sensitive items close to your competitors' prices.
217. Make up profit margin on your blind items.
218. Put prices on inventory in your store. Customers complain that the new breed doesn't do this.

Kaizen Your Financial Statements

219. If you aren't already, begin producing and analyzing financial statements every month.
220. Get financial statements from your trade association so you can have a benchmark for yours.
221. Set goals to increase your sales by a specific amount this year.
222. Communicate those goals with everyone in your business.
223. Record your progress toward your goals every day, every week, and every month. Make it a game. You are keeping score.
224. Establish goals to improve your profit by a specific amount. (Read Kaizen Your Costs and Kaizen Your Pricing, both above.)
225. Reduce your accounts receivable as a percentage of your sales.
226. Reduce your accounts receivable collection time.
227. Take all discounts offered on invoices.
228. Analyze profit margins on the individual lines you sell.
229. Promote the lines with the highest margin to increase overall margins.
230. Try to decrease your inventory as a percentage of sales this year.
231. Try to turn your inventory more times than your industry's average.
232. Reduce your debt to equity ratio.
233. Common-size your financial statements for the last three years. Look for trends.

234. Work hard to improve your current ratio (liquidity).
235. Produce a cash flow statement and monitor where your cash is going.
236. Lower your cost of goods sold percentage by buying better and pricing right.
237. Know your cash position and try to lower your expenses to improve your position.

Kaizen Resources

238. Get ideas for improving your business from other businesses like yours in other trade areas. Visit their stores; invite them to yours.
239. Visit your library at least once each month. Go during a slow morning or afternoon and look for new books on topics related to your business.
240. While at the library, pick out two or three trade publications in industries unrelated to your own. Look for improvement ideas to *borrow*.
241. Read advertisements in out-of-town newspapers.
242. When you network with other people, go armed with some questions, such as, What's the most successful promotion you ever had? or, If you were in my shoes how would you try to get more customers?
243. Attend trade shows and industry meetings. If you can't attend, at least order the tapes of relevant seminars and speeches.
244. Visit your state fair and spend a day talking to business vendors and exhibitors. Check out the displays.
245. Visit the megastores regularly. They are the cutting edge—see what's new.
246. Contact your trade association for training materials, publications, and recent studies. Learn from each source.
247. Visit your local bookstore. Try to find at least one book with new ideas.
248. Visit with college or university business deans, department heads, and professors.

Personal Kaizen

249. Build your personal communication skills by joining a Toastmaster's club. (Learn to speak, listen, and think on your feet.)
250. Get computer smart. If you're still illiterate, take a beginning applications class.
251. Listen to motivational tapes while you are traveling.
252. Read *How to Win Friends and Influence People* by Dale Carnegie.
253. Write down three personal desires you want to accomplish this year. Complete open-ended statements like, "I've always wanted to . . . ," "I'd like to learn . . . ," or "I want to be. . . ."
254. Spend some time with someone who understands and uses the goal-setting process in his life; then . . .
255. Set at least one personal goal to achieve this year in the following areas: spiritual renewal, physical renewal, family relationships, career growth, education, and finances.
256. Read *Seeds of Greatness* by Denis Waitley.
257. Resolve to improve your physical fitness. A little conditioning can improve your health, restore vitality, increase your mental alertness, and improve your attitude.
258. Read Don Taylor's *Minding Your Own Business* newspaper column every week. If it's not in your local paper, ask them to get it. For information, write to: Data Staar Communications, P.O. Box 67, Amarillo, TX 79105.
259. Take a course in the art of negotiating. Learn how to create win-win situations.
260. Build your personal selling skills.
261. Spend one hour alone every week doing something you really enjoy.
262. Read *See You at the Top* by Zig Ziglar.
263. Divide a clean white sheet of paper into two columns. List your strengths on the left and your weaknesses on the right. Pick two weaknesses to turn into strengths this year.

264. Nurture your family and friendships.
265. Don't fear failure. Some of the most successful people we know experienced failures at some point in their lives.
266. Don't be afraid to try the "ready, fire, aim" approach. If you wait until you're sure beyond all doubt, it'll probably be too late to shoot.
267. Surround yourself with funny people. Laughter is good for your soul and is a terrific stress reliever.
268. Take your work seriously, but don't take yourself too seriously. The world will go on after we're gone. Try to enjoy the time you have. Happiness is not in the destination, but in the journey itself.
269. Accentuate the possible. Since we become what we think about, emphasize the possible.
270. Never say any of the following: "I can't," "I quit," "I'll get even," or "That won't work; I tried it once."
271. Say these words often: "I can," "I will," "I love you," and "How may I help?"
272. Live every day as if there were no tomorrow. For indeed we have no guarantee, except that we shall reap whatever we sow. Today's decisions are tomorrow's realities.
273. Mistakes are the building blocks of experience. Experience is the foundation of success. Don't be afraid of making mistakes, but don't stop there. Use each mistake as a step toward success.

A Final Thought

Someday soon, someone will update what we've written in this book. Our guess is that some of you who are reading this chapter right now will become the role models for a new epistle describing yet another generation of successful entrepreneurs. It will be *your* success story that will appear in that new work.

We only hope that our book will have played a small role in your story. Many small businesses are going to be successful competing with the giants, and we can't think of any reason why yours shouldn't be one of them.

Index